IMAGES
of America

FILIPINOS IN NEW YORK CITY

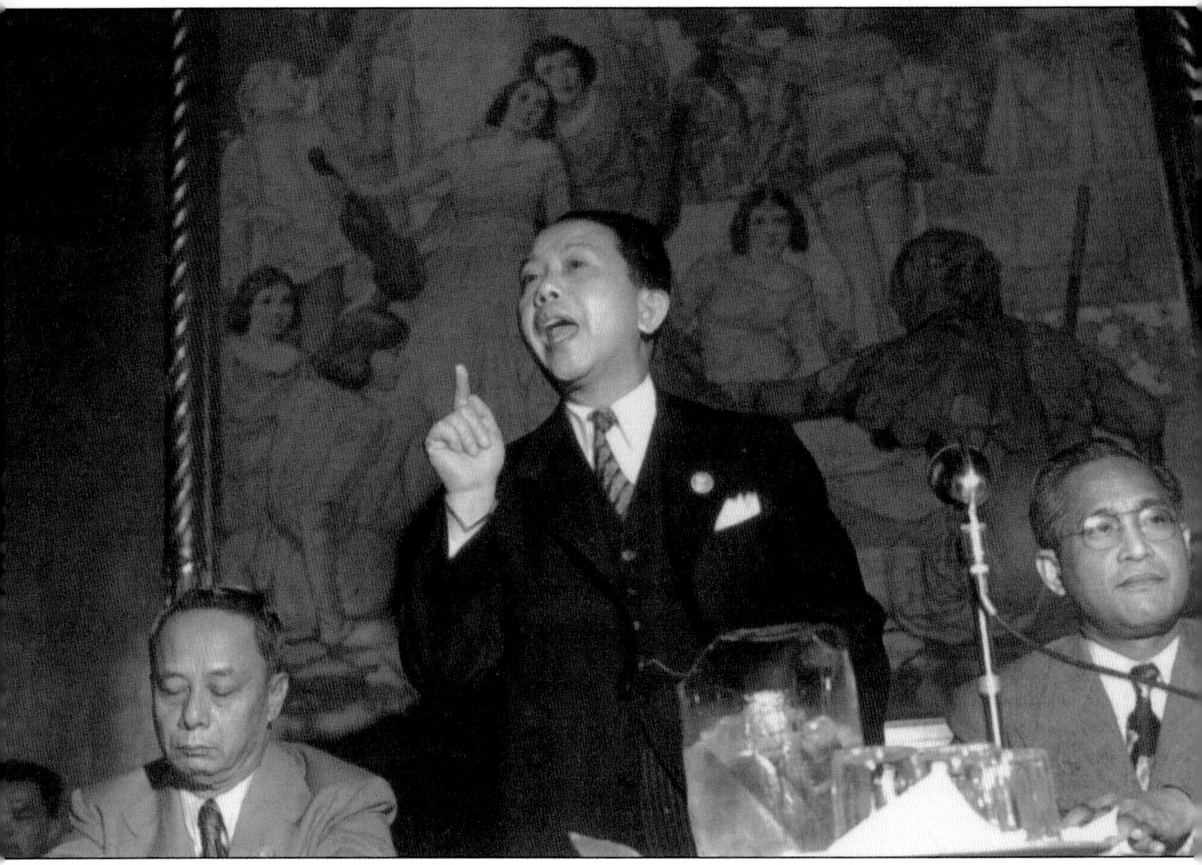

Carlos Romulo was a Filipino diplomat who served as the president of the Fourth Session of the United Nations General Assembly from 1949 to 1950, as well as the chairman of the United Nations Security Council. In this photograph, Romulo is presiding at a press conference as chairman of the Philippine delegation in 1945, with Carlos P. Garcia to his left. (Courtesy of the Carlos P. Romulo Foundation for Peace and Development.)

On the Cover: Cecilia Espinosa first came to New York in 1953 with her sister Carmen to attend graduate school at Columbia University. Here, she is in Times Square, which is often viewed as the center of Manhattan. While Times Square has gone through significant changes throughout the years, its signature billboards and ambiance have made it a tourist attraction for decades. Bienvenido Sison Jr., her future husband, captured this photograph. (Courtesy of the Sison family.)

IMAGES
of America

FILIPINOS IN NEW YORK CITY

Kevin L. Nadal and the Filipino American
National Historical Society
Metropolitan New York Chapter

ARCADIA
PUBLISHING

ISBN 978-1-4671-2308-2

Published by Arcadia Publishing
Charleston, South Carolina

Printed in the United States of America

Library of Congress Control Number: 2014949512

For all general information, please contact Arcadia Publishing:
Telephone 843-853-2070
Fax 843-853-0044
E-mail sales@arcadiapublishing.com
For customer service and orders:
Toll-Free 1-888-313-2665

Visit us on the Internet at www.arcadiapublishing.com

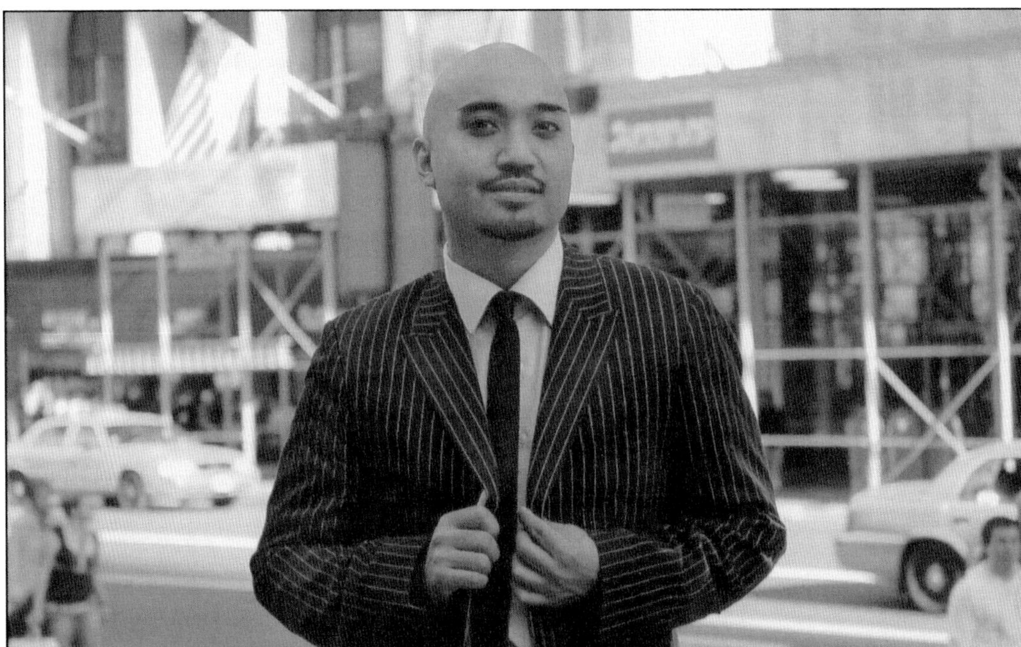

Dr. Kevin Nadal is a national trustee of the Filipino American National Historical Society (FANHS) and a board member of the FANHS Metropolitan New York chapter. He is an associate professor of psychology at the City University of New York, the executive director of CLAGS (the Center for LGBTQ Studies), the president-elect of the Asian American Psychological Association, and one of the leading researchers in Filipino American psychology and mental health. He is pictured here in midtown Manhattan. (Courtesy of JoAnn Garcia.)

Contents

Acknowledgments

I would like to thank so many amazing people who helped this book to happen and who have helped to promote and preserve Filipino American history in New York. First, I would like to acknowledge the hard work and dedication of the past and present board members of the Metropolitan New York Chapter of the Filipino American National Historical Society, particularly Dolores "Dolly" Fernandez Alic, Daniel Ballesteros, Kilusan Bautista, Lorial Crowder, Andre Dimapilis, Brenda Gambol, RJ Mendoza-Nadal, Gail Tamayo Prado, Pamela Santos, Cecile Sison, Joey and Jackie Tabaco, Alexandra Thomas, and Rose-Ann Ubarra-Cunanan. Thank-yous go especially to the Alic-Fernandez family, the Campano family, the Prado-Tamayo family, the Sison family, and the Tabaco family for sharing so much of your family histories with us. Sincere thanks also go to so many others who contributed their family photographs and histories to this project. Their names are credited throughout the book.

I would like to thank FANHS National, particularly our founder, Auntie Dorothy Laigo Cordova, and our founding president, the late Uncle Fred Cordova, who taught Filipino Americans across the country to be proud of where they came from, to document our histories, and to tell our stories. Thank-yous go to all FANHS National Trustees from all over the country for your continued support and for keeping Uncle Fred and Auntie Dorothy's dreams alive.

Thanks are extended to our many local FANHS members and supporters who have been vital in keeping our organization alive through numerous programs and events. *Maraming salamat*—to Ryan Abugan, Sonny Ago, Marissa Aroy, Joe Bataan, Paul Beaubrun, Nancy Bulalacao-Leung, Ana Liza Caballes, Michelle Camaya, Michael Capito, Cynthia Casasola, Liz Casasola, Stephanie Chrispin, Debralee Daco, Mathilda de Dios, Ben de Guzman, Claro de los Reyes, Lily Divino, Maria Doherty, Kara Mia Escobar, Kirklyn Escondo, Allison Joy Faelnar, Renee Floresca, Luis Francia, Randy Gener, Rio Guerrero, Mark Habana, Jaygee Macapugay, Agnes "Bing" Magtoto, Corinne Manabat, Jake Manabat, Venessa Manzano, Loida Nicolas-Lewis, Marie Obaña, Leah Obias, Rachelle Ocampo, Riya Ortiz, John Pasquarello, Nicole Ponseca, Ryan Punzalan, Steve Raga, Monette Rivera, Jamie Rojo, Anisa Tabaco, Air Tabigue, Julian Tamayo, Pamela Tamayo, Leezel Tanglao, Larry Tantay, Angela Tolosa, Rhodora Ursua, Jose Antonio Vargas, Ermena Vinluan, and Tristan Vizconde.

Finally, I want to pay tribute to the founder of the FANHS Metropolitan New York Chapter—the late Reynaldo "Ronnie" Alejandro, who initiated our official chapter in 1990. We are eternally grateful for your passion, your commitment, and your trailblazing achievements.

Introduction

New York City is known as many things—the Big Apple, the City that Never Sleeps, the Concrete Jungle, the Melting Pot, the Greatest City in the World, and the Center of the Universe. Most people know that Frank Sinatra sang that if you could make it here, you could make it anywhere. And many people may be familiar with the state of mind that Billy Joel, Jay-Z, and Alicia Keys have belted about. Despite this, what people may not realize is that New York City has been the home of hundreds of thousands of Filipino Americans for the past 100 years, including me, a transplant originally from California.

I first joined the Filipino American National Historical Society as a 19-year-old college student in California. I was encouraged by a mentor at UC Irvine to attend the biennial FANHS national conference in Portland, Oregon, in 1998, and I began to volunteer with the FANHS Los Angeles chapter shortly after. When I moved to New York in 2002, I had heard that there was a local FANHS chapter. But alas, I did not have time to join the organization until I had completed my doctoral studies at Columbia University. Plus, the chapter began to dissolve when chapter founder Ronnie Alejandro became ill. After Alejandro's passing, Joey Tabaco began to revive the New York chapter in 2009, and I was ready to get involved. Over the next five years, we were able to recruit several committed members, and the chapter regenerated strongly.

As chapter president, it became my mission to educate people about the history of Filipino Americans in New York City. Because most studies on Filipino Americans focused on communities on the West Coast and in Hawai'i, it was important for me to learn and educate others about the experiences of Filipinos on the East Coast. And when I finally delved into the process of documenting this rich history of Filipinos in New York, I had no idea how much I would uncover.

The story of Filipinos in New York City begins with the national hero of the Philippines, Dr. Jose Rizal, who first visited New York in 1888 and stayed at the Fifth Avenue Hotel (which overlooked Madison Square Park in Manhattan). While he did not stay for long, he did write about how he was impressed with the buildings and even drew a sketch of the Brooklyn Bridge, which had just been built a few years earlier. There is something very humbling about knowing that Dr. Rizal wandered the streets of Manhattan over a century before us. Perhaps this is why the annual Philippine Independence Day Parade and celebration has been held at Madison Square Park—the neighborhood where Dr. Rizal stayed—since 1990.

For the next decade or two, there was not any documentation of Filipinos who came to New York until the first Filipinos who landed in Ellis Island in the early 1900s. During this time, Filipino *pensionados* (sponsored students) came to the United States and studied at various universities across the country. Those students who immigrated through New York were required to register at Ellis Island. Several Filipinos who entered through Ellis Island became famous politicians in the Philippines and around the world. These notable Filipinos include Sergio Osmena and Manuel Quezon, who both later became presidents of the Philippines; Carlos Romulo, who later became the president of the United Nations General Assembly; and Camilo Osias, who twice served as the senate president of the Philippines.

When I was doing my research at the FANHS National Archives in Seattle, Washington, with Dorothy and Fred Cordova in 2010, I discovered the *Filipino Student Bulletin*—a newsletter from the 1920s and 1930s that was created to document the experiences of the pensionados. Students from all over the country would send photographs and short stories to its home office on Madison Avenue in Manhattan, and these newsletters would be published several times a year. It is truly amazing to know that these young immigrants knew how to stay connected decades before the Internet and social media were invented.

During my search, I learned about the Filipinos who were treated as circus animals at the Dreamland amusement park at Brooklyn's Coney Island around 1911. While I had learned about Filipinos who were on display at the St. Louis World's Fair in 1904, I had not ever known that this same tragic treatment occurred on the East Coast too. While it was mortifying and sad to learn this part of our history, it was a reminder that discrimination towards Filipinos was just as much a part of New York City as it has been in other parts of the country.

The histories of Filipinos in New York City have come from our FANHS members and other affiliates who have shared their family stories with us. For example, Dolores Fernandez Alic's photographs and stories of her father, Pio Fernandez, have helped us to see what life was like for Filipino seafarers in the 1920s who worked as stewards for the US Navy and who settled in the Brooklyn Navy Yards. Gerald Campano shared photographs of his grandfather Freddy, who immigrated sometime in the 1930s and lived his dream as a musician in the big city. Joey Tabaco's family history showed us what it was like for the first Filipinos to be employed by the US government, as well as what it was like to be one of the few Filipinos in certain New York neighborhoods in the 1940s and 1950s. Cecile Sison revealed the stories of her parents, who were students at Columbia University in the 1950s, while Gail Prado offered the accounts of her parents, who were among the first to arrive after the 1965 Asian Immigration Act. Together, all of these personal histories have helped us to further understand the history of a larger community of Filipino Americans in New York.

From the 1970s forward, the Filipino American community has grown significantly across all five boroughs. Many immigrants came as a college-educated professionals who worked as doctors and nurses in hospitals across the city. Some arrived as migrant workers searching for job opportunities so that they could send money back to their families in the Philippines. Some artists came to New York to pursue theater, music, writing, fashion, and more, and many became stars in the City of Dreams. And dozens of community organizations were formed, gathering Filipinos of all backgrounds to serve a variety of interests and needs.

The individual stories about New Yorkers who found success can surely inspire current and future generations of Filipino New Yorkers. For instance, I have been fortunate enough to have many conversations with Prof. Luis Francia, an esteemed poet, author, and professor who has lived in New York since 1970. He educated me about many notable Filipinos like Manuel Rodriguez Sr., also known as the "father of Philippine printmaking," who moved to New York in the 1960s to pursue a Rockefeller printmaking scholarship. Professor Francia also shared personal recollections about Jose Garcia Villa, a renowned Filipino American poet and writer, who had an apartment in Greenwich Village where he would gather many local poets, including Professor Francia, to share their work. Through my research, I also learned about Sugar Pie De Santo, a Filipina R&B singer of the 1950s who was discovered by James Brown at the Apollo Theater.

Present-day Filipino American New Yorkers are just as inspirational as those who came before them. Loida Nicolas-Lewis immigrated to New York in the 1960s and has become one of the most successful businesswomen of color in all of the United States. Lea Salonga, who is revered as one of the most successful Filipino actresses and singers, has called New York her home since she first starred in Broadway's *Miss Saigon*. Joe Bataan, the Afro Filipino "King of Latin Soul," grew up in Spanish Harlem, and Agnes "Bing" Magtoto is a community leader and professor who taught young Filipino Americans Tagalog and Filipino culture for years.

The photographs and stories that you will read about are just a glimpse of the many Filipino Americans who have lived in New York. We have documented everything from the Filipinos who served in the Navy or military to some of the successful Filipino restaurants (of the past and present). We will introduce you to some extraordinary Filipinos who have made their marks on New York City, as well as those we lost on September 11, 2001.

What I love most about Filipino New Yorkers is that we are both Filipino and New Yorker. As Filipinos, we are proud of where we come from, and we hold onto cultural values like *kapwa* (collective being), *utang ng loob* (debt of reciprocity), and *pakikasama* (social connectedness). As New Yorkers, we work hard, we are resilient, we are assertive, we chase after dreams, and we get things done. We hope that this photographic journal will inspire others to educate future generations about the 100 years of Filipino American history in this great city. We also hope that the stories will inspire Filipino American New Yorkers to flourish over the next 100 years and beyond.

One

Our Early History

Ellis Island to the Brooklyn Navy Yards

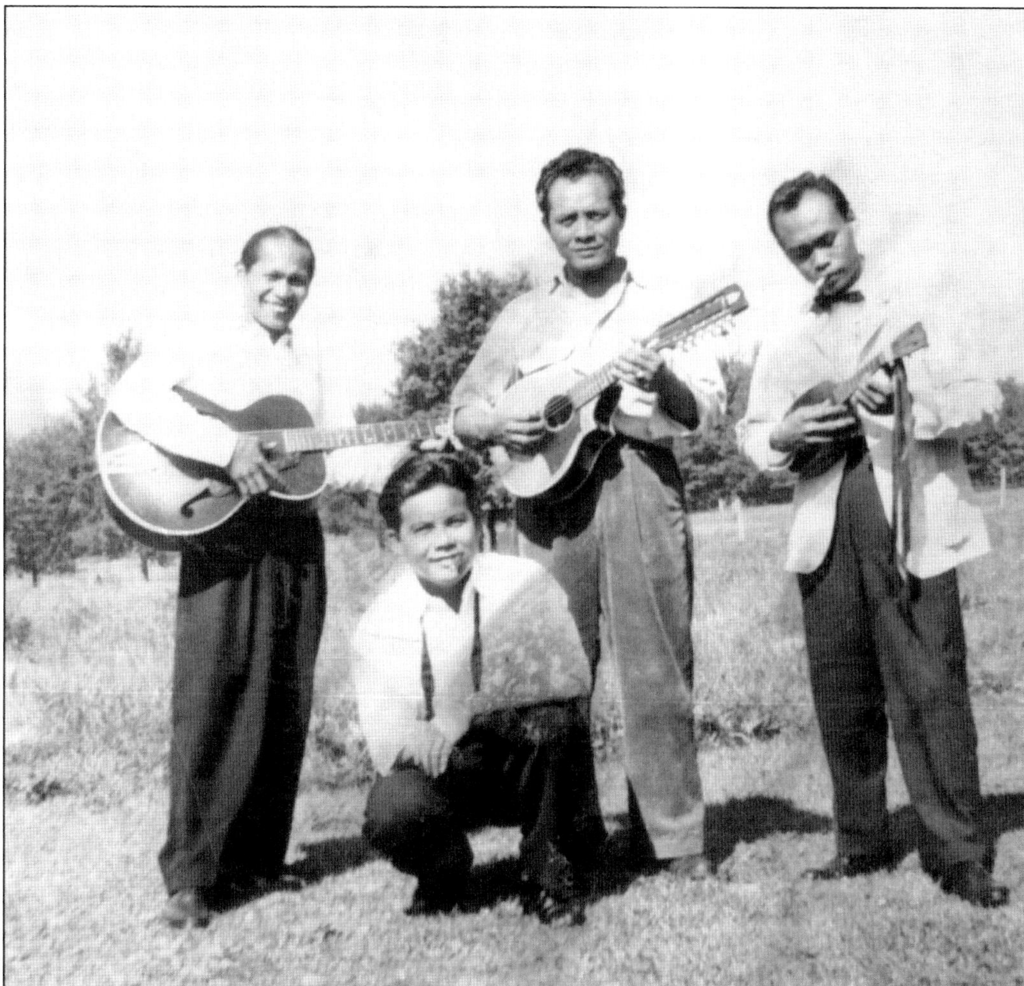

Many of the Filipino seafarers who lived in the Brooklyn Navy Yards liked to take weekend trips outside of New York City to enjoy some fresh air. Pictured here are Pio Fernandez (far left) and three friends in the Catskills in the 1920s. (Courtesy of the Alic-Fernandez family.)

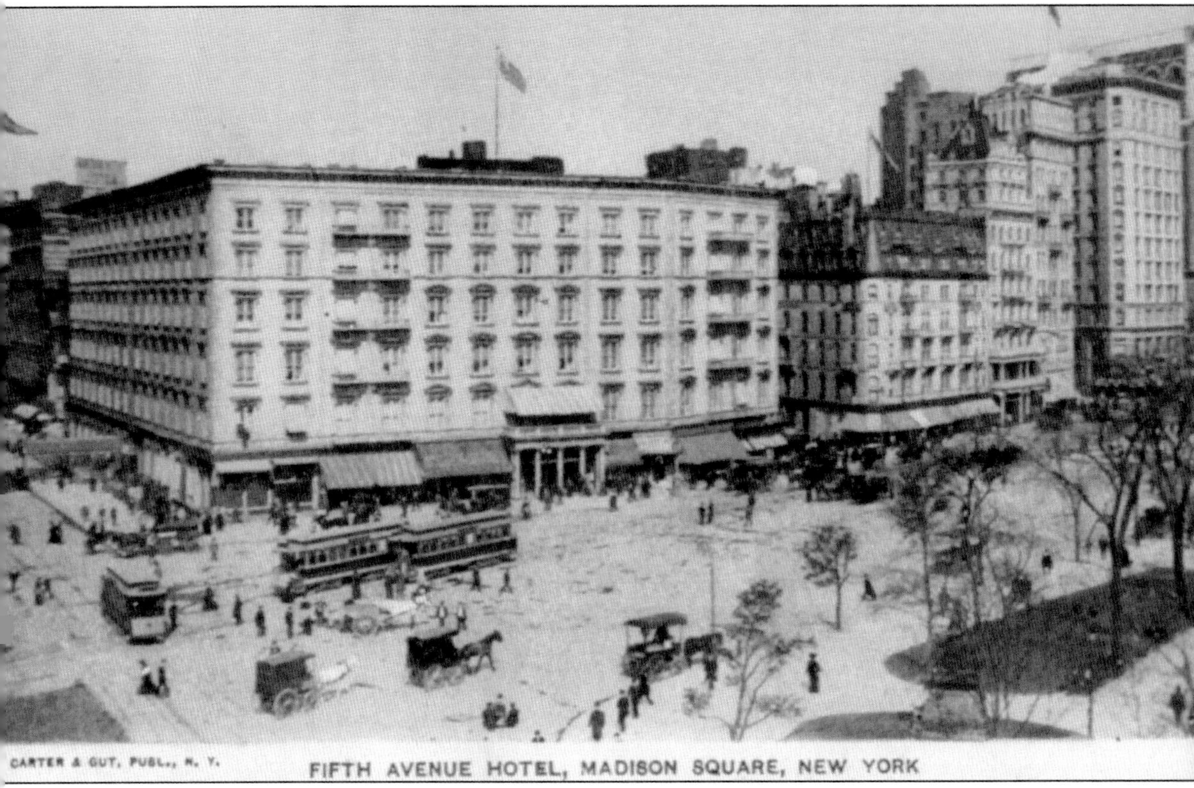

Jose Rizal, national hero of the Philippines, is documented as one of the first Filipinos to visit New York City. After stops in California and other parts of the West Coast, Rizal landed in New York on May 13, 1888, for a three-day visit. He stayed at the Fifth Avenue Hotel (pictured here), a luxury establishment that was located at 200 Fifth Avenue (between Twenty-third and Twenty-fourth Streets) in Manhattan. Rizal wrote of his stay in New York: "Was in New York; big town, but there everything is new. I visited some memorials to Washington, the great man who, I think, has no equal in this century." (Courtesy of New York Company Postcards.)

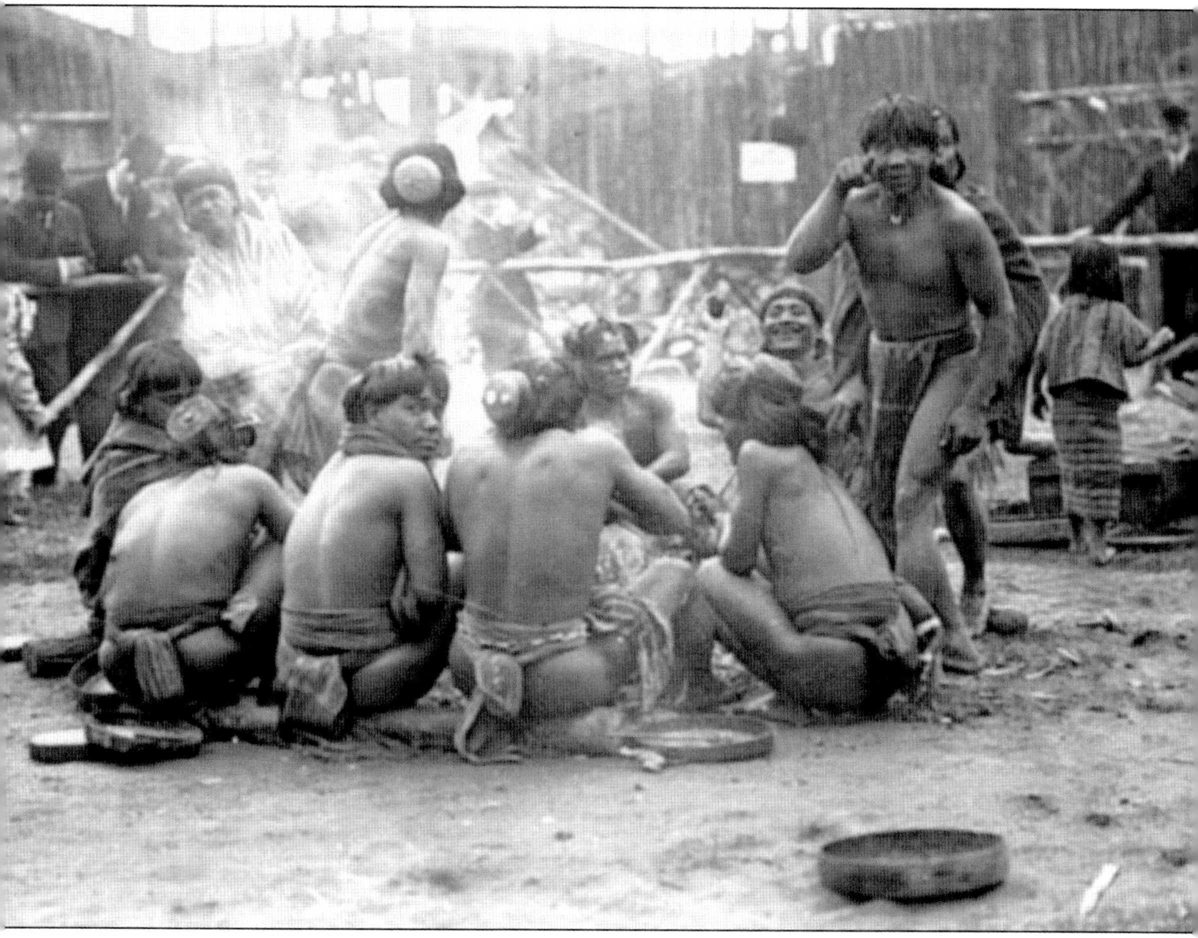

In 1911, Filipinos came to New York to entertain visitors at the Dreamland amusement park on Coney Island in Brooklyn. They were forced to wear native Igorot costumes, even though many were not from that region and few Filipino people dressed this way at the time. Similar to the Filipinos who entertained tourists at the St. Louis World's Fair in 1904 as uncivilized savages, these Filipinos lived in a fake village at the amusement park while visitors viewed what they believed life was like for the typical Filipino savage. (Courtesy of FANHS National Archives.)

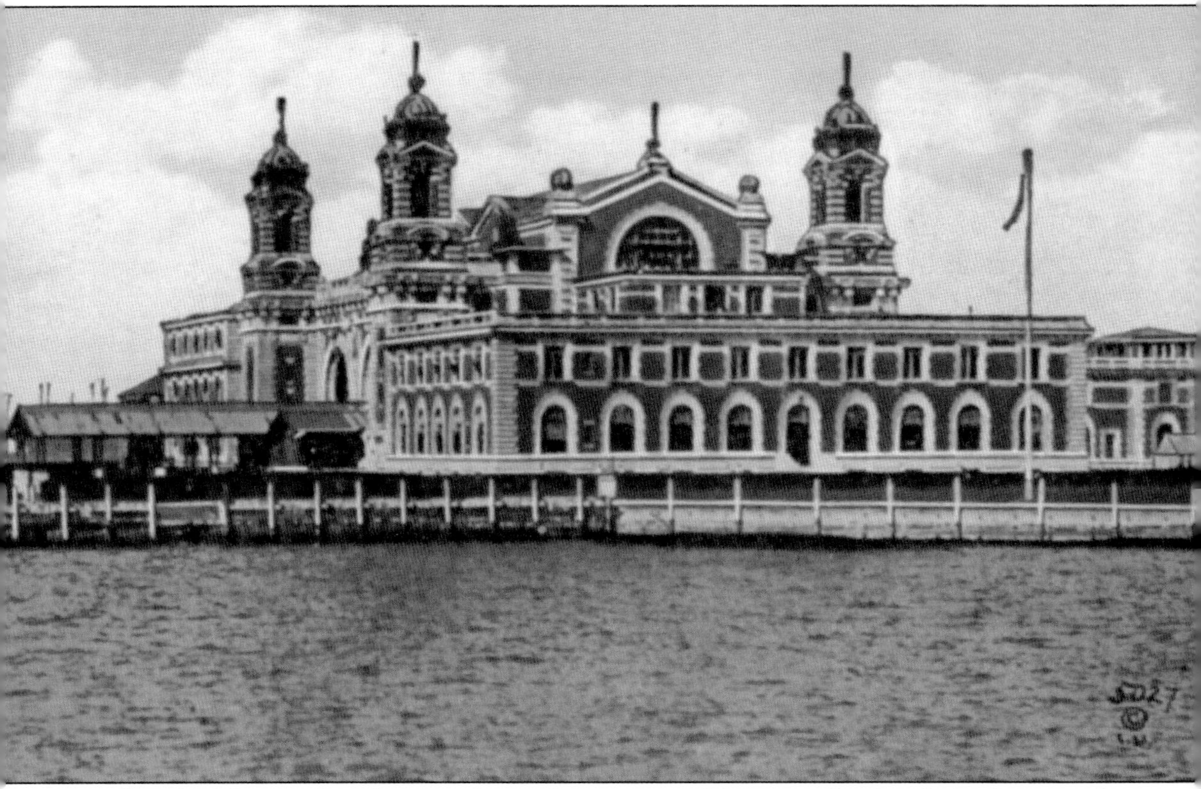

Ellis Island (pictured in this c. 1915 image) is a treasured American landmark that has served as a gateway for millions of immigrants into the United States. While it may be common knowledge that many European immigrants arrived in Ellis Island from the 1890s to the 1950s, most Americans may not realize there were also smaller amounts of Filipinos who arrived through Ellis Island from 1908 through the 1930s. Most of these Filipinos to arrive were pensionados, or students sponsored by the US government to study at schools like Columbia University and New York University. (Courtesy of Manhattan Post Card Company.)

One of the earliest Filipinos to arrive through Ellis Island was Carlos Romulo (right). On the morning of July 23, 1919, Romulo boarded the Japanese ship SS *Suwa Maru* as a government-sponsored pensionado on his way to attend Columbia University. The 45-day journey took him to several places, including Hong Kong, China, Japan, Seattle and Chicago. (Courtesy of the Carlos P. Romulo Foundation for Peace and Development.)

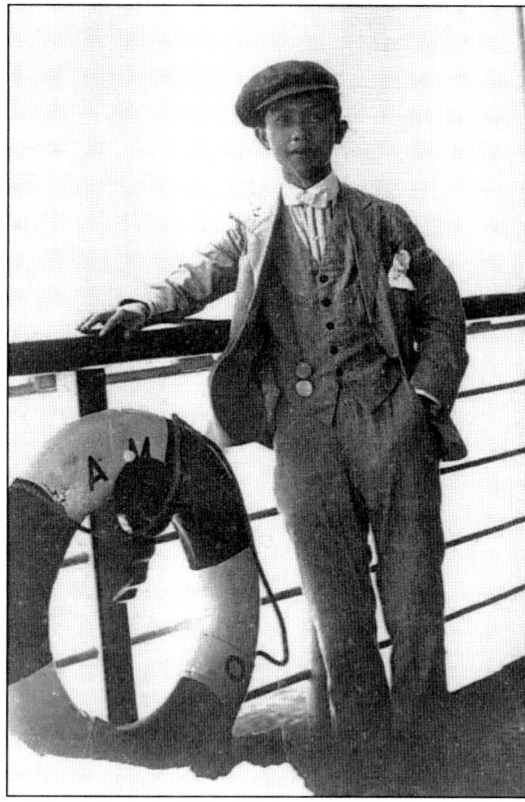

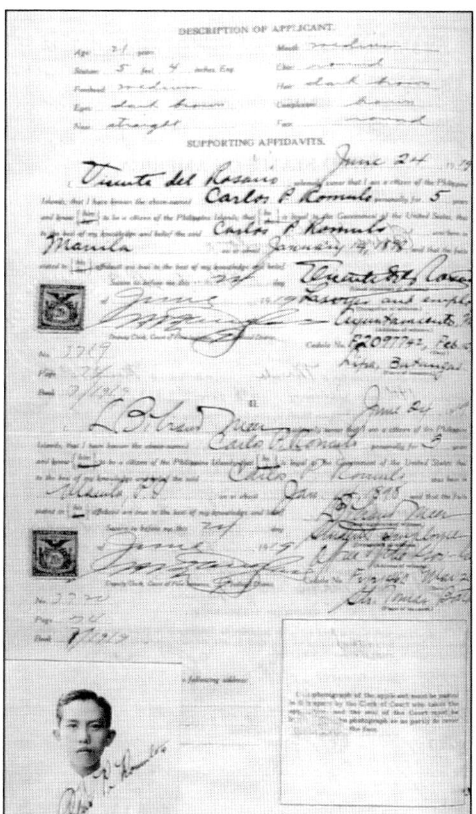

DESCRIPTION OF APPLICANT.

SUPPORTING AFFIDAVITS.

Carlos P. Romulo

Manila

Pictured here is Carlos Romulo's passport application from 1919. (Courtesy of the Carlos P. Romulo Foundation for Peace and Development.)

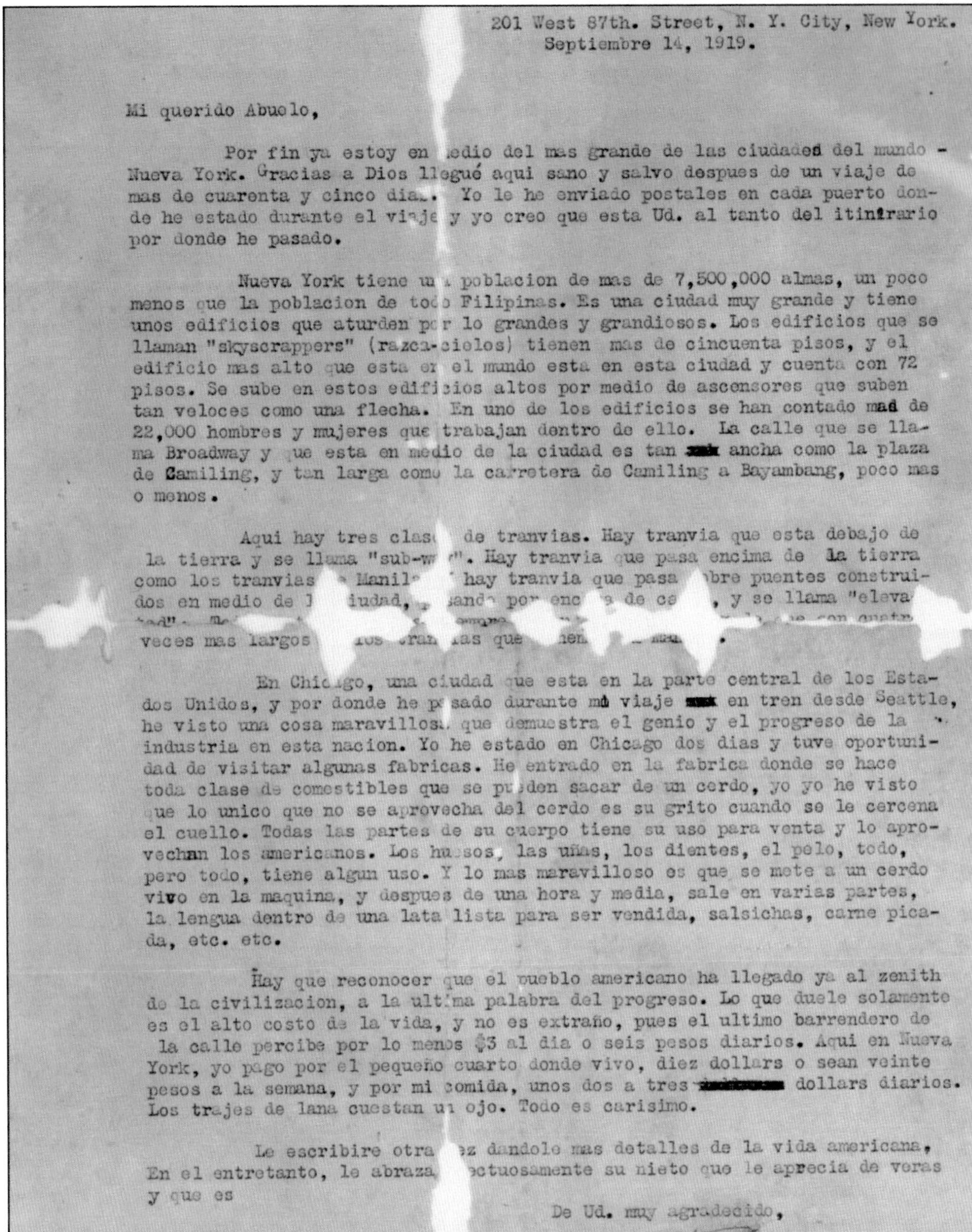

201 West 87th. Street, N. Y. City, New York.
Septiembre 14, 1919.

Mi querido Abuelo,

Por fin ya estoy en medio del mas grande de las ciudades del mundo - Nueva York. Gracias a Dios llegué aqui sano y salvo despues de un viaje de mas de cuarenta y cinco dias. Yo le he enviado postales en cada puerto donde he estado durante el viaje y yo creo que esta Ud. al tanto del itinerario por donde he pasado.

Nueva York tiene una poblacion de mas de 7,500,000 almas, un poco menos que la poblacion de todo Filipinas. Es una ciudad muy grande y tiene unos edificios que aturden por lo grandes y grandiosos. Los edificios que se llaman "skyscrappers" (razca-cielos) tienen mas de cincuenta pisos, y el edificio mas alto que esta en el mundo esta en esta ciudad y cuenta con 72 pisos. Se sube en estos edificios altos por medio de ascensores que suben tan veloces como una flecha. En uno de los edificios se han contado mas de 22,000 hombres y mujeres que trabajan dentro de ello. La calle que se llama Broadway y que esta en medio de la ciudad es tan ancha como la plaza de Camiling, y tan larga como la carretera de Camiling a Bayambang, poco mas o menos.

Aqui hay tres clas[illegible] de tranvias. Hay tranvia que esta debajo de la tierra y se llama "sub-w[illegible]". Hay tranvia que pasa encima de la tierra como los tranvias [illegible] Manil[illegible] hay tranvia que pasa [illegible]bre puentes construidos en medio de [illegible] iudad, [illegible] por enc[illegible] de ca[illegible], y se llama "eleva[illegible] [illegible] con cuatro veces mas largos [illegible] que [illegible].

En Chicago, una ciudad que esta en la parte central de los Estados Unidos, y por donde he pasado durante mi viaje en tren desde Seattle, he visto una cosa maravillosa que demuestra el genio y el progreso de la industria en esta nacion. Yo he estado en Chicago dos dias y tuve oportunidad de visitar algunas fabricas. He entrado en la fabrica donde se hace toda clase de comestibles que se pueden sacar de un cerdo, yo yo he visto que lo unico que no se aprovecha del cerdo es su grito cuando se le cercena el cuello. Todas las partes de su cuerpo tiene su uso para venta y lo aprovechan los americanos. Los huesos, las uñas, los dientes, el pelo, todo, pero todo, tiene algun uso. Y lo mas maravilloso es que se mete a un cerdo vivo en la maquina, y despues de una hora y media, sale en varias partes, la lengua dentro de una lata lista para ser vendida, salsichas, carne picada, etc. etc.

Hay que reconocer que el pueblo americano ha llegado ya al zenith de la civilizacion, a la ultima palabra del progreso. Lo que duele solamente es el alto costo de la vida, y no es extraño, pues el ultimo barrendero de la calle percibe por lo menos $3 al dia o seis pesos diarios. Aqui en Nueva York, yo pago por el pequeño cuarto donde vivo, diez dollars o sean veinte pesos a la semana, y por mi comida, unos dos a tres dollars diarios. Los trajes de lana cuestan un ojo. Todo es carisimo.

Le escribire otra vez dandole mas detalles de la vida americana. En el entretanto, le abraza afectuosamente su nieto que le aprecia de veras y que es

De Ud. muy agradecido,

On this page is a letter from Carlos Romulo to his grandfather, written in Spanish and dated September 14, 1919. It reads in part: "New York has a population of more than 7,500,000 souls, a little less than the population of the entire Philippines. It is a very big city and has buildings that are stunning . . . One goes up these buildings by means of elevators that rise with so much velocity, like that of an arrow. In one of the buildings they have counted more than 22,000 men and women who work inside of it." (Courtesy of the Carlos P. Romulo Foundation for Peace and Development.)

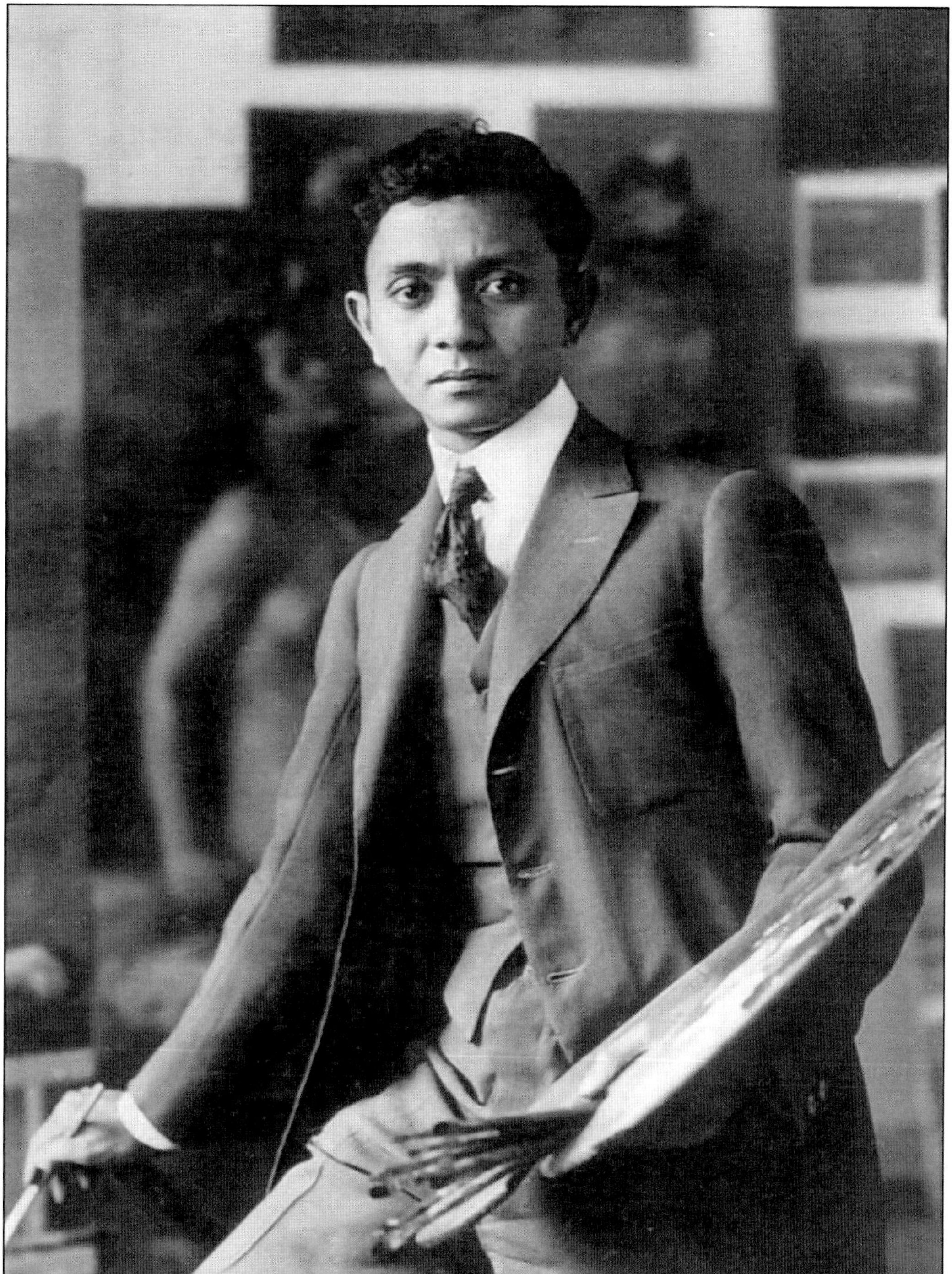

Fernando Amorsolo (May 30, 1892–April 24, 1972) is known as one of the most influential Filipino artists of all time. He specialized as a portrait artist and painter of rural Philippine landscapes. He first traveled through Ellis Island in 1919 and lived in New York for several years. (Courtesy of Fernando C. Amorsolo Art Foundation.)

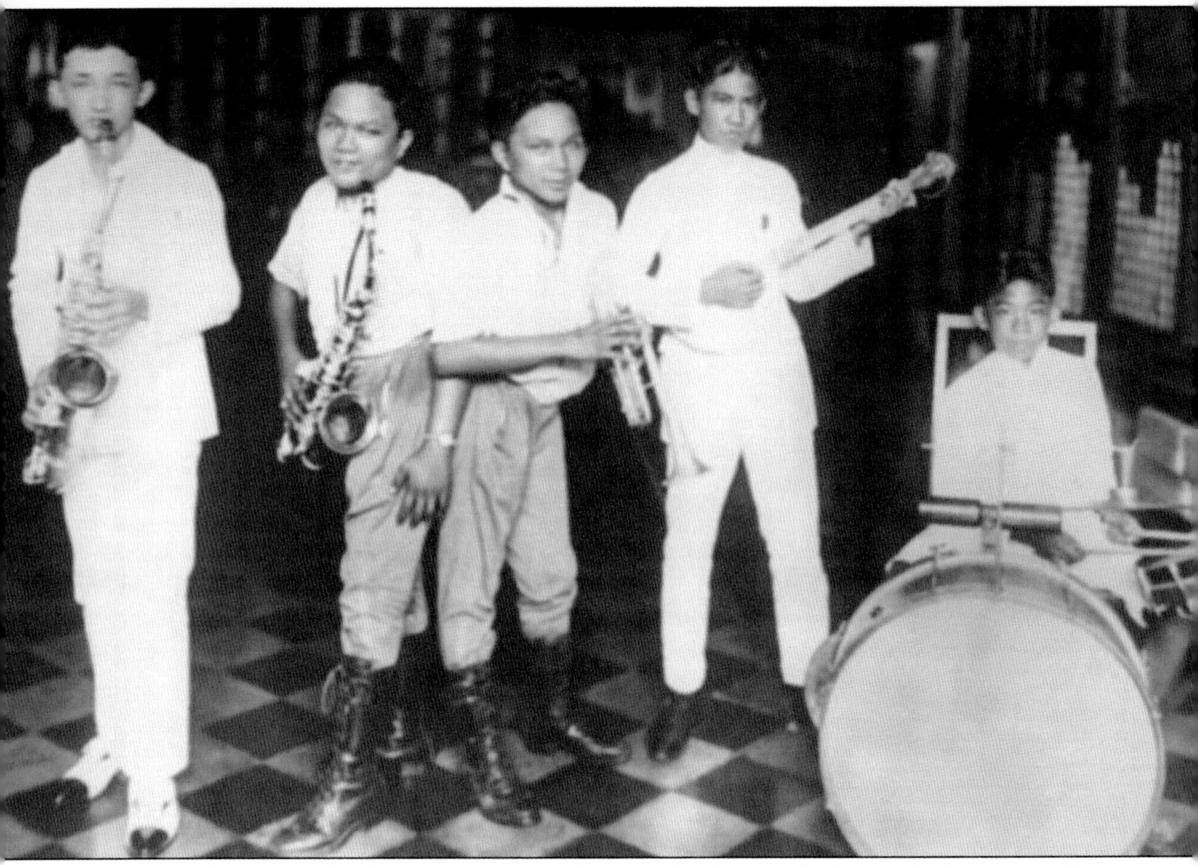

Lucio and Simplicio Godino were conjoined twins who first worked as a sideshow act at Coney Island when they were 11 years old. While it is unclear when they first arrived, Ellis Island records indicate that they came back to New York in 1924 when they were 16 years old. This photograph was taken in 1926, when they were approximately 18 years old. They later returned to the Philippines, where they met and married identical twin sisters. The two couples later returned to New York City, where they continued to work in the vaudeville scene. Unfortunately, one of the Godino twins developed pneumonia and died, and the other passed away shortly after. (Courtesy of Kadel and Herbert News.)

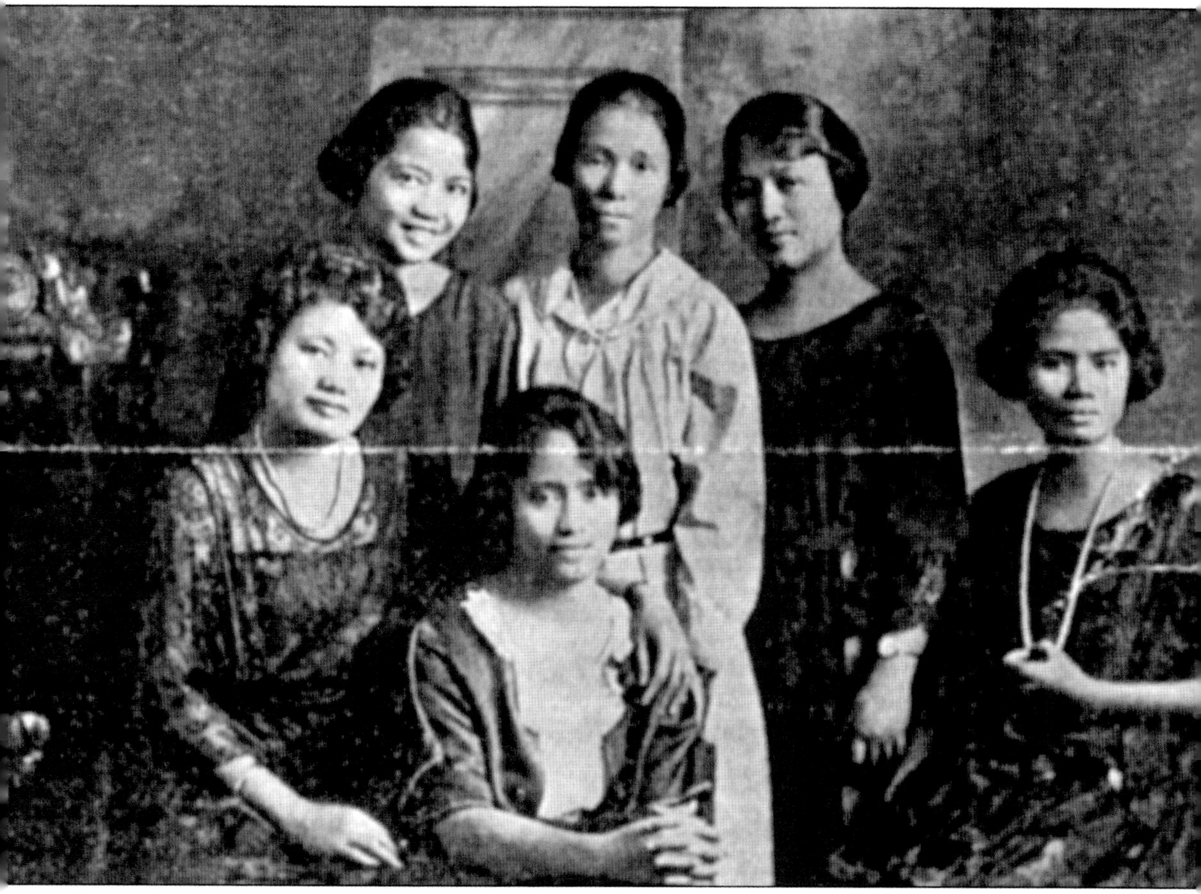

While the sponsored students who came to New York were predominantly male, this photograph indicates that there were some Filipina students as well. These Filipina students attended Teachers College, Columbia University, about 1922. The US government sponsored two of these students, while the Red Cross and Rockefeller Foundation sponsored the others. Pictured here, from left to right, are (first row) Romana Bumanglag, Josefa Abaya, and Irene Abelgas; (second row) Alberta Cabanos, Socorro Salamanca, and Paciencia Cornista. (Courtesy of FANHS National Archives.)

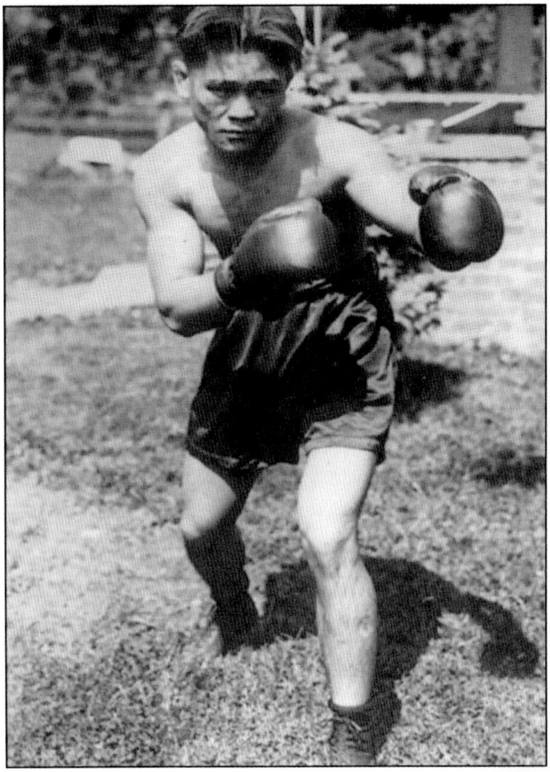

Pancho Villa (born Francisco Guilledo) was a Filipino professional boxer who resided in Brooklyn, New York, in the early 1920s. Pictured here about 1923, he first became popular when he won the World Flyweight Championship in 1923 at the Polo Grounds in New York. He died suddenly at the age of 23 following complications from a tooth extraction. Some still claim he was the "greatest Asian fighter in history." (Courtesy of Topical Press Agency/Getty Images.)

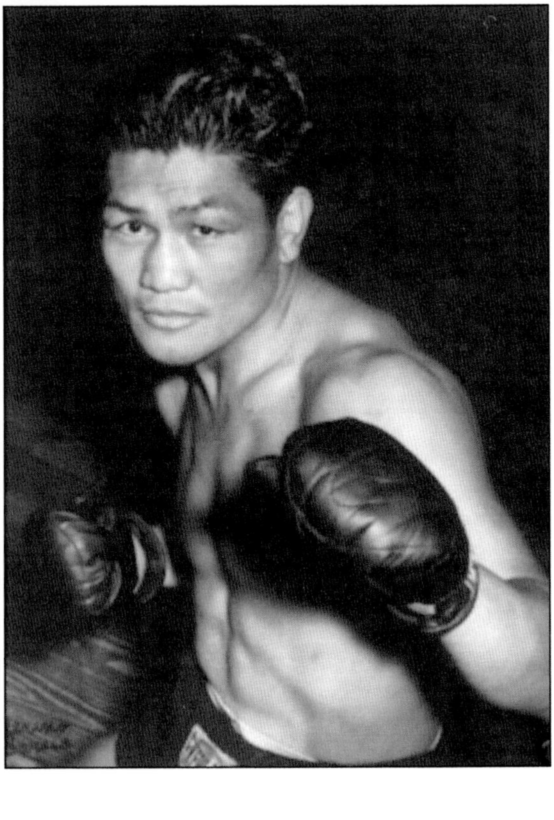

Cerefino Garcia was another Filipino boxer who spent time in New York in the 1930s and 1940s. Pictured here in 1939, he is known for holding the most victories ever achieved by a Filipino boxer and is also the only boxer from the Philippines to become world champion in the middleweight division. He won the NYSAC World Middleweight Title at Madison Square Garden on October 2, 1939. (Courtesy of Topical Press Agency/Getty Images.)

The *Philippine Herald* was a monthly journal published in New York City from 1920 to 1922 by the Filipino Students' Federation of America. The Filipino Students' Federation first gathered in at the apartment of Arsenio N. Luz (201 West Eighty-seventh Street), with participants Vicente Villamin, Dr. M.V. Arguelles, Issac Barza, and Carlos Romulo. Issues of the journal contain articles that were of interest to Filipino students who were studying abroad in the United States. (Both, courtesy of FANHS National Archives.)

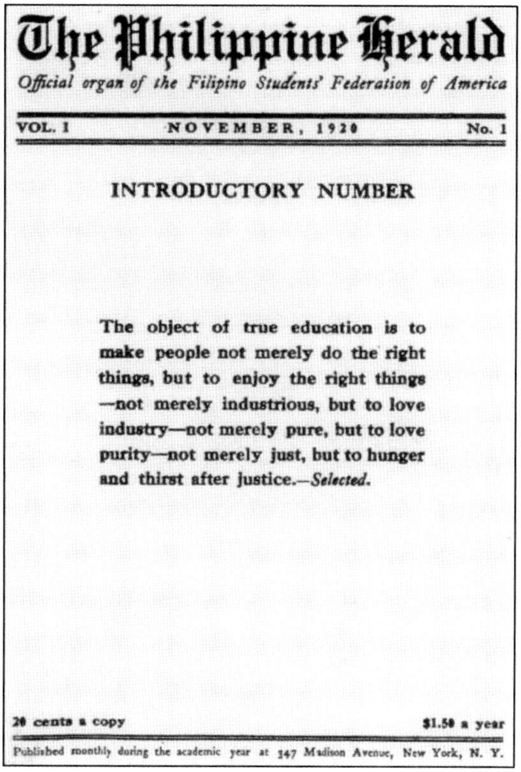

The Philippine Herald

Official organ of the Filipino Students' Federation of America

VOL. I — NOVEMBER, 1920 — No. 1

INTRODUCTORY NUMBER

The object of true education is to make people not merely do the right things, but to enjoy the right things —not merely industrious, but to love industry—not merely pure, but to love purity—not merely just, but to hunger and thirst after justice.—*Selected.*

20 cents a copy — $1.50 a year

Published monthly during the academic year at 347 Madison Avenue, New York, N. Y.

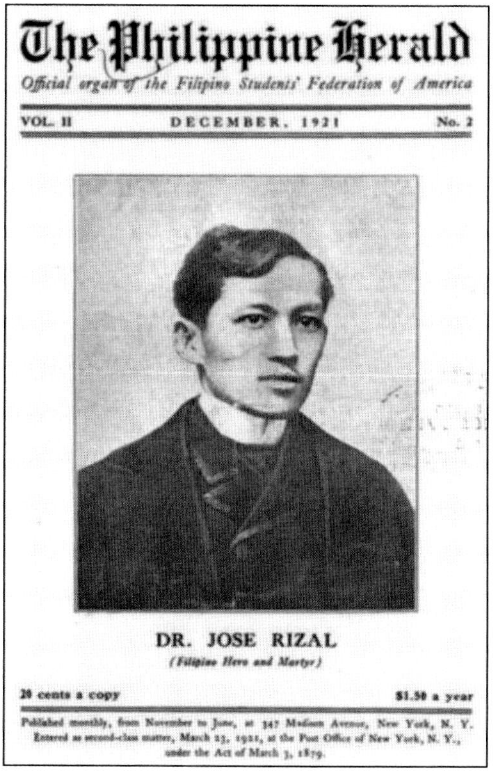

The Philippine Herald

Official organ of the Filipino Students' Federation of America

VOL. II — DECEMBER, 1921 — No. 2

DR. JOSE RIZAL

(Filipino Hero and Martyr)

20 cents a copy — $1.50 a year

Published monthly, from November to June, at 347 Madison Avenue, New York, N. Y. Entered as second-class matter, March 23, 1921, at the Post Office of New York, N. Y., under the Act of March 3, 1879.

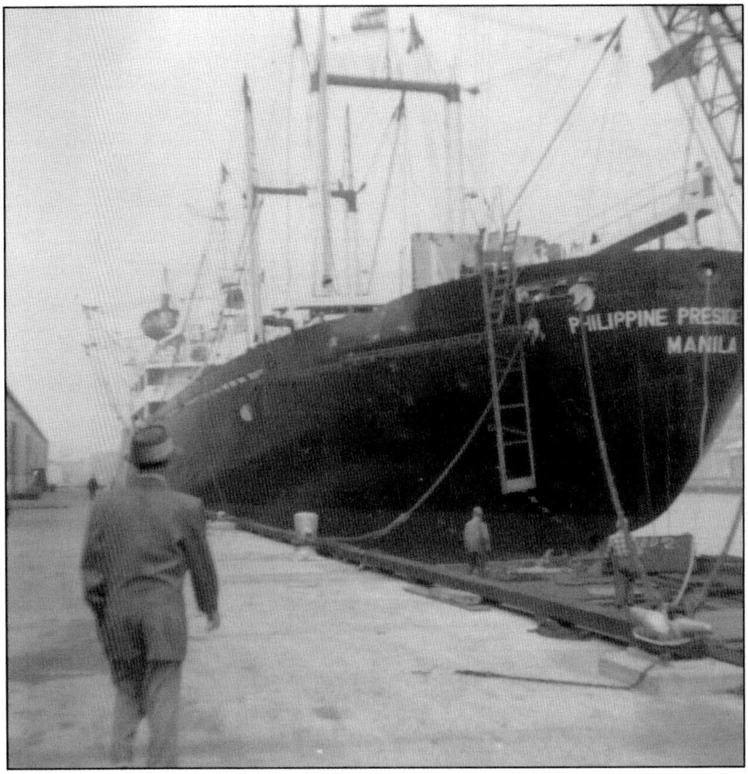

Some of the earliest Filipino Americans in New York were Navy seafarers who settled near the Brooklyn Navy Yards in the early 1920s. When they were not on ships, many of the sailors liked to dress in fancy suits and go dancing in the city. Pictured at left is one of the Navy ships that many Filipino sailors were aboard. Pictured below in the 1940s are, from left to right, John Rayola, Pio Fernandez, and Chris Modina in Long Island, New York. (Both, courtesy of the Alic-Fernandez family.)

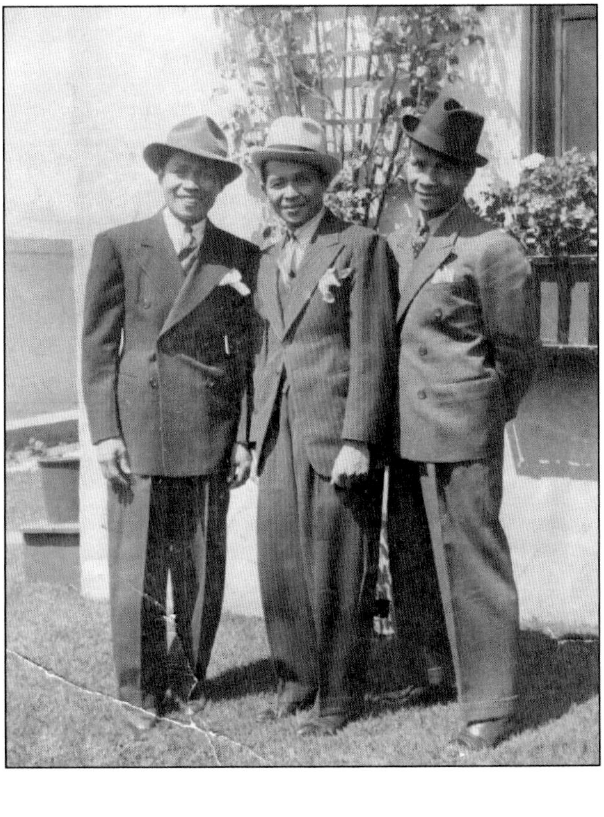

Pio Fernandez immigrated to the United States in the late 1930s after joining the US Army and serving directly under Gen. Douglas MacArthur as a houseboy or personal valet. Fernandez traveled on 10 different ships before finally landing in New York City. When General MacArthur died in 1964, Fernandez was quoted in the newspaper, describing his personal experiences with the general. At right is Fernandez in Pelham, New York, in the 1920s; below, he is with friends in the Catskills. (Both, courtesy of the Alic-Fernandez family.)

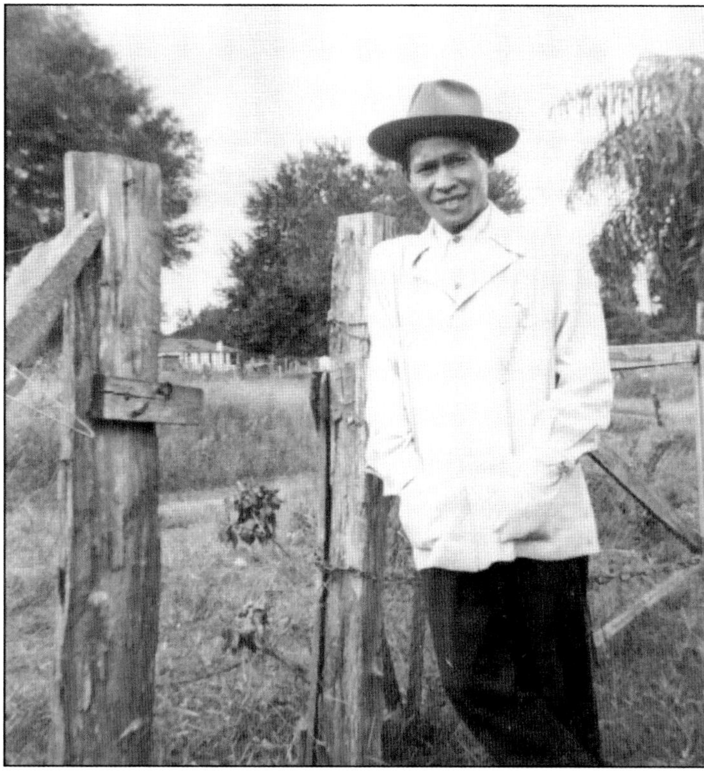

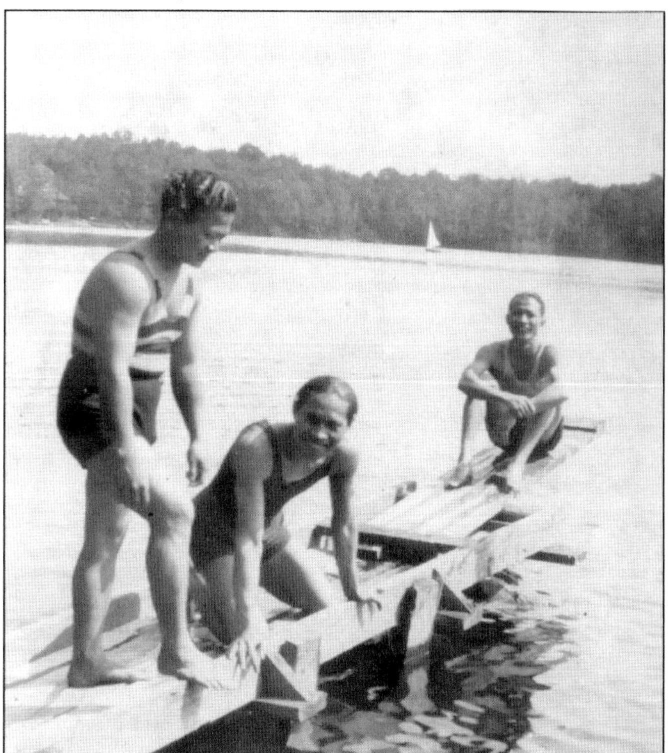

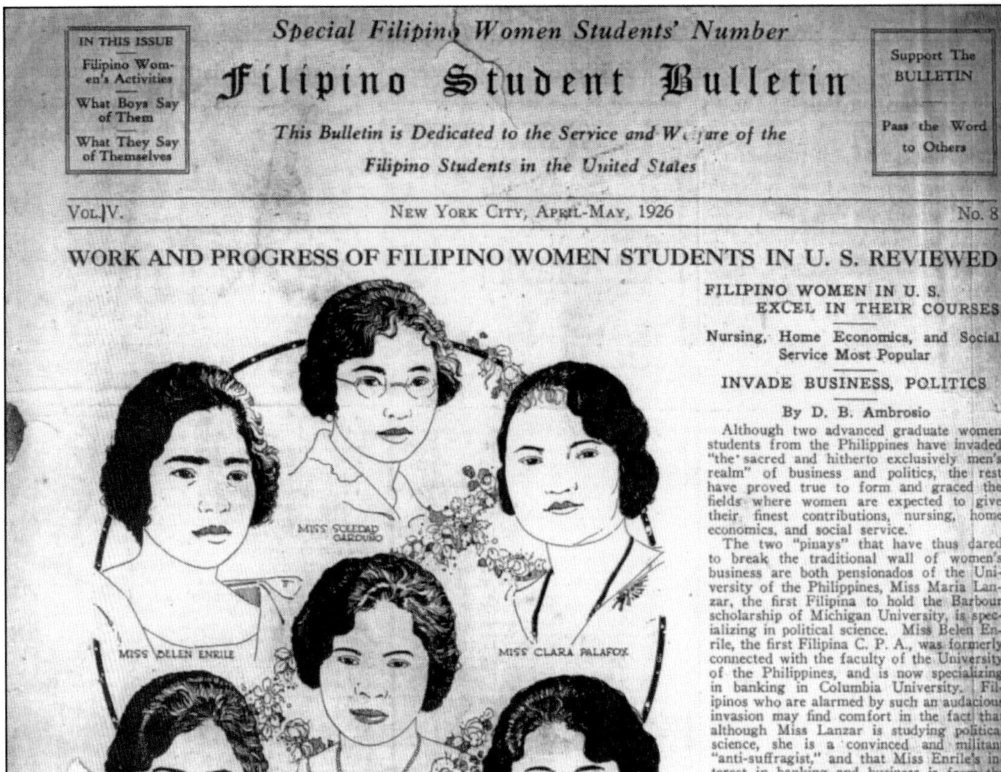

IN THIS ISSUE
Filipino Women's Activities
What Boys Say of Them
What They Say of Themselves

Special Filipino Women Students' Number

Filipino Student Bulletin

This Bulletin is Dedicated to the Service and Welfare of the Filipino Students in the United States

Support The BULLETIN

Pass the Word to Others

VOL. IV. NEW YORK CITY, APRIL-MAY, 1926 No. 8

WORK AND PROGRESS OF FILIPINO WOMEN STUDENTS IN U. S. REVIEWED

MISS SOLEDAD CARDUNO
MISS BELEN ENRILE
MISS CLARA PALAFOX
MISS DAMIANA DOLORICO
MISS IDA MC ILROY
MISS AMPARO FERNANDEZ

"PHILIPPINE FLOWERS" of NEW YORK CITY *As a Filipino Artist Sees Them*

Courtesy of MR. MANUEL REY. ISIP, *Filipino Artist*

FILIPINO WOMEN IN U. S. EXCEL IN THEIR COURSES

Nursing, Home Economics, and Social Service Most Popular

INVADE BUSINESS, POLITICS

By D. B. Ambrosio

Although two advanced graduate women students from the Philippines have invaded "the sacred and hitherto exclusively men's realm" of business and politics, the rest have proved true to form and graced the fields where women are expected to give their finest contributions, nursing, home economics, and social service.

The two "pinays" that have thus dared to break the traditional wall of women's business are both pensionados of the University of the Philippines, Miss Maria Lanzar, the first Filipina to hold the Barbour scholarship of Michigan University, is specializing in political science. Miss Belen Enrile, the first Filipina C. P. A., was formerly connected with the faculty of the University of the Philippines, and is now specializing in banking in Columbia University. Filipinos who are alarmed by such an audacious invasion may find comfort in the fact that although Miss Lanzar is studying political science, she is a convinced and militant "anti-suffragist," and that Miss Enrile's interest in banking and business is from the academic and scientific interest of a professorial chair. Anyway, they can both assure that they have not entirely abandoned "woman's highest ambition" of being some day "queen of the home," and that Cupid is not intimidated by apparently unromantic callings as business and politics.

(*Continued on Page* 2)

PEN-PICTURES OF NEW YORK "PINAYS"

By Vicente Mabakiao

"Women do not often have it in their power to give like men," said Mme. Necker, "but they forgive like heaven." What I shall say about our Filipino women was not given to me, but I trust I will be forgiven for my bold attempt.

An Apostle of Happiness

By a curious accident of birth a baby was born some years ago with this sign upon her forehead: "Keep Smiling." That was baby Clarita, now Miss Clara Palafox, a graduate student in Home Economics at Columbia University. Miss Palafox radiates cheer and sunshine. Let any one who doubts this statement read her article in the January issue of the FILIPINO STUDENT BULLETIN. She is a member of the Editorial Board of the Bulletin and an active member of the Filipino Students' Christian Movement.

(*Continued on Page* 2)

PINAYS CONSTITUTE ELEVATING INFLUENCE AMONG FILIPINOS

Lead in Social, Religious and Cosmopolitan Club Activities

SERVE ADOBO TO HOMESICK BOYS

That the Filipino girls constitute a very helpful and elevating moral influence among Filipino student communities in America is the consensus of opinion revealed in an unofficial study made by some members of the editorial board of the FILIPINO STUDENT BULLETIN. The "Pinays" generally assume the leading role in most social, religious, and cosmopolitan club activities in campuses and

WHAT OUR WOMEN ARE STUDYING

Home Economics	14
Social and Religious Work	6
Nursing Education	6
Special Students	6
Medicine	2
Music	2
Pharmacy	1
Banking	1
Political Science	1
High School	1

Manila, P. I.—Judge Jose Abad Santos, chairman of the committee of publicity of the National Supreme Council has been

The *Filipino Student Bulletin* was published by the Committee on Friendly Relations Among Foreign Students. The bulletin was "dedicated to the service and welfare of Filipino students in the United States." The earliest discovered issue was February 1923 (Volume 1, Number 3), and the last discovered issue was November–December 1937 (Volume 16, Number 1). (Courtesy of FANHS National Archives.)

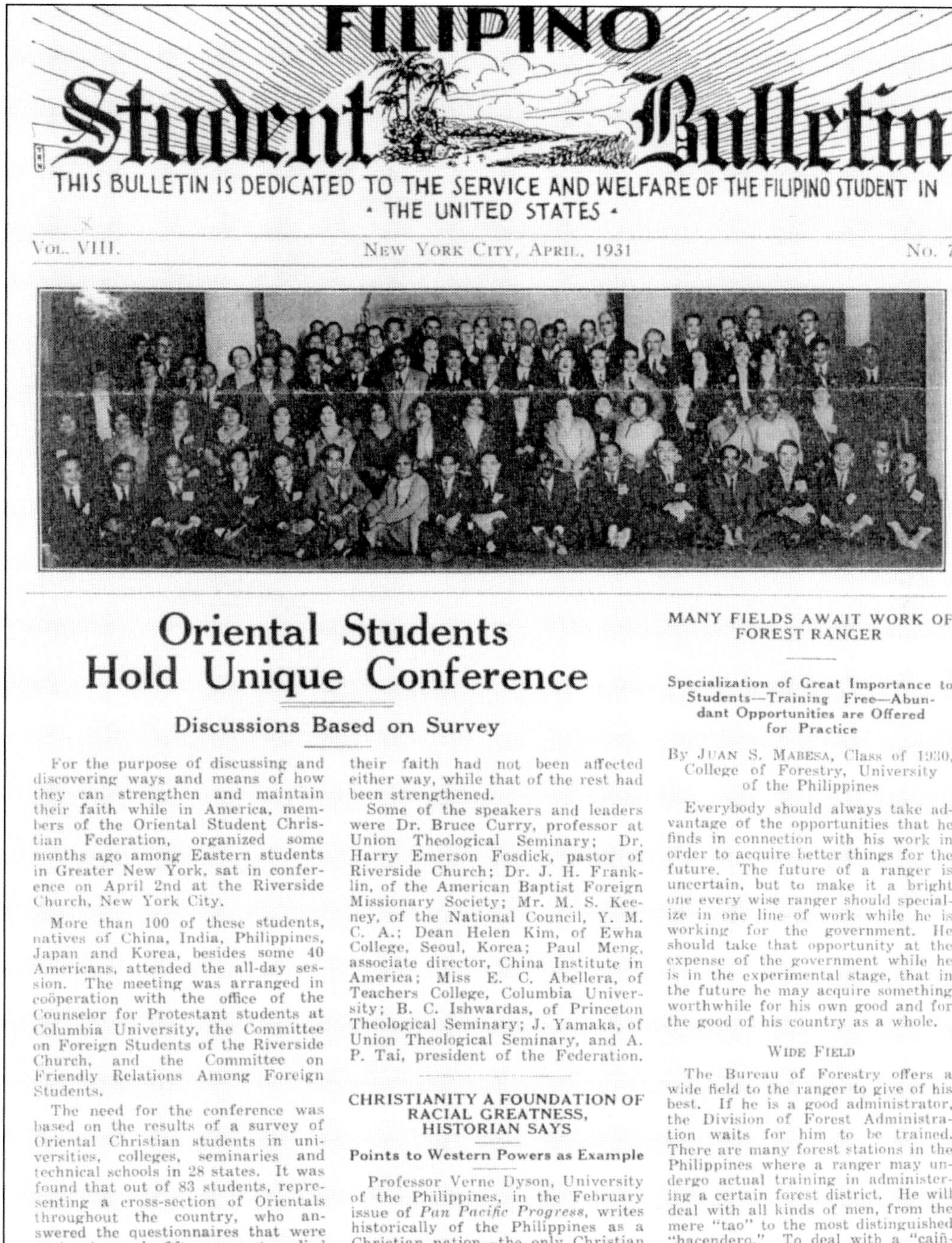

FILIPINO Student Bulletin

THIS BULLETIN IS DEDICATED TO THE SERVICE AND WELFARE OF THE FILIPINO STUDENT IN • THE UNITED STATES •

VOL. VIII. NEW YORK CITY, APRIL, 1931 NO. 7

Oriental Students Hold Unique Conference

Discussions Based on Survey

For the purpose of discussing and discovering ways and means of how they can strengthen and maintain their faith while in America, members of the Oriental Student Christian Federation, organized some months ago among Eastern students in Greater New York, sat in conference on April 2nd at the Riverside Church, New York City.

More than 100 of these students, natives of China, India, Philippines, Japan and Korea, besides some 40 Americans, attended the all-day session. The meeting was arranged in coöperation with the office of the Counselor for Protestant students at Columbia University, the Committee on Foreign Students of the Riverside Church, and the Committee on Friendly Relations Among Foreign Students.

The need for the conference was based on the results of a survey of Oriental Christian students in universities, colleges, seminaries and technical schools in 28 states. It was found that out of 83 students, representing a cross-section of Orientals throughout the country, who answered the questionnaires that were sent out, nearly fifty per cent replied that their faith had been weakened, their faith had not been affected either way, while that of the rest had been strengthened.

Some of the speakers and leaders were Dr. Bruce Curry, professor at Union Theological Seminary; Dr. Harry Emerson Fosdick, pastor of Riverside Church; Dr. J. H. Franklin, of the American Baptist Foreign Missionary Society; Mr. M. S. Keeney, of the National Council, Y. M. C. A.; Dean Helen Kim, of Ewha College, Seoul, Korea; Paul Meng, associate director, China Institute in America; Miss E. C. Abellera, of Teachers College, Columbia University; B. C. Ishwardas, of Princeton Theological Seminary; J. Yamaka, of Union Theological Seminary, and A. P. Tai, president of the Federation.

CHRISTIANITY A FOUNDATION OF RACIAL GREATNESS, HISTORIAN SAYS

Points to Western Powers as Example

Professor Verne Dyson, University of the Philippines, in the February issue of *Pan Pacific Progress*, writes historically of the Philippines as a Christian nation—the only Christian nation in Asia. He says:

(Continued on Page 5)

MANY FIELDS AWAIT WORK OF FOREST RANGER

Specialization of Great Importance to Students—Training Free—Abundant Opportunities are Offered for Practice

By JUAN S. MABESA, Class of 1930, College of Forestry, University of the Philippines

Everybody should always take advantage of the opportunities that he finds in connection with his work in order to acquire better things for the future. The future of a ranger is uncertain, but to make it a bright one every wise ranger should specialize in one line of work while he is working for the government. He should take that opportunity at the expense of the government while he is in the experimental stage, that in the future he may acquire something worthwhile for his own good and for the good of his country as a whole.

WIDE FIELD

The Bureau of Forestry offers a wide field to the ranger to give of his best. If he is a good administrator, the Division of Forest Administration waits for him to be trained. There are many forest stations in the Philippines where a ranger may undergo actual training in administering a certain forest district. He will deal with all kinds of men, from the mere "tao" to the most distinguished "hacendero." To deal with a "caiñginero" is a very different matter

(Continued on Page 4)

Each issue of the *Filipino Student Bulletin* contained images and updates that were submitted from all over the country. Because the bulletin was published in New York City, a majority of the articles focused on Filipino Americans in New York and on the East Coast. The address of the bulletin was listed as 347 Madison Avenue in Manhattan. Today, this address is the home of Metropolitan Transit Authority (MTA). (Courtesy of FANHS National Archives.)

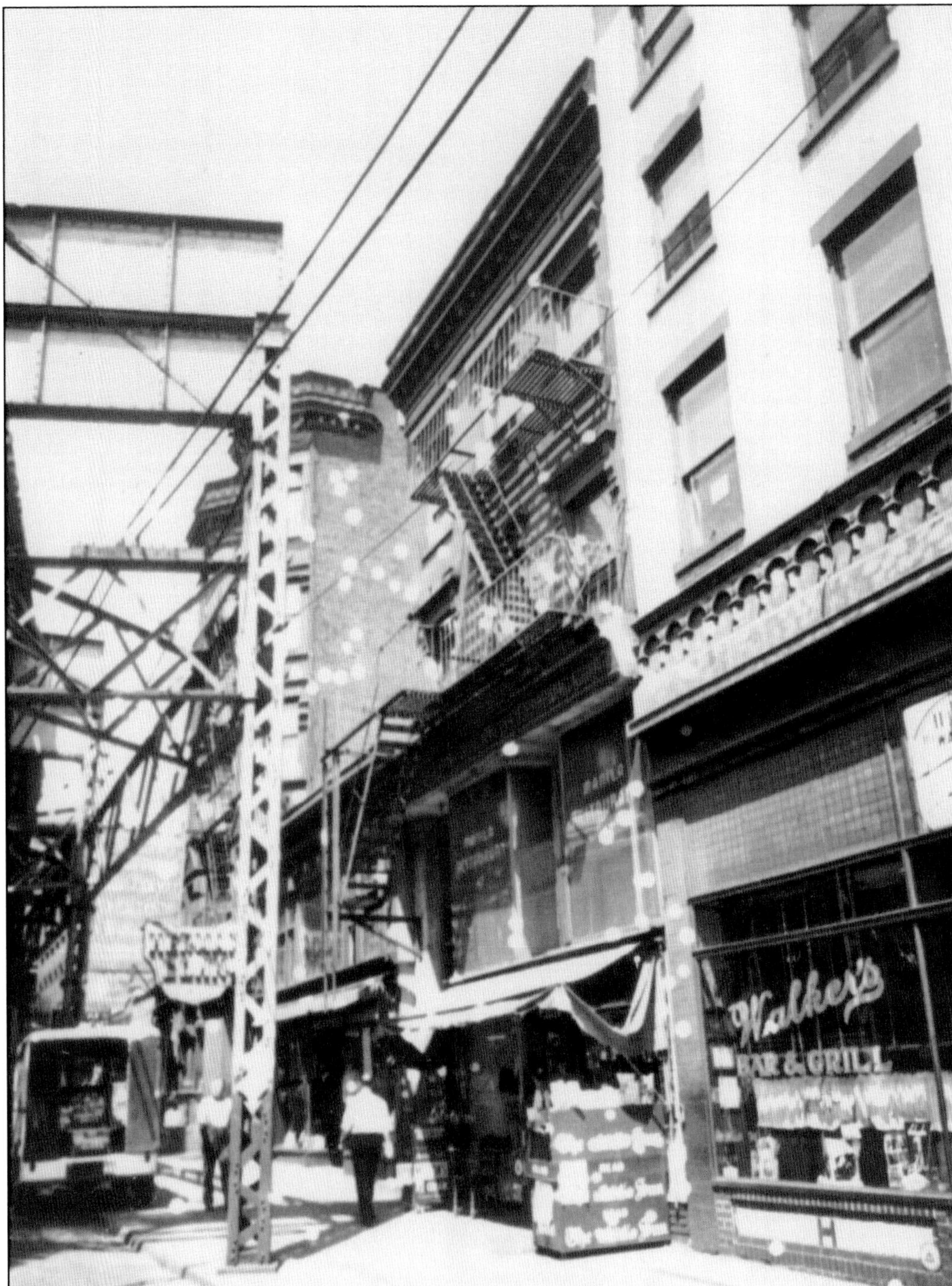

One of the first documented Filipino restaurants in the United States was the Manila Karihan Restaurant, located at 47 Sands Street in Brooklyn. Sands Street was located near the Brooklyn Navy Yards and was where many Filipino seafarers resided at the time. One famous resident of 47 Sands Street was Claudio Manela, a Filipino baseball player who was on the All-Cuban traveling team from 1921 to 1922. (Courtesy of the New York City Municipal Archives.)

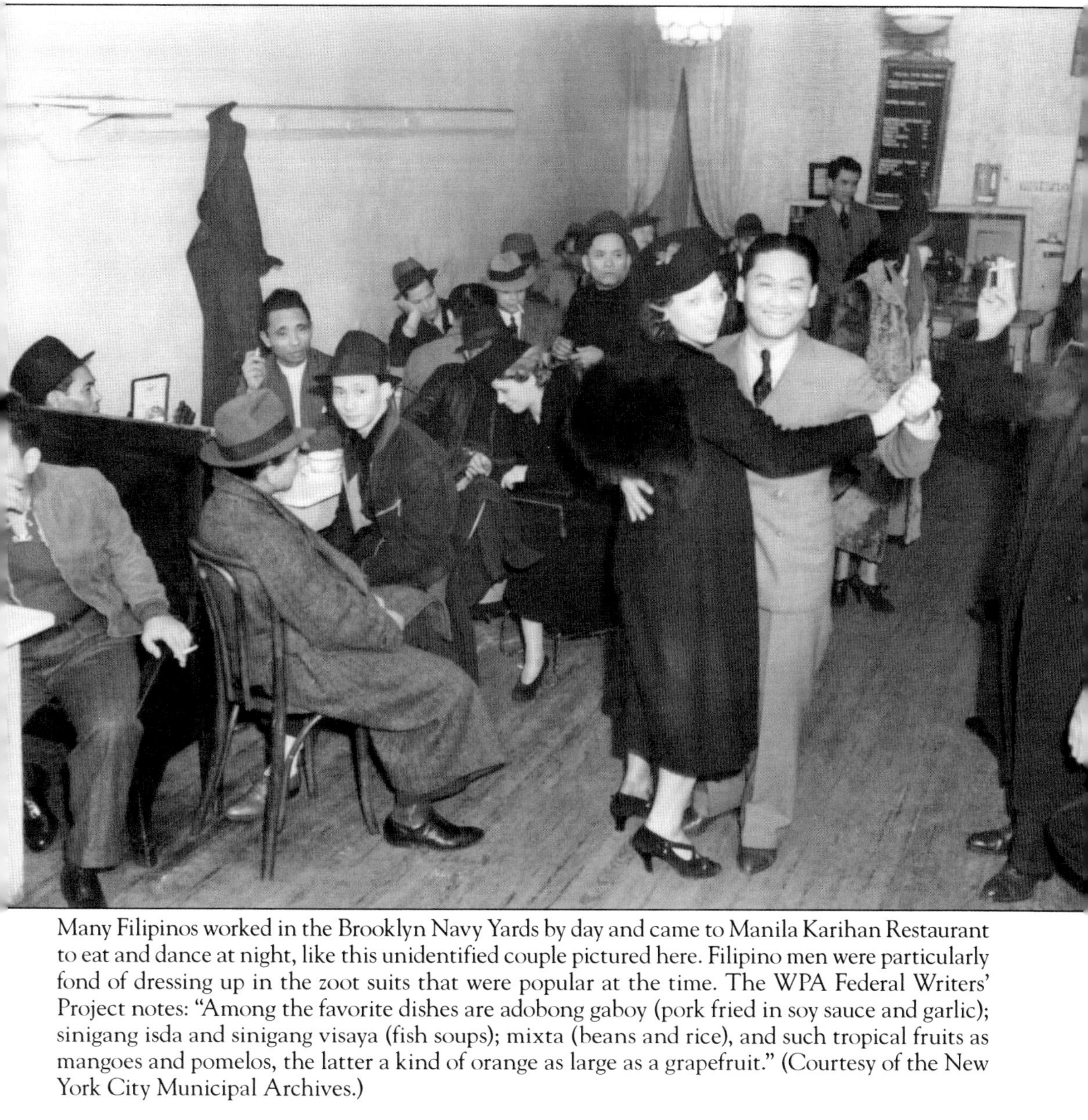

Many Filipinos worked in the Brooklyn Navy Yards by day and came to Manila Karihan Restaurant to eat and dance at night, like this unidentified couple pictured here. Filipino men were particularly fond of dressing up in the zoot suits that were popular at the time. The WPA Federal Writers' Project notes: "Among the favorite dishes are adobong gaboy (pork fried in soy sauce and garlic); sinigang isda and sinigang visaya (fish soups); mixta (beans and rice), and such tropical fruits as mangoes and pomelos, the latter a kind of orange as large as a grapefruit." (Courtesy of the New York City Municipal Archives.)

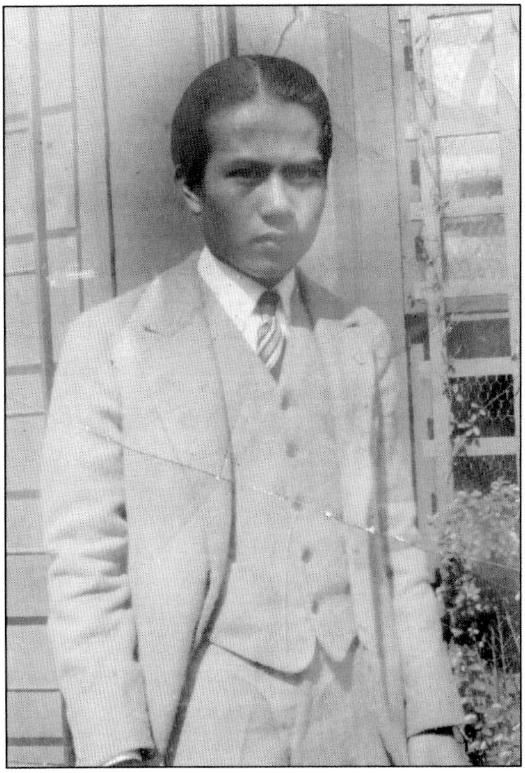

Faustino "Freddy" Yamba Campano was an immigrant from Mindanao who came to the United States and found homes in Brooklyn, Queens, and Manhattan from the 1930s until his death in 2000. Born in 1910 and orphaned as a child, Campano found his way on a US Navy ship as a steward and eventually fulfilled his dream of moving to New York City. He met and married an Italian immigrant, Anne, and they had seven children. In the photograph at left, Freddy is approximately 20 years old, about 1930; below, Freddy is pictured with his friend Richard in the 1930s. (Both, courtesy of Gerald Campano.)

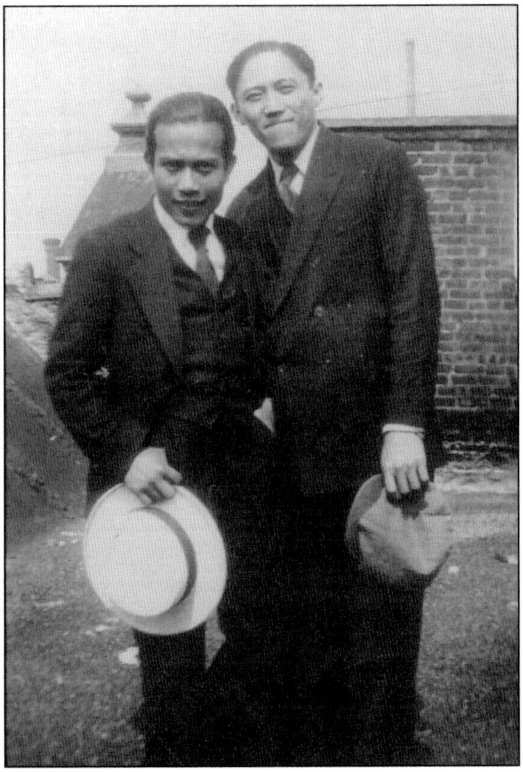

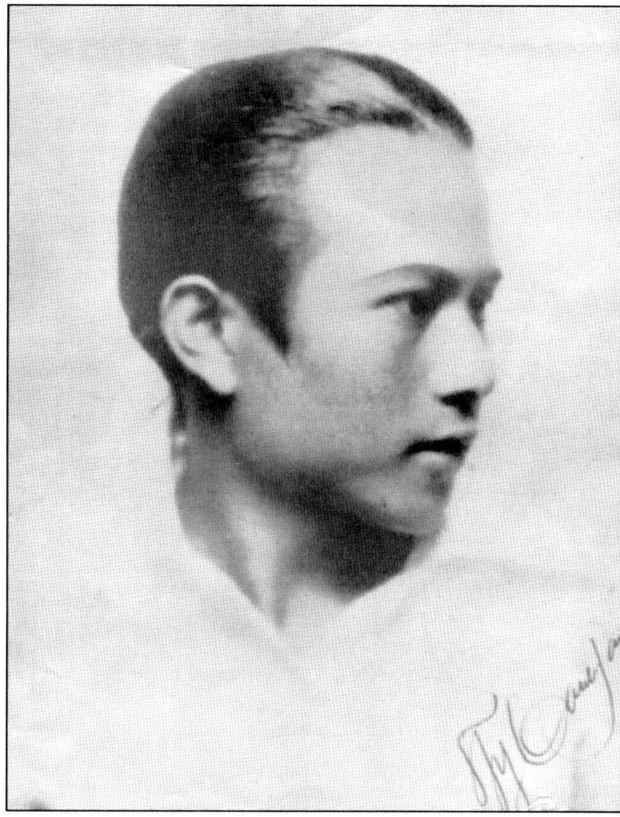

Freddy Campano formed two bands when he was in New York—the Luzon Travelers and Freddy Campano's Filipino Swing Orchestra. Pictured at right is a flyer from one of his shows in Sunnyside, Queens. Below, he is pictured with one of his bands in the 1940s. (Both, courtesy of Gerald Campano.)

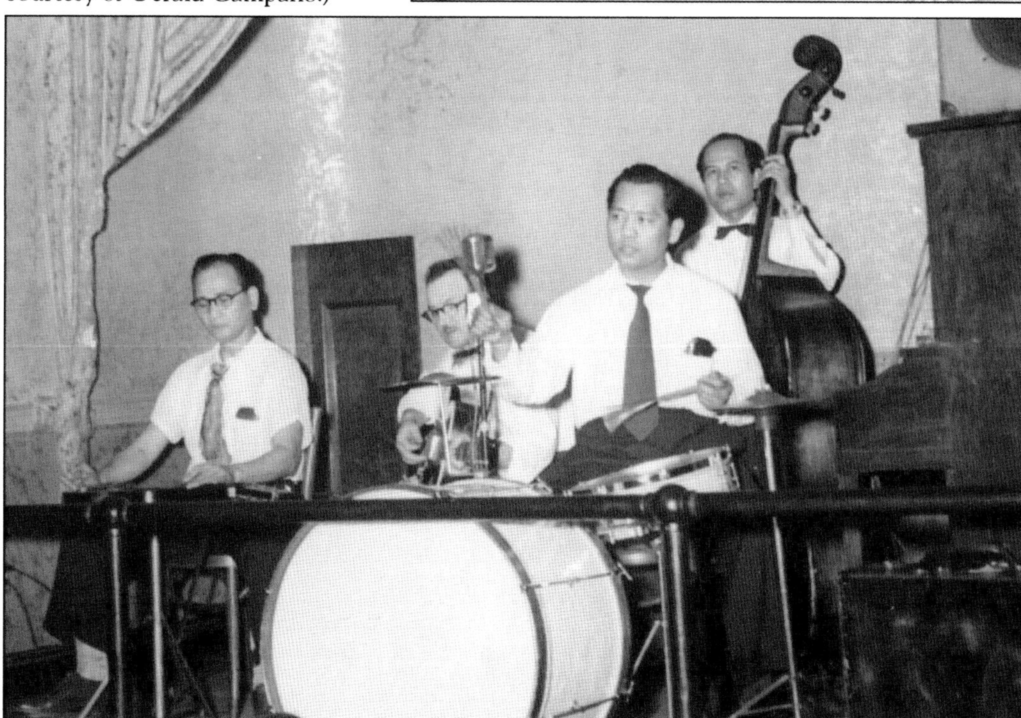

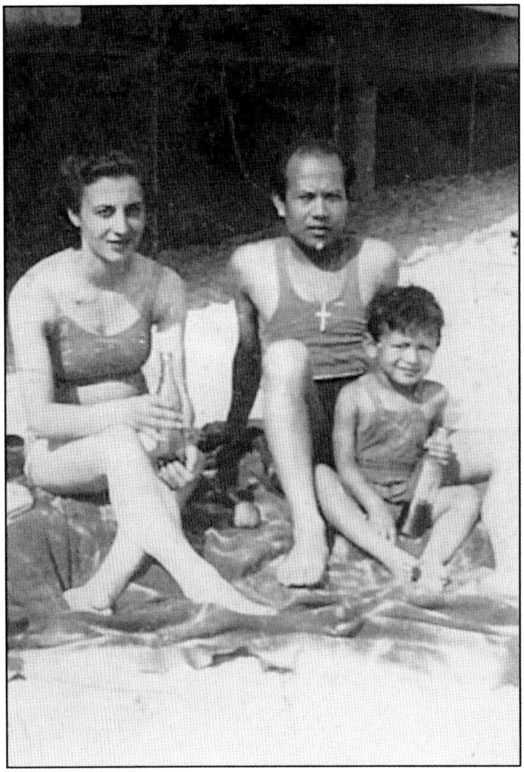

Campano raised his family mostly in Queens, New York. Pictured at left are Campano, his wife, Anne, and his eldest son, Fred Jr., at Coney Island around 1939. Pictured below are Campano and his son Fred Jr. on a rooftop in Harlem in 1938. (Both, courtesy of Gerald Campano.)

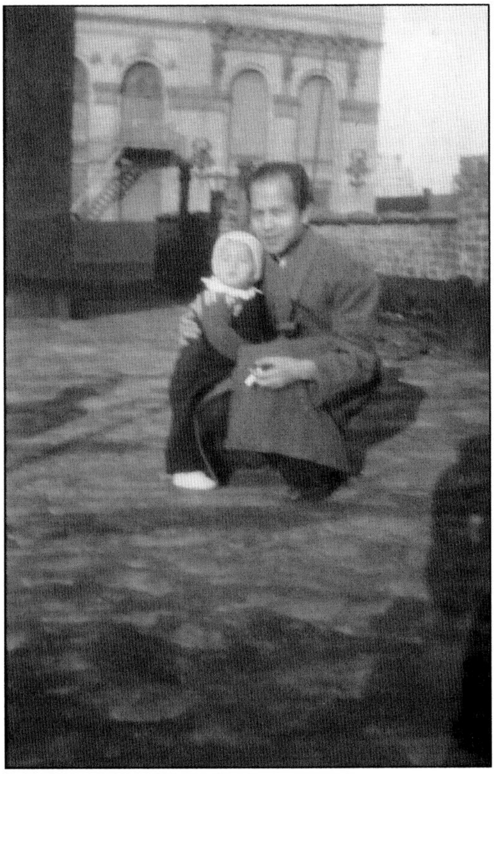

Two

Planting Roots in the Big City

World War II to the Immigration Act

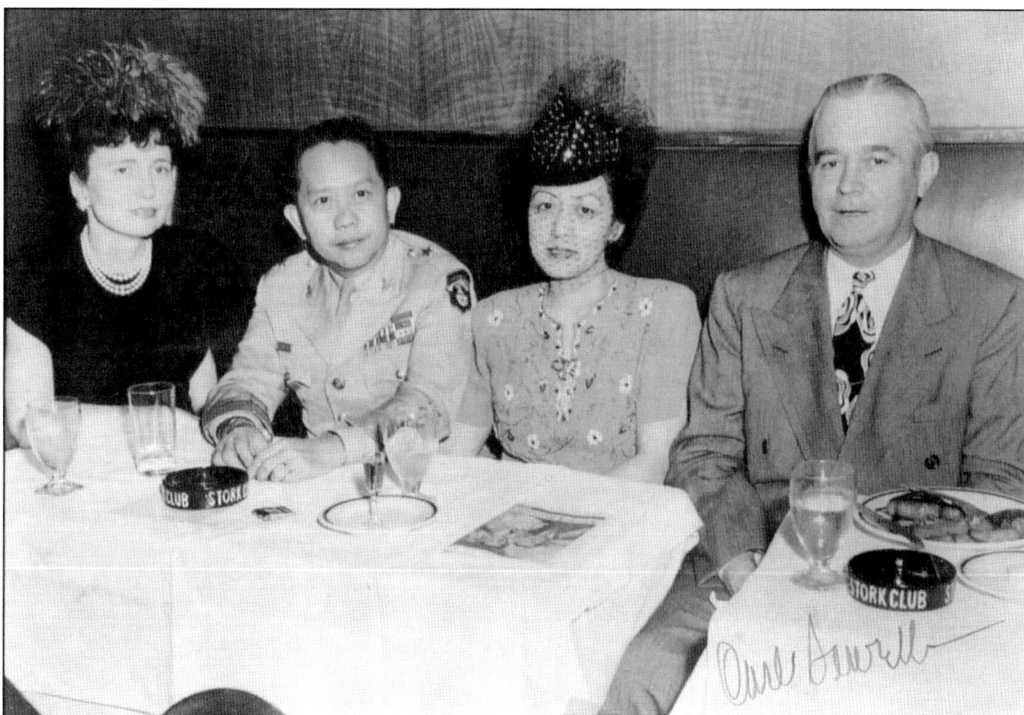

While there were a few Filipino Americans that immigrated to New York prior to World War II as students or as seafarers, many went back to the Philippines once they completed their studies or tours. There were some Filipinos who did settle in New York during this time and many who began to raise their families. From 1946 to 1965, there were still some Filipinos who came to New York as students and found employment in the United Nations. Pictured is Gen. Carlos Romulo at the Stork Club, about 1947, with his wife, Virginia Llamas Romulo (center), and Mr. and Mrs. Carl Sewell Sr. Mr. Sewell was a onetime deputy US marshal. (Courtesy of the Carlos P. Romulo Foundation for Peace and Development.)

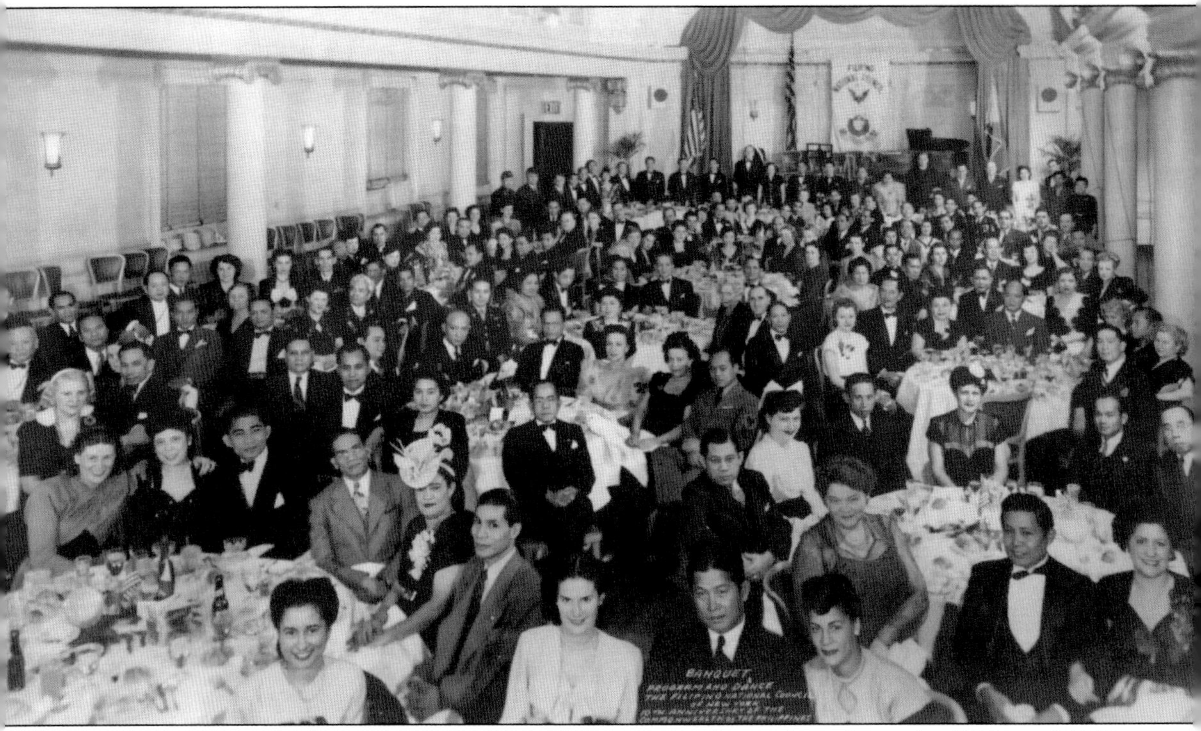

Filipinos continued to come to the United States as students throughout the 1930s and 1940s. Because there were very few Filipinos in the area, Filipinos tended to gravitate toward each other and form organizations, often inviting their other *kababayan* (countrymen) from different local states and cities. This photograph is of the Filipino National Council of New York at the Hotel McAlpin in the 1940s. (Courtesy of Angel Agesta.)

As personal guests of Thomas J. Watson of IBM and his wife, Jeanette, Carlos Romulo is pictured at the opening night of the Metropolitan Opera in November 1949. (Courtesy of the Carlos P. Romulo Foundation for Peace and Development.)

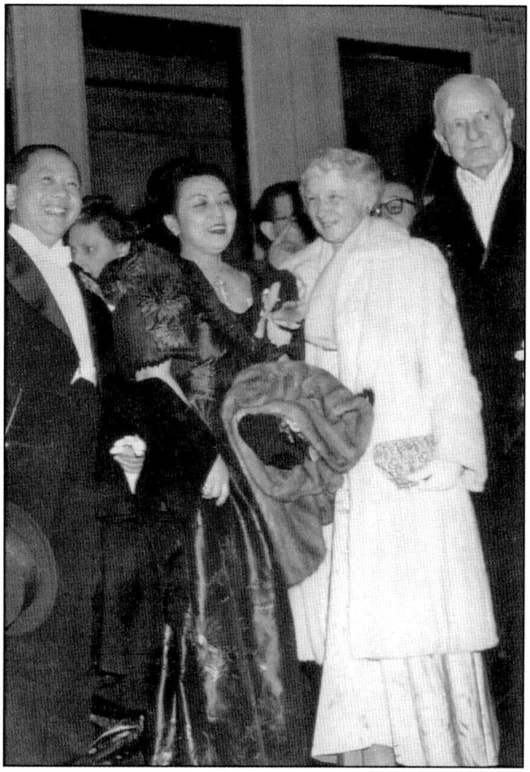

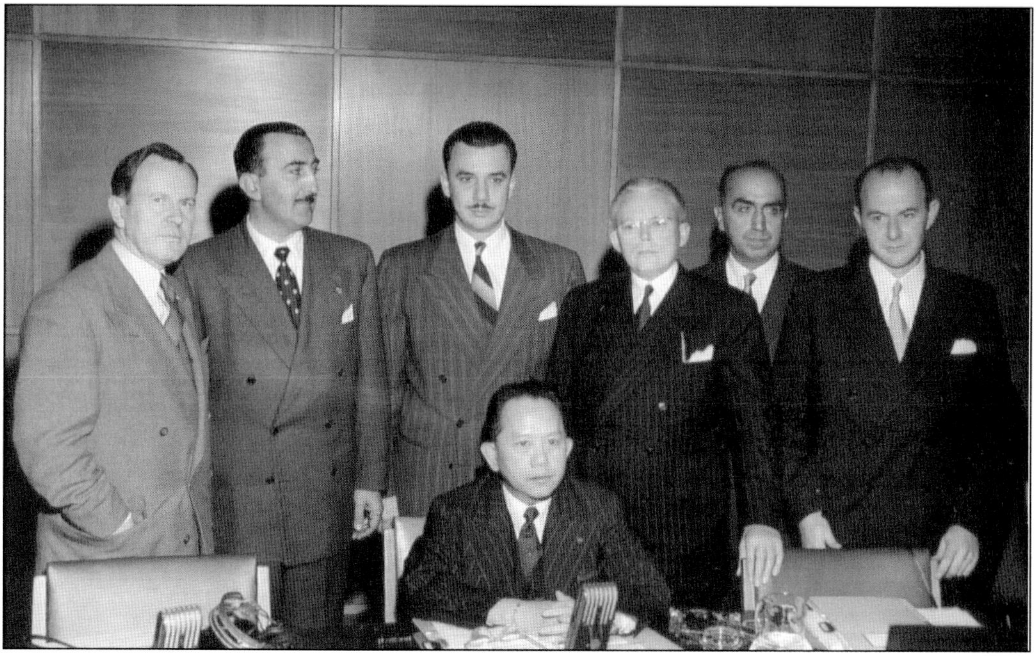

In 1948, Romulo was elected president of the general assembly to preside over the next session, with an overwhelming majority of 53 to 6. He envisioned "a world in which the conditions of peace and the conditions of life would be understood and upheld." (Courtesy of the Carlos P. Romulo Foundation for Peace and Development.)

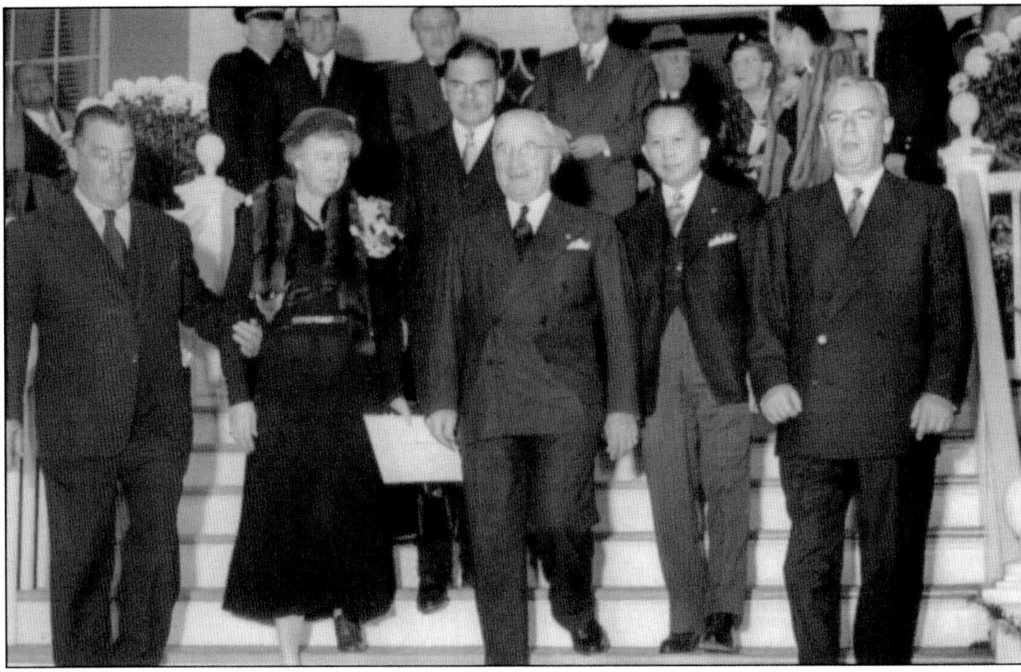

This photograph was taken outside of Gracie Mansion (the mayor's home) in Manhattan after a luncheon hosted by Mayor William O'Dwyer in honor of Pres. Harry S. Truman on October 24, 1949. Pictured here in the front row, from left to right, are Grover A. Whalen assisting Eleanor Roosevelt, President Truman, Carlos Romulo, and Mayor O'Dwyer. Following them is Gov. Thomas E. Dewey, and at top of steps, center, is Secretary of State Dean Acheson. (Courtesy of the Carlos P. Romulo Foundation for Peace and Development.)

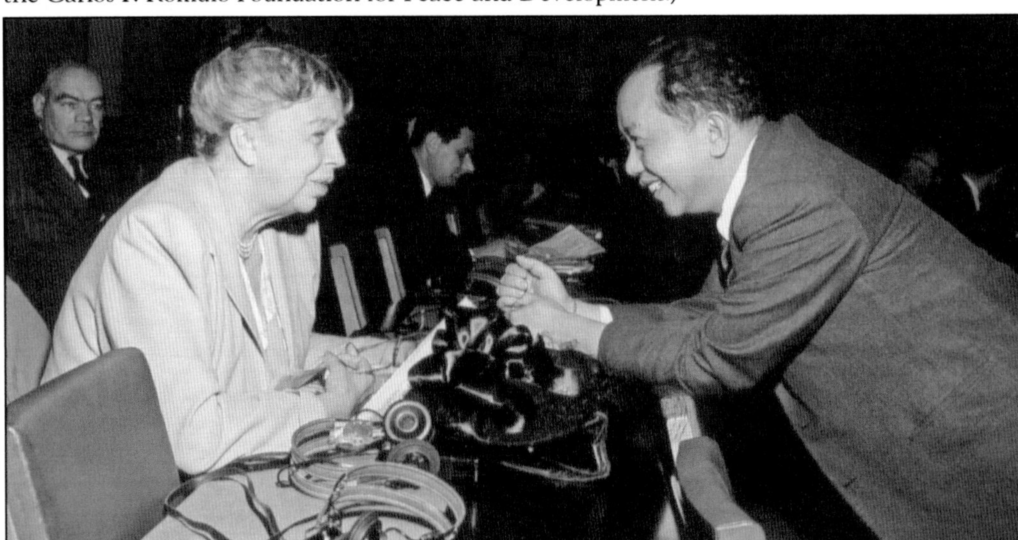

Pictured here is an informal meeting between Carlos Romulo and Eleanor Roosevelt in November 1947. Roosevelt had been chairman of the United Nations' Human Rights Commission since June 1946; her ambitious task was to draft a bill of human rights. Romulo served on the commission until the UN General Assembly finally adopted the Universal Declaration of Human Rights at the end of 1948. (Courtesy of the Carlos P. Romulo Foundation for Peace and Development.)

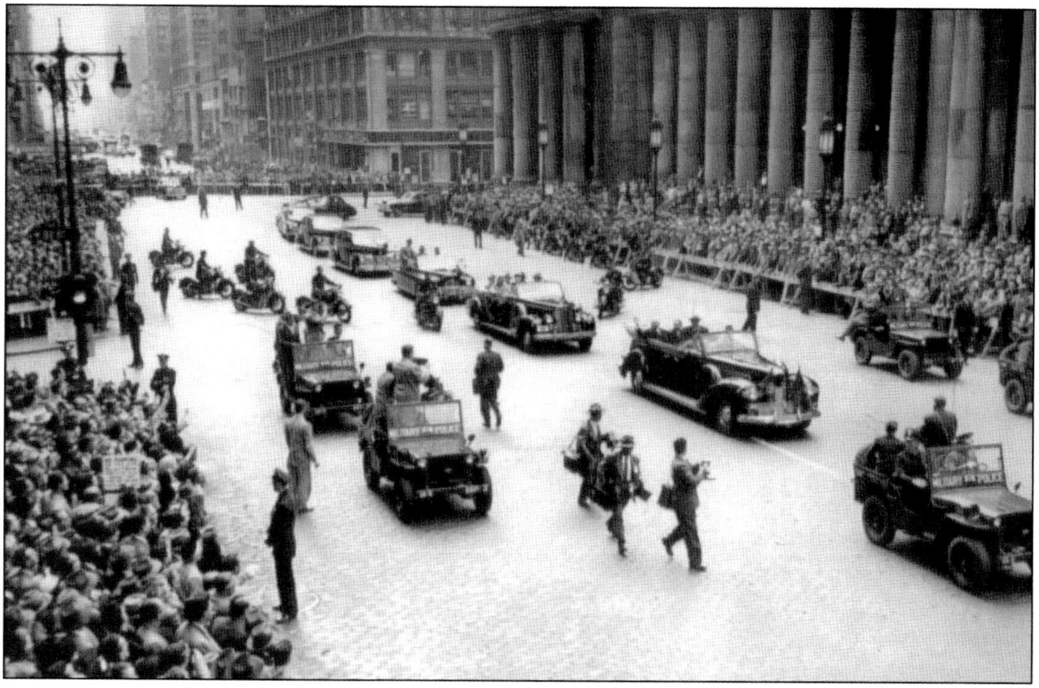

Pres. Harry S. Truman, Carlos Romulo, and New York's mayor William O'Dwyer (second car) ride in a ticker tape parade that ended at the site of the cornerstone-laying ceremonies for the permanent headquarters of the United Nations on October 24, 1949. As president of the general assembly, Romulo sat between Truman and O'Dwyer. Truman said to the mayor, "Do you realize you are the mayor of the greatest city in the world?" Truman looked at Romulo. "And the general here is the president of the world." (Courtesy of the Carlos P. Romulo Foundation for Peace and Development.)

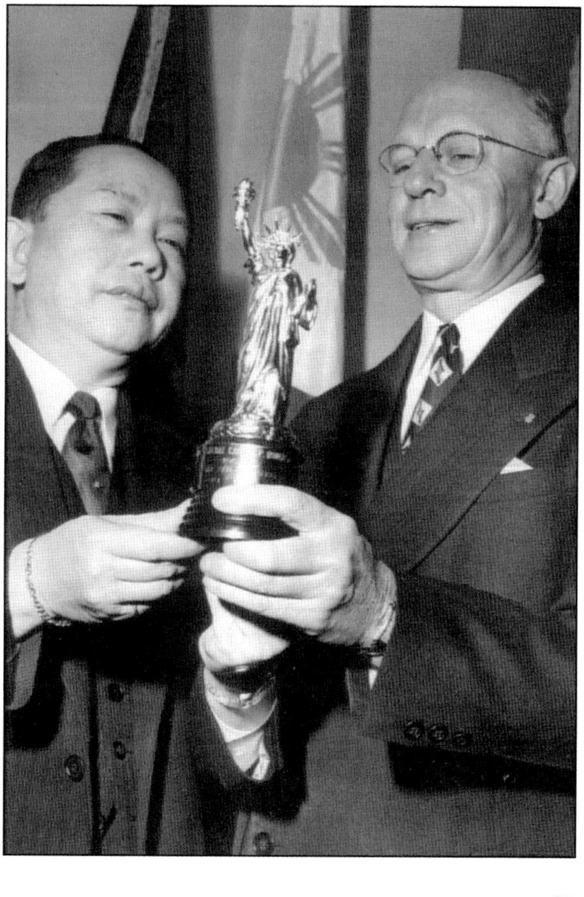

Chief Scout executive Arthur A. Shuck presented Carlos Romulo with a miniature of the Statue of Liberty in April 1950. The Philippines was the first independent nation to receive one of the 4,000 eight-inch statues—a gift to the Philippine Scouts from the Boy Scouts of America. (Courtesy of the Carlos P. Romulo Foundation for Peace and Development.)

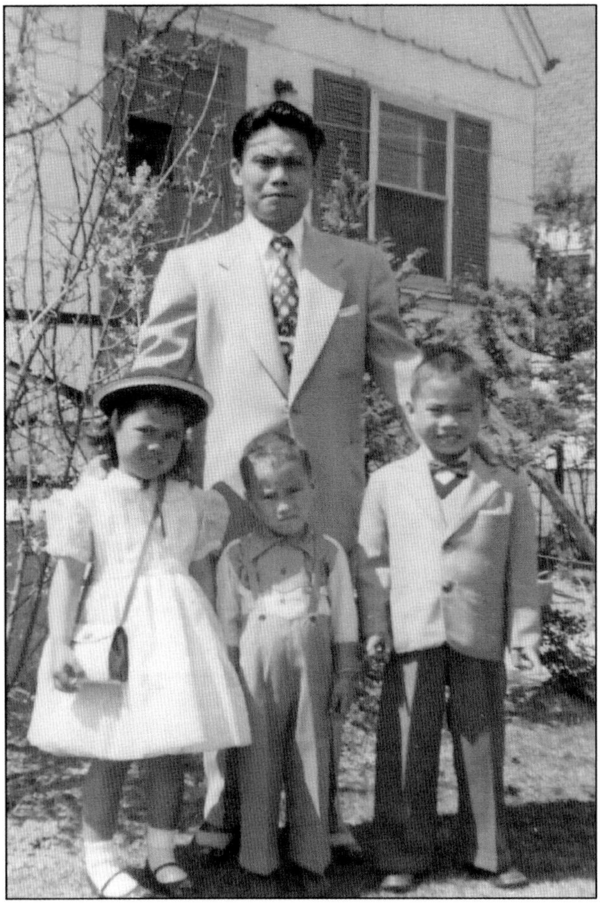

Natalio D. Tabaco was the first Filipino citizen employed by the UN Secretariat at Lake Success, New York, in 1946. Here, he is pictured standing in front of his home in New Hyde Park with his first three children, Joanne, Robert (center), and Joseph. Pictured below is Venancia Catay Tabaco, Natalio's wife, who first arrived to New York from Ubujan, Bohol, in 1947. This photograph was taken at the UN Building, which was then located in Lake Success. (Both, courtesy of the Tabaco family.)

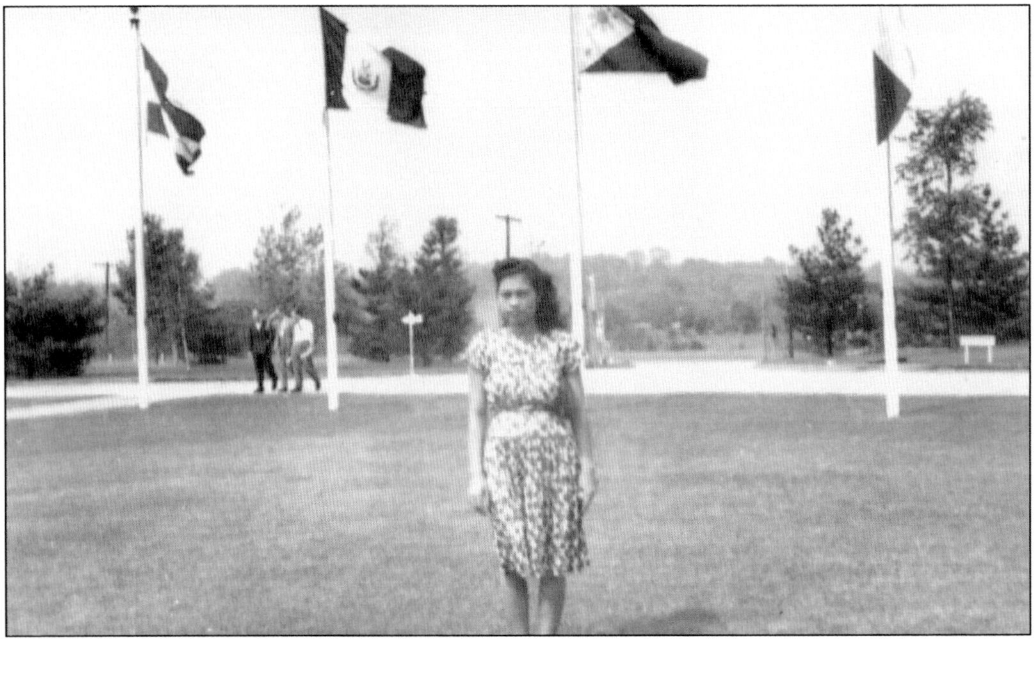

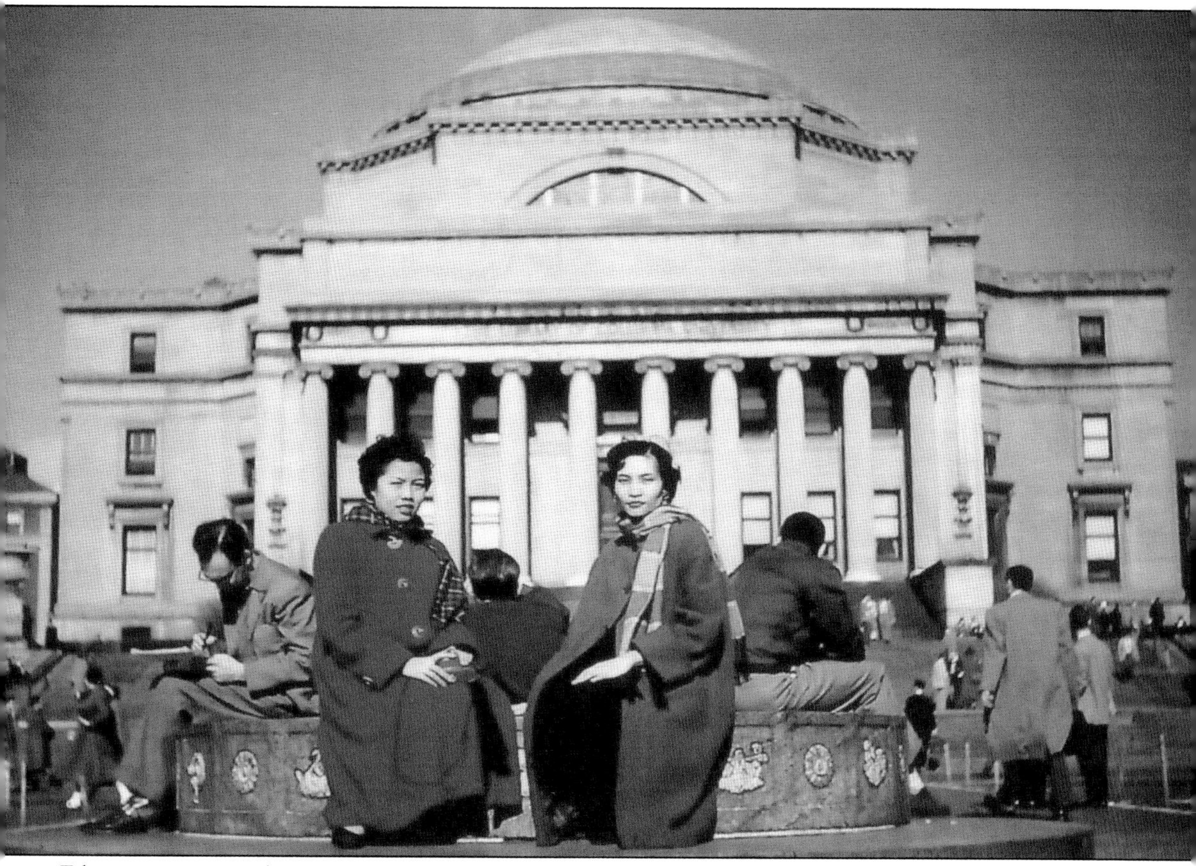

Filipinos continued to migrate to New York City as students at some of New York's prestigious universities. Pictured at Columbia University are two Filipina students, Mary Caluya (left) and Cecilia Espinosa, who were roommates there in the early 1950s. (Courtesy of the Sison family.)

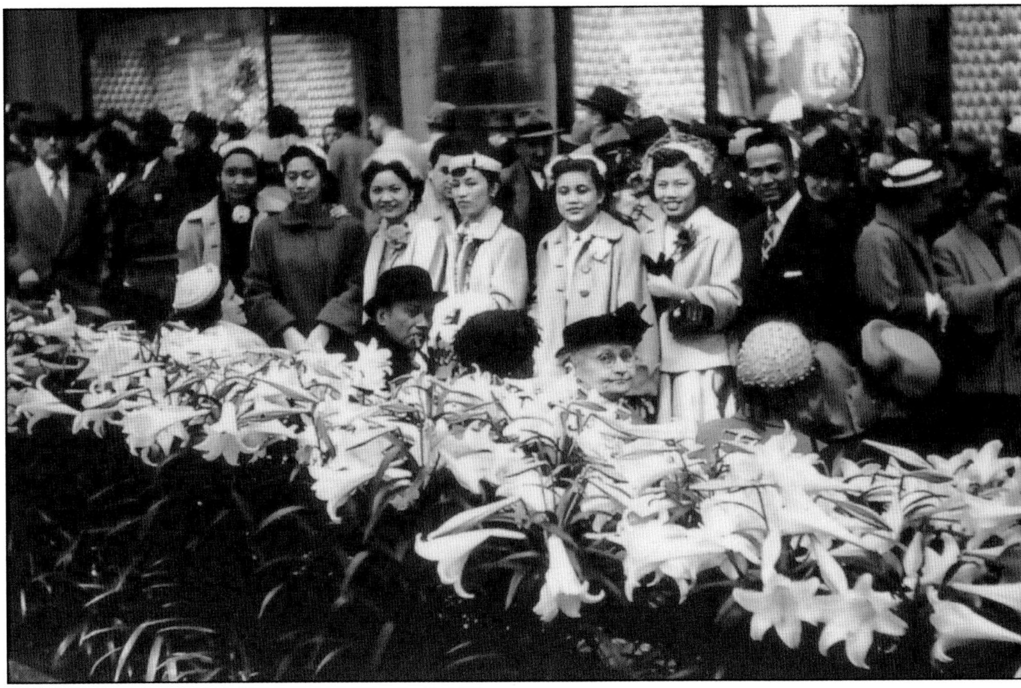

These photographs are from the annual Easter Parade at New York City's Rockefeller Center. Built by the Rockefeller family, Rockefeller Plaza is known for many things, including Radio City Music Hall, the annual Christmas tree, and the bronze statue of the Greek legend Prometheus. In the photograph above are sisters Cecilia (first on left) and Carmen Espinosa (fifth from left), and their friends at the Easter Parade in 1953. In the image below are Carmen (left) and Cecilia Espinosa (third from left), along with their other sister Pacita and Cecilia's future husband Bienvenido Sison Jr. (Both, courtesy of the Sison family.)

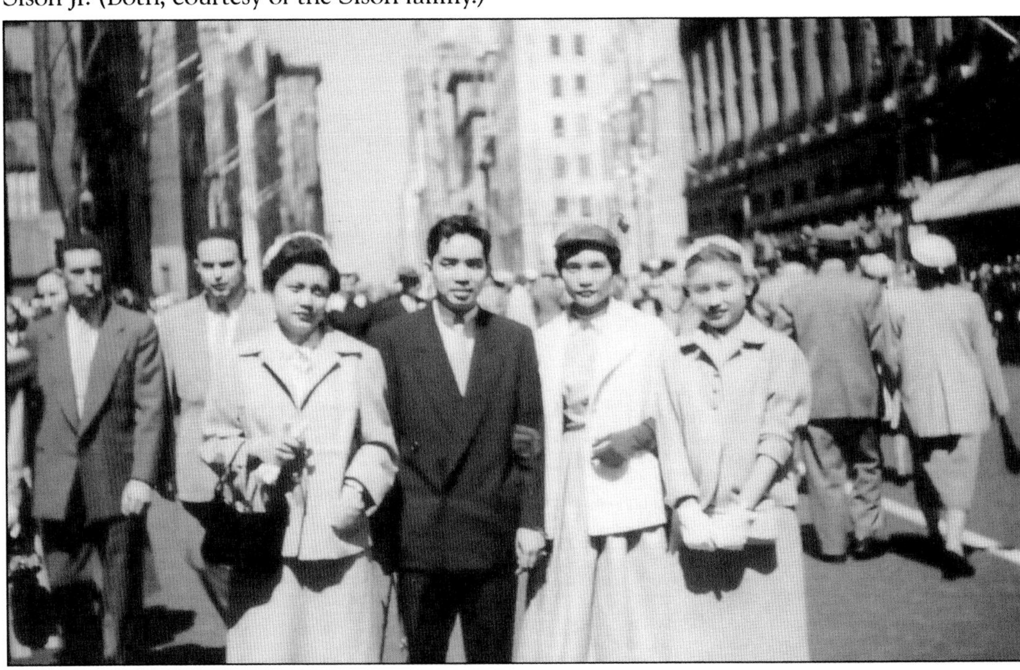

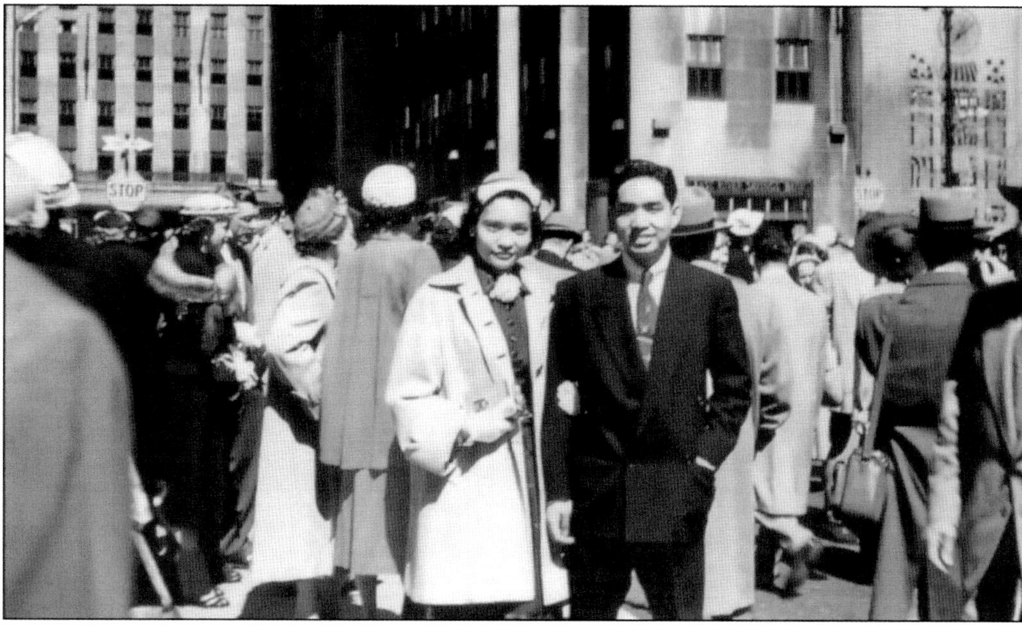

Pictured here are Cecilia Espinosa and Bienvenido C. Sison Jr. in Rockefeller Center after the Easter Parade in 1953. They were dating at the time the photograph was taken and later married and had several children. (Courtesy of Sison family.)

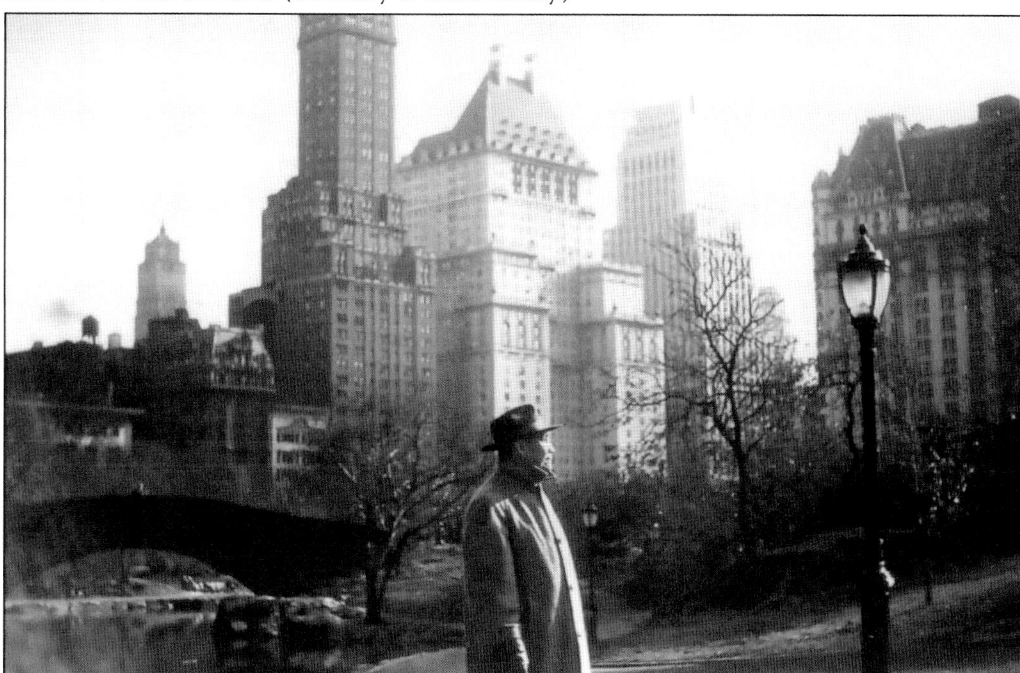

This is a photograph that Cecilia Espinosa-Sison took of her father, Jose Espinosa, also known as "Lolo Pepe," a Filipino who worked at the registrar's office as a student at MIT and was a 1922 graduate. He returned to the Philippines to become a pioneering chemical engineer. In 1952, he took his daughters back to the United States to attend graduate school at Columbia University. (Courtesy of the Sison family.)

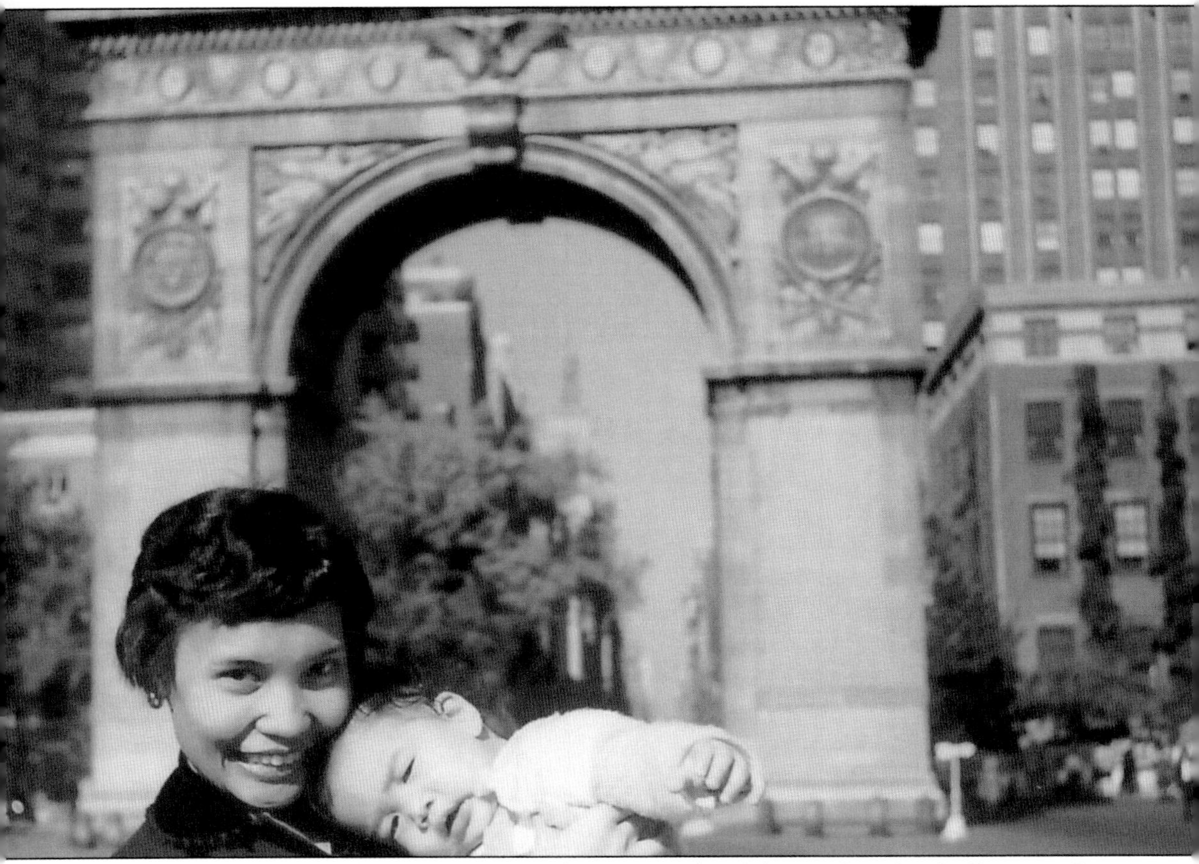

Jose Espinosa Sison was born in 1955. Here, he is pictured with his mother, Cecilia Espinosa-Sison, at Washington Square Park in Manhattan's Greenwich Village. The Washington Arch, located in the northern part of the park, was constructed in 1892 to celebrate the centennial anniversary of George Washington as president of the United States. The Washington Arch still stands today, near New York University, and serves as a classic monument in New York City. Bienvenido Sison Jr., proud father and husband, captured this photograph. (Courtesy of the Sison family.)

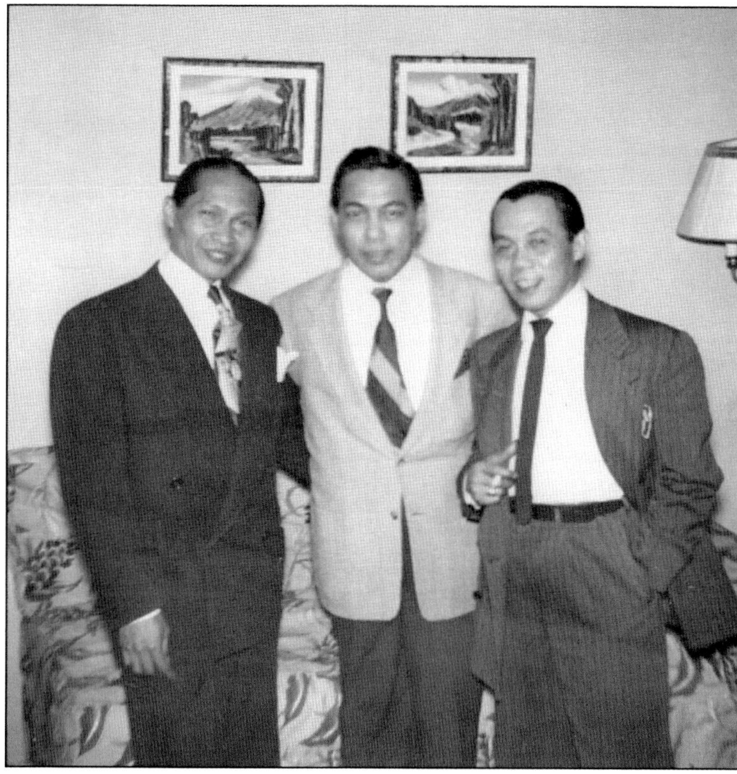

Filipino seafarers traveled all over the world on Navy ships, working predominantly as stewards and assistants. When they docked in the United States, a majority resided near the Brooklyn Navy Yards; however, several found homes in other boroughs of New York as well. Pictured here are Pio Fernandez (left), Gene Caro (center), and Jay Matapang at Fernandez's apartment in Astoria, Queens, about 1952. (Courtesy of the Alic-Fernandez family.)

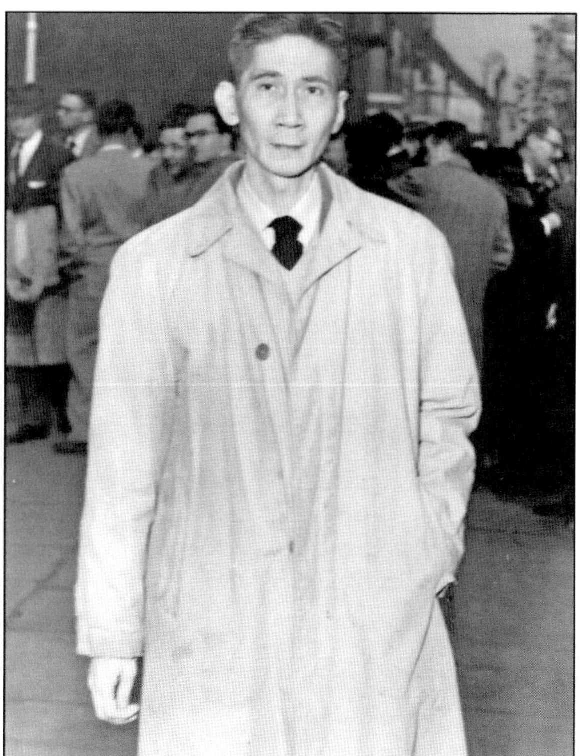

Jose Garcia Villa was a Filipino poet, writer, and literary critic who resided in the West Village of New York City for most of his adult life. He was awarded the National Artist of the Philippines title for literature in 1973 as well as a Guggenheim Fellowship in creative writing. Some of his books include *Philippine Short Stories* (1929), *Footnote to Youth* (1933), *Have Come, Am Here* (1941), and *A Doveglion Book of Philippine Poetry* (1962). This photograph was taken in 1953. (Photograph by Walter Albertin, courtesy of *New York World-Telegram*.)

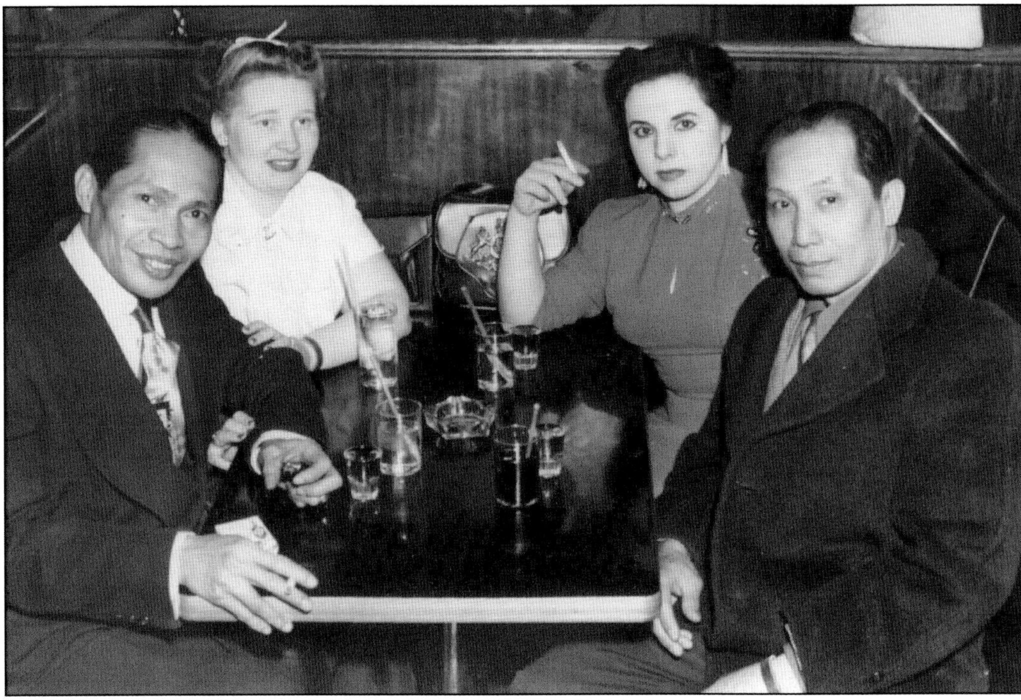

Pio Fernandez met his future wife, Agnes, at the Plaka Restaurant in Manhattan. Agnes, a redheaded Scandinavian American, was the hatcheck girl at the restaurant. Fernandez came in every day until she finally noticed him. He asked her on a date, and they were married shortly after. While interracial marriages were illegal in other parts of the country, there were never any laws banning interracial marriages in New York. Above is a photograph of Pio and Agnes when they were dating (left side of the table); below is a photograph of Pio and Agnes with their friends and their daughter Dolores in 1953. (Both, courtesy of the Alic-Fernandez family.)

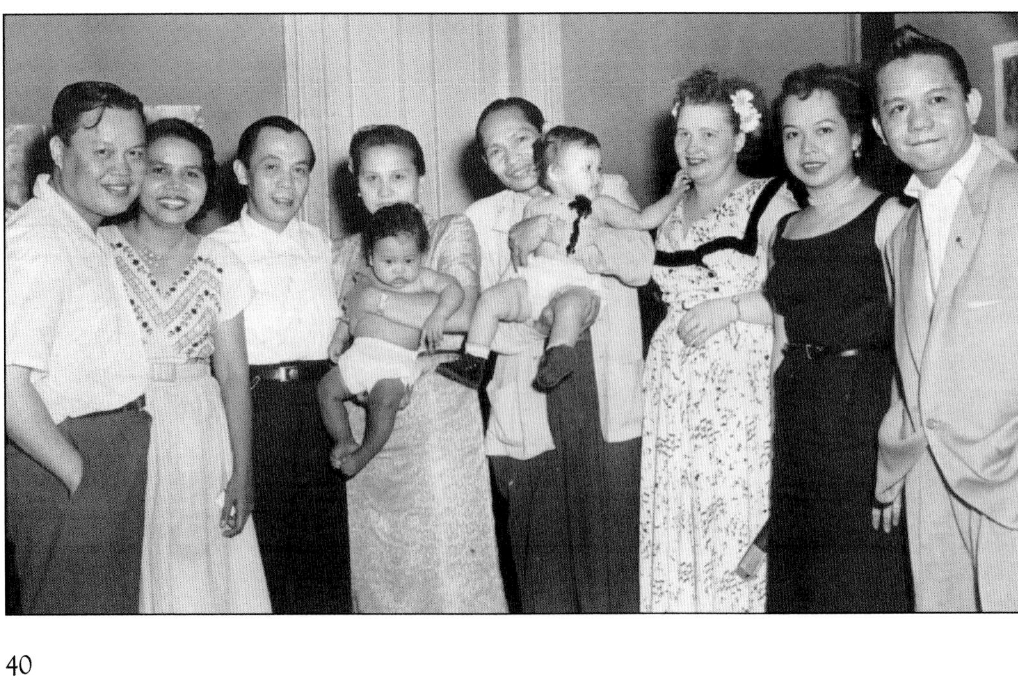

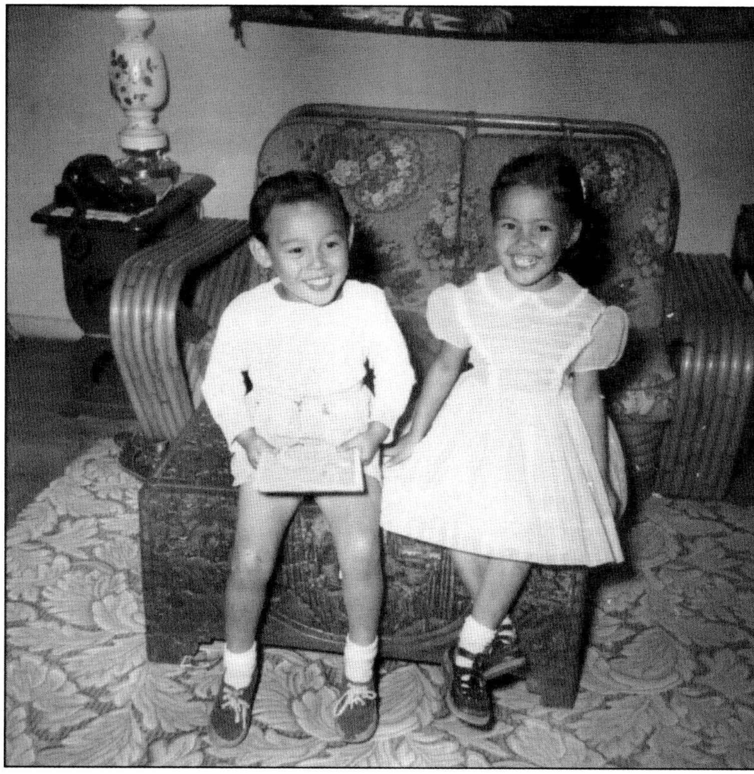

Dolores Fernandez and her cousin Frank Rocco celebrate her fifth birthday in 1957. Dolores remembers that her father had many friends she considered her uncles, and their children were her cousins, which is still a common practice in Filipino American culture. (Courtesy of the Alic-Fernandez family.)

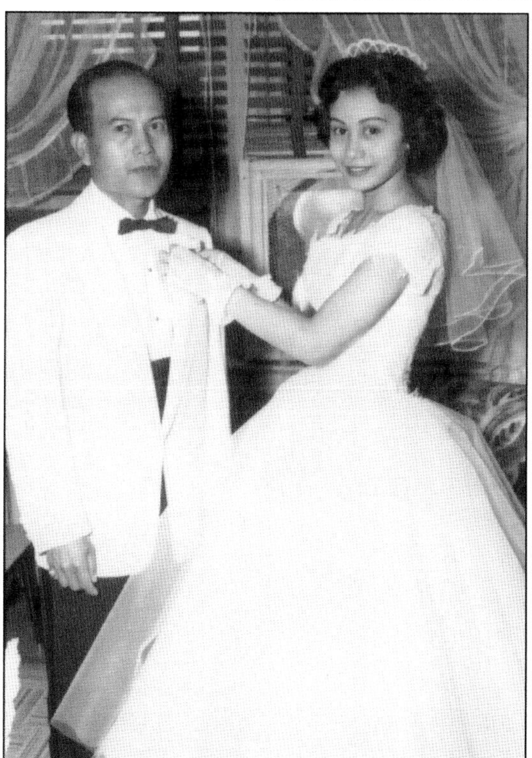

Freddy Campano and his wife, Anne, raised all seven of their children in New York. Pictured here are Freddy and his daughter Gloria on her wedding day, about 1957. (Courtesy of Gerald Campano.)

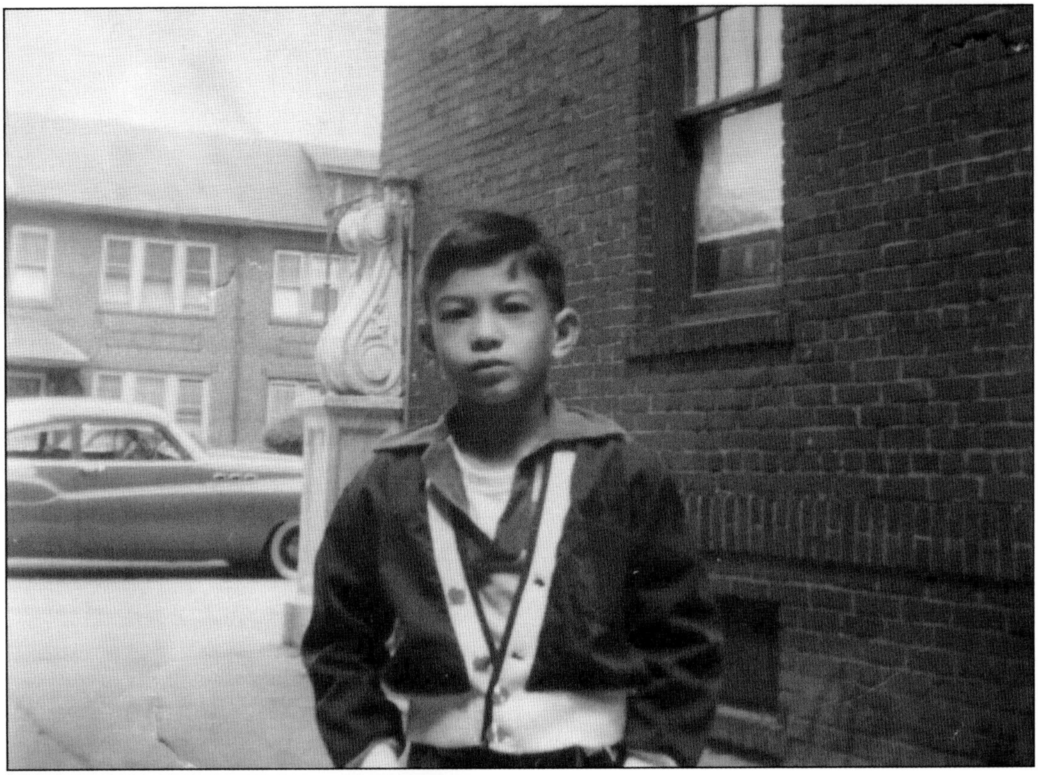

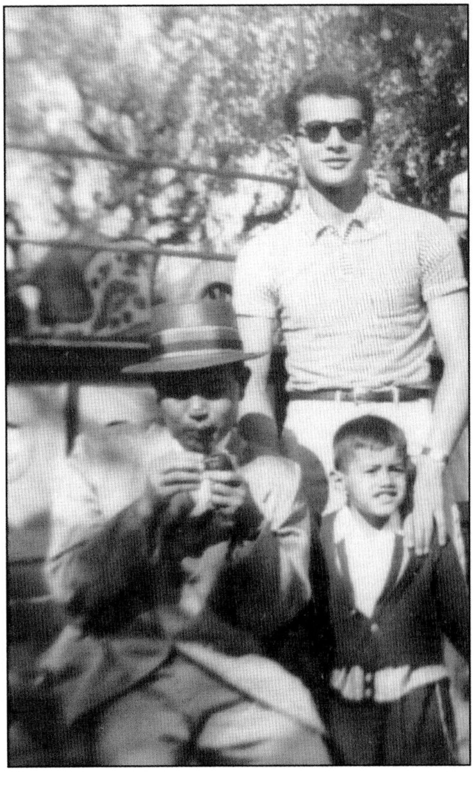

Pictured above is a young Dennis Campano, around 1959, outside of his family's walk-up apartment at 47-17 Thirty-ninth Street in Long Island City, Queens. Dennis was one of seven children raised by Freddy and Anne Campano. Pictured at left are Freddy Campano, his eldest son, Fred Jr., and his youngest son, John, around 1958. (Both, courtesy of Gerald Campano.)

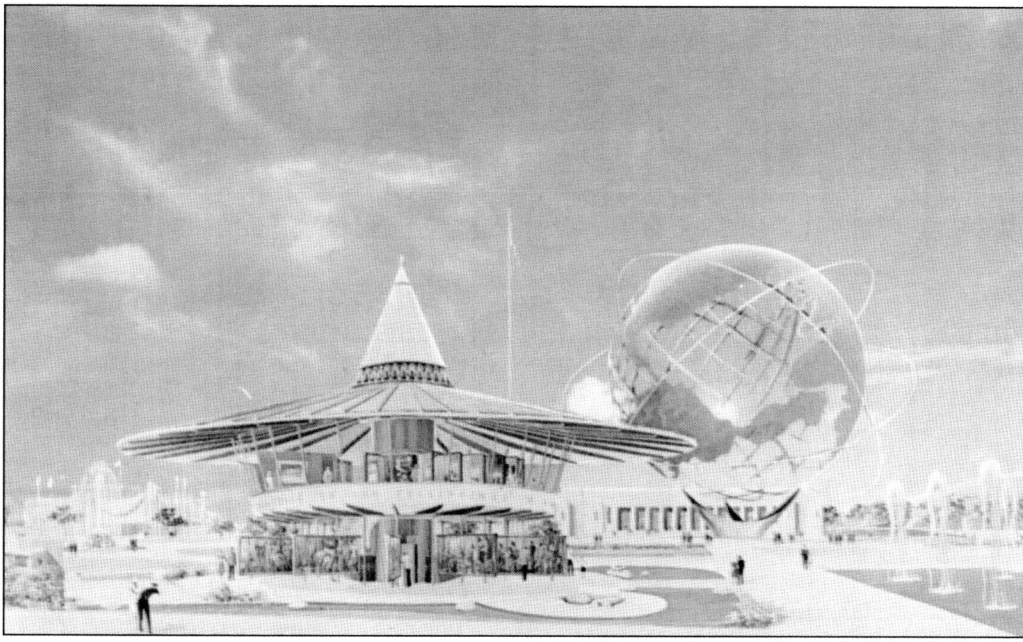

The 1964 New York World's Fair was the second world's fair to be held in New York City. One of its features was the Philippine Pavilion, which presented the history of the Philippines in paneled wood carvings, a lagoon surrounding the circular building, and scale replicas of Bataan and Corregidor. (Courtesy of Dexter Press Postcards.)

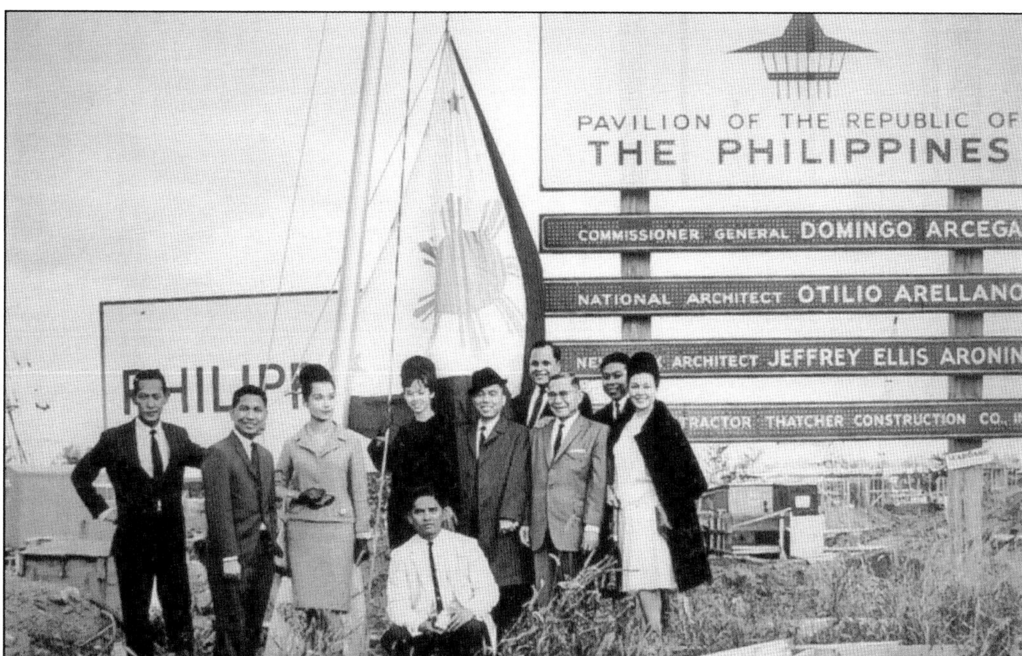

Pictured here is a group of Filipino Americans at the construction of the Philippine Pavilion for the 1964 World's Fair in New York. Art Valenzuela Jr. was a supervising architect. (Courtesy of Bel Molina.)

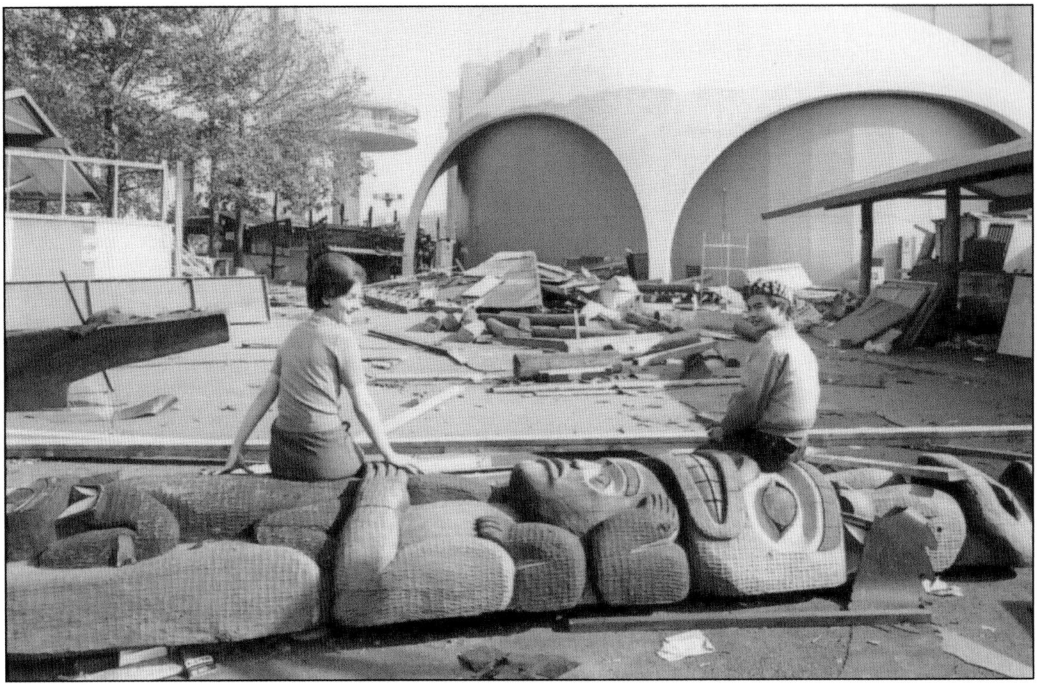

The 1964 World's Fair was located in Flushing, Queens, New York. Sitting on the right, Joseph Tabaco, eldest son of Natalio Tabaco, worked at the Alaska Pavilion and participated in the closure of the world's fair. (Courtesy of the Tabaco family.)

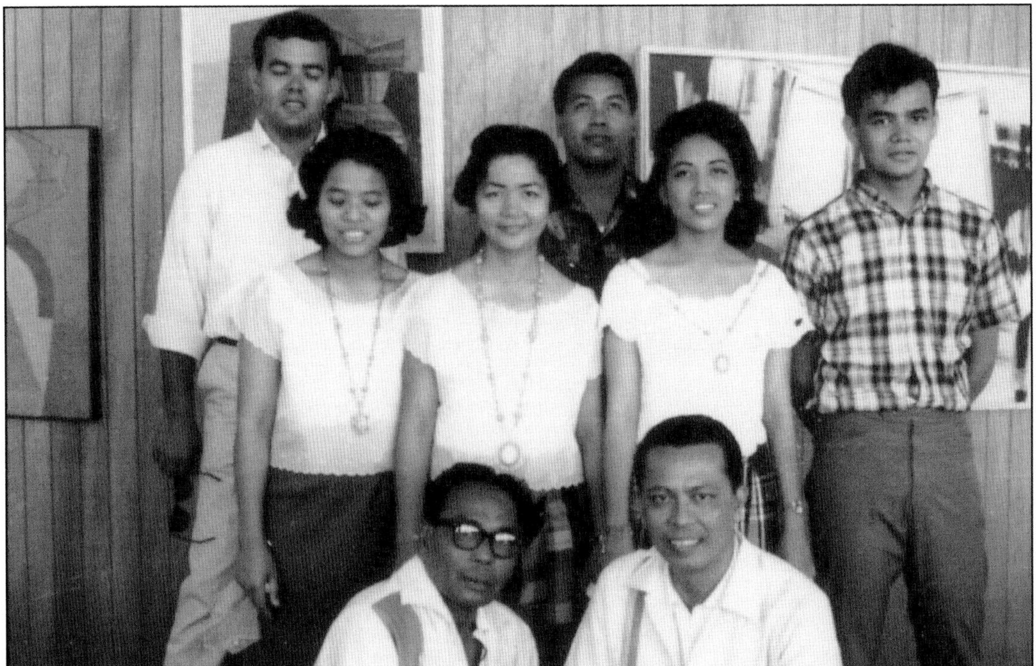

This group of young Filipino Americans worked at the 1964 World's Fair. (Courtesy of FANHS Metro New York Archives.)

Carlos Soriano was a Filipino who served in the military during the 1930s and settled in New York afterwards. He met his wife, Elaine, in New York, and they had two children—Carlos Jr. and Judie. Soriano was active in the Filipino National Council in the 1940s. (Courtesy of Angel Agesta.)

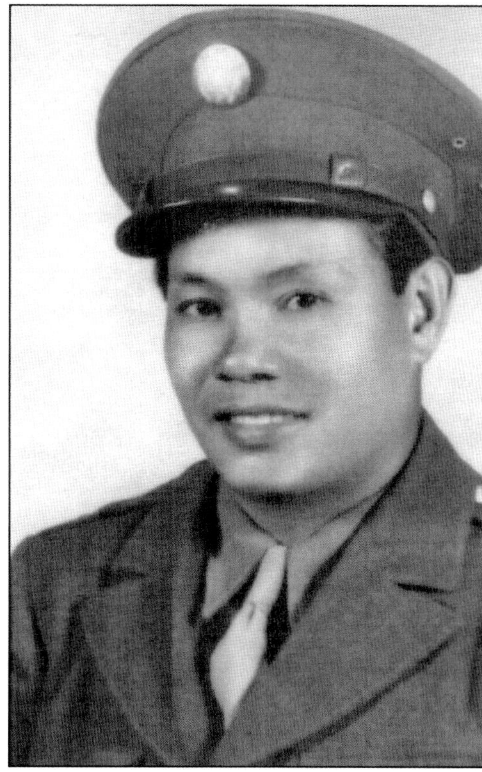

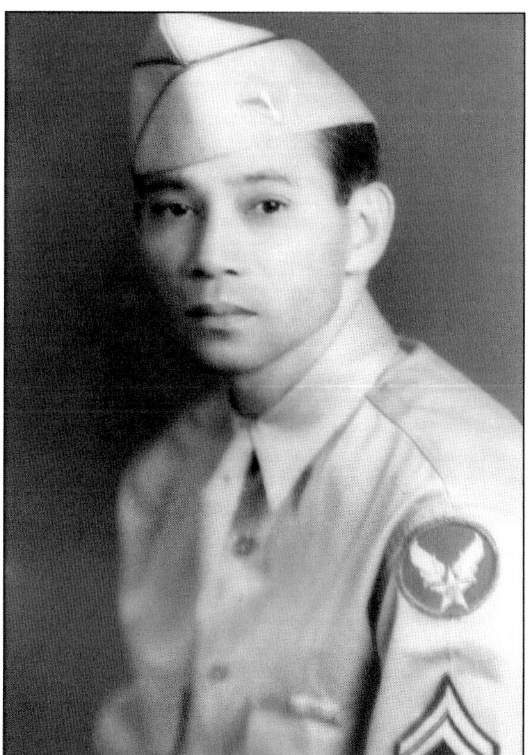

Dolores Fernandez Alic remembers her Uncle Jay, a friend of her father's who served in the military and eventually opened up his own barbershop on Pell Street in Chinatown, where he died. Pictured here is Uncle Jay around 1940. (Courtesy of the Alic-Fernandez family.)

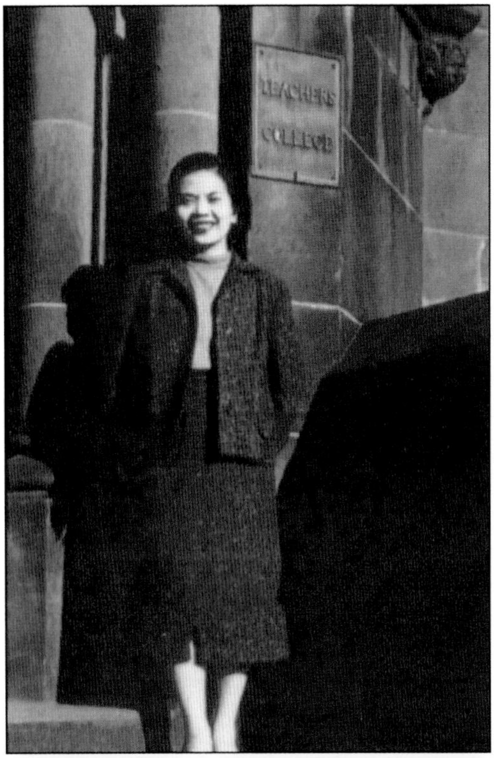

Pictured here in 1955 at Teachers College, Columbia University, Ceferina Madlangbayan Gonzales was a 28-year-old student who studied science and nutrition. Gonzales returned to live in the Philippines, but she visited Teachers College again in 2009. (Courtesy of Cynthia Marfori-Gordon.)

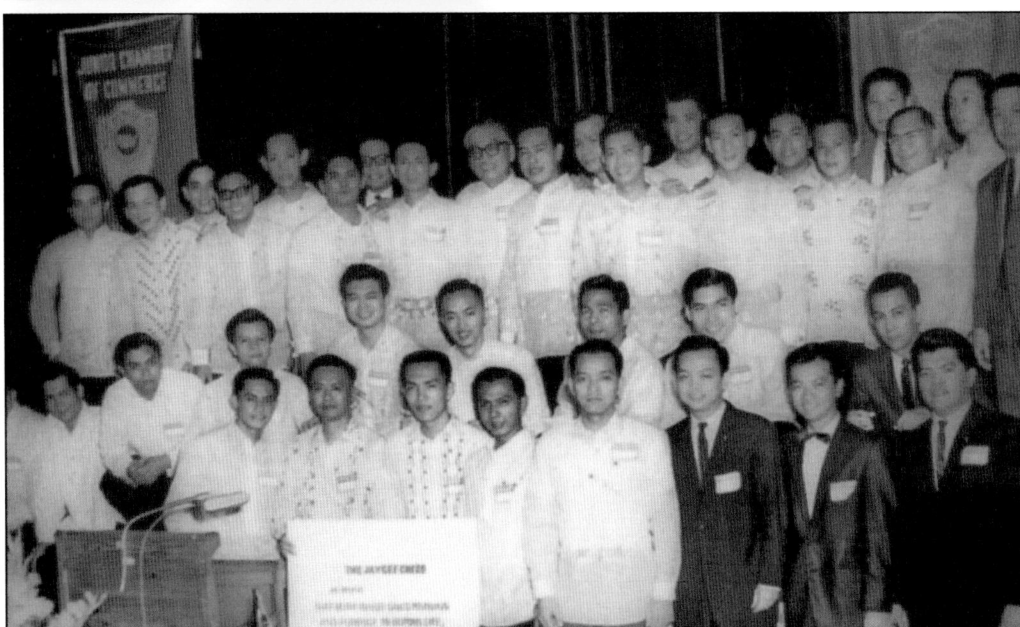

In this photograph are the charter members of Philippine-New York Jaycees, about 1963, who sought to serve the civic and social needs of the then-fledgling Filipino community in New York. They founded the first Filipino Jaycees chapter in a foreign land and eventually opened the door to the formation of other chapters outside the Philippines. Ernesto Pilares (third row, 10th from left) was the founding president. (Courtesy of Bel Molina.)

Three

A Growing Community
The Post-1965 Immigrants Arrive

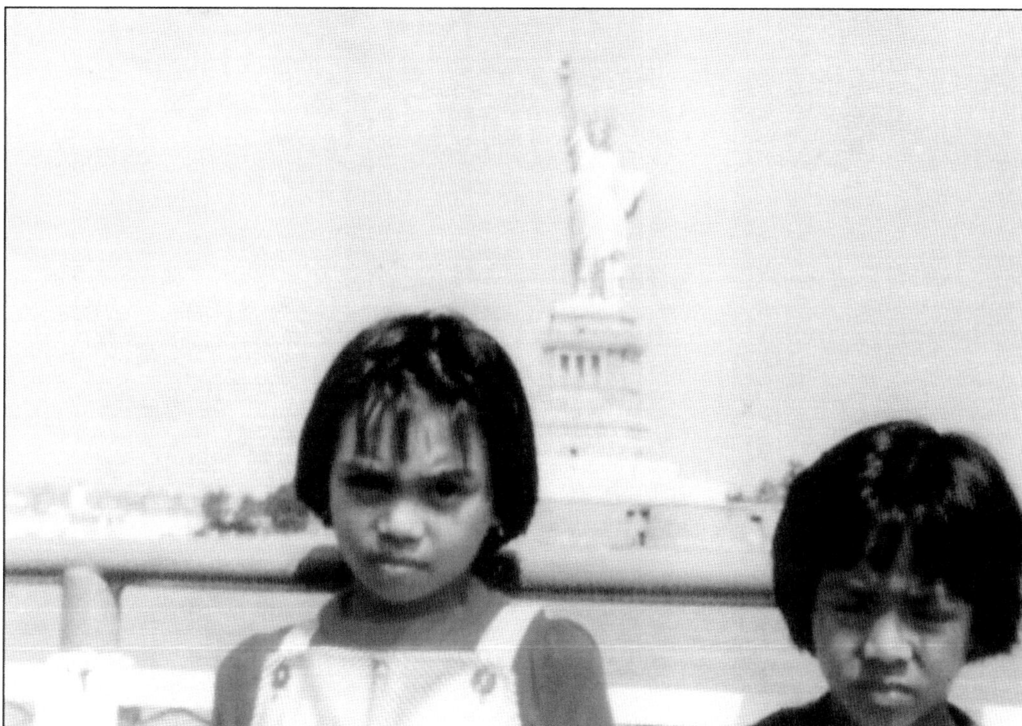

The Immigration and Nationality Act of 1965 was a significant moment in Asian American history, as it put an end to immigration quotas. It also allowed for Filipino Americans to immigrate in search of opportunities that they would not have in the Philippines. Many Filipino Americans moved to New York as professionals (such as physicians, nurses, and engineers) and often petitioned for their relatives to follow suit. Many of these immigrants were married prior to arrival, while some met their husbands or wives in the United States. Pictured here are Gail and Jed Prado on a ferry on their way to Liberty Island in 1980. Gail and Jed are the American-born children of Evan and Elna Prado, who immigrated in the 1960s. The children are standing in front of the Statue of Liberty, which is often viewed as one of the most prominent symbols of America—representing freedom, liberty, and the American dream. (Courtesy of the Prado family.)

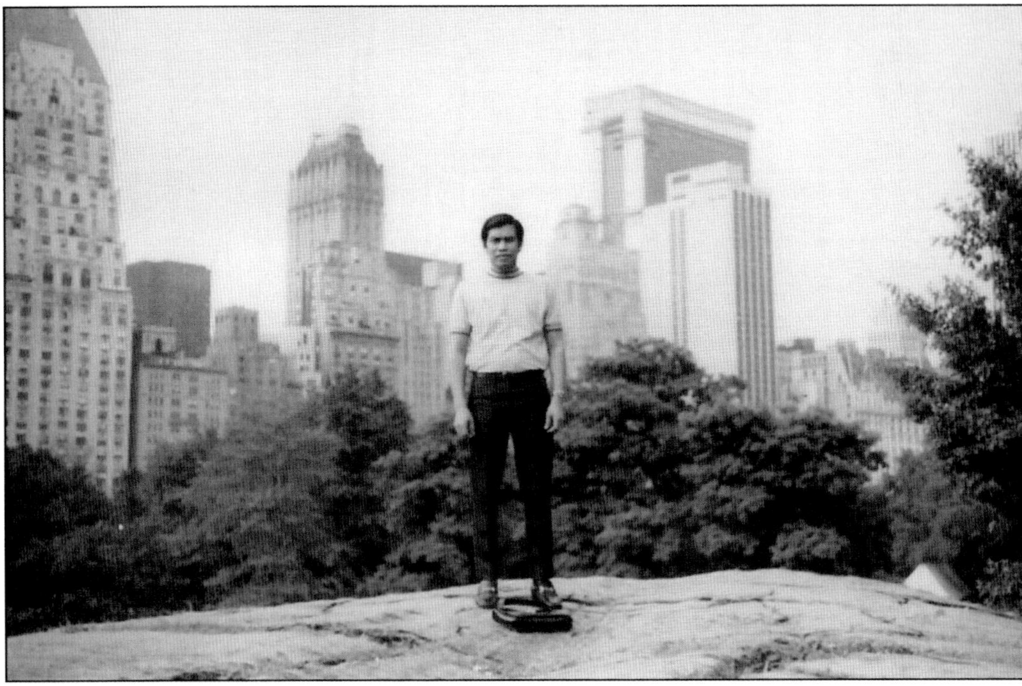

Evan Prado (above) and Elna Tamayo Prado (below) immigrated to New York in the late 1960s as professionals. They lived in midtown Manhattan before they settled down in Jamaica, Queens. Here, they are pictured in Central Park in 1969. (Both, courtesy of the Prado family.)

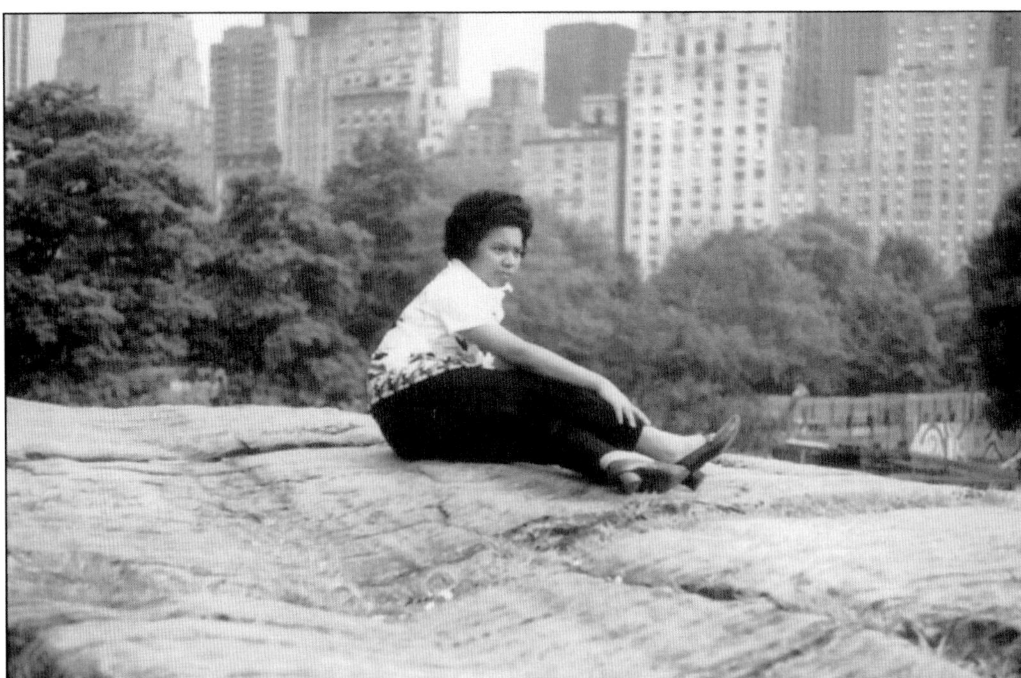

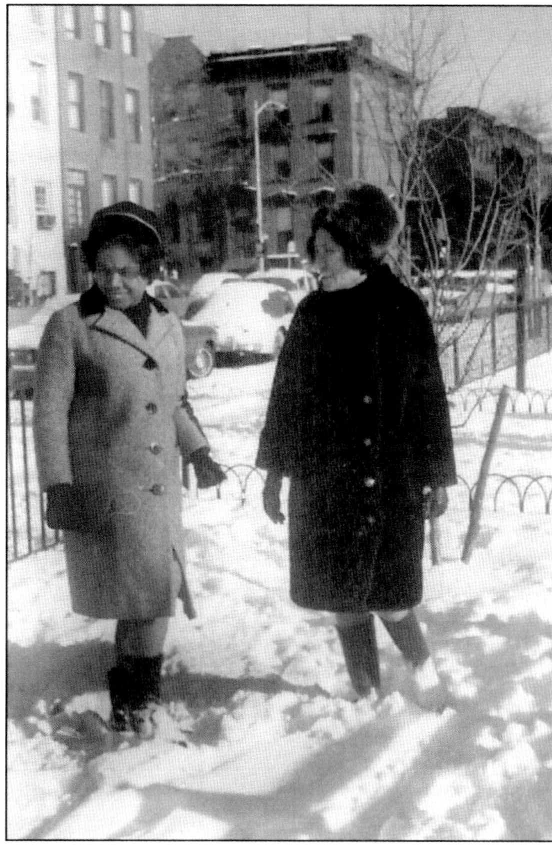

Having finished her medical degree in the Philippines, Dr. Elna Tamayo Prado came to the United States to practice medicine. One of the biggest culture shocks for many Filipinos upon arriving in New York (during this time and even today) is adjusting to the cold weather and the snow. At right are Dr. Prado (left) and her colleague experiencing snow for one of the first times; below is a photograph of Dr. Prado (right) and friends from her job at the hospital. (Both, courtesy of the Prado family.)

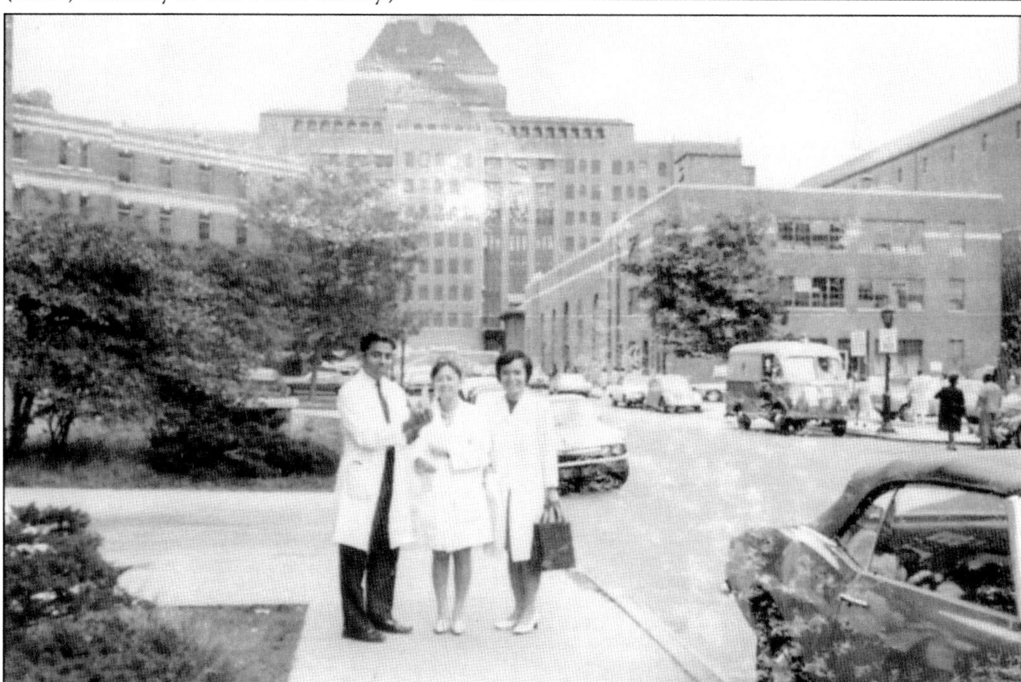

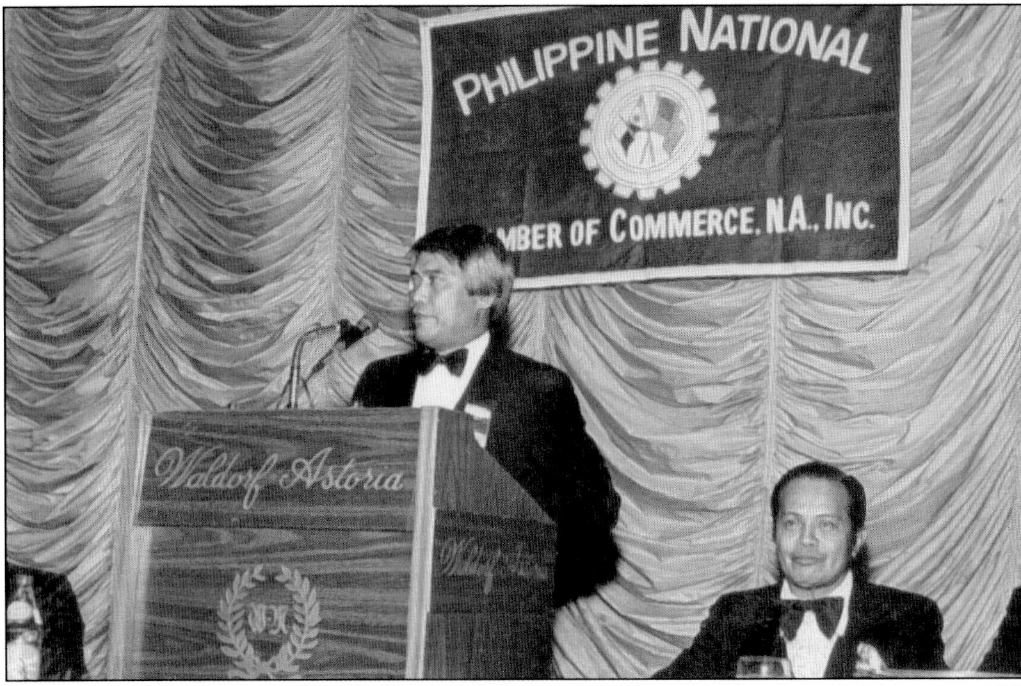

Evan Prado delivers a speech at a gala of the Philippine National Chamber of Commerce, NA, Inc., which was held at the Waldorf Astoria in the 1970s. The Waldorf Astoria continues to be one of New York City's most famous and glamorous luxury hotels. (Courtesy of the Prado family.)

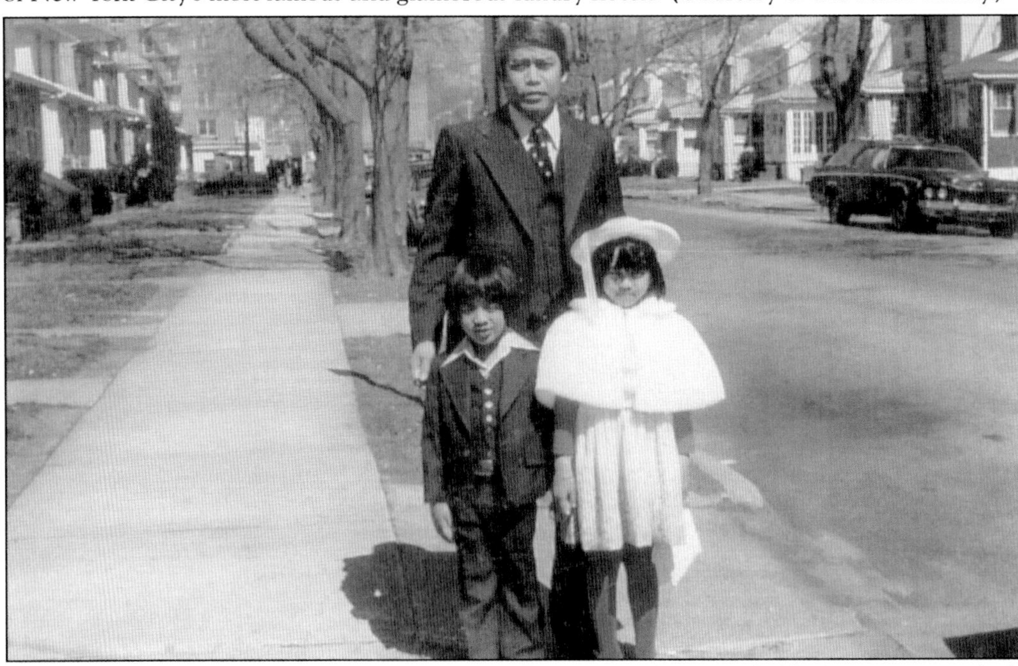

Many Filipino families moved to Queens, particularly in neighborhoods like Jamaica, Woodside, and Jackson Heights. While many of these Filipinos worked in Manhattan and other boroughs, they took the subway as a main mode of transportation. In this photograph is Evan Prado with his two children, Gail and Jed, around 1977. (Courtesy of the Prado family.)

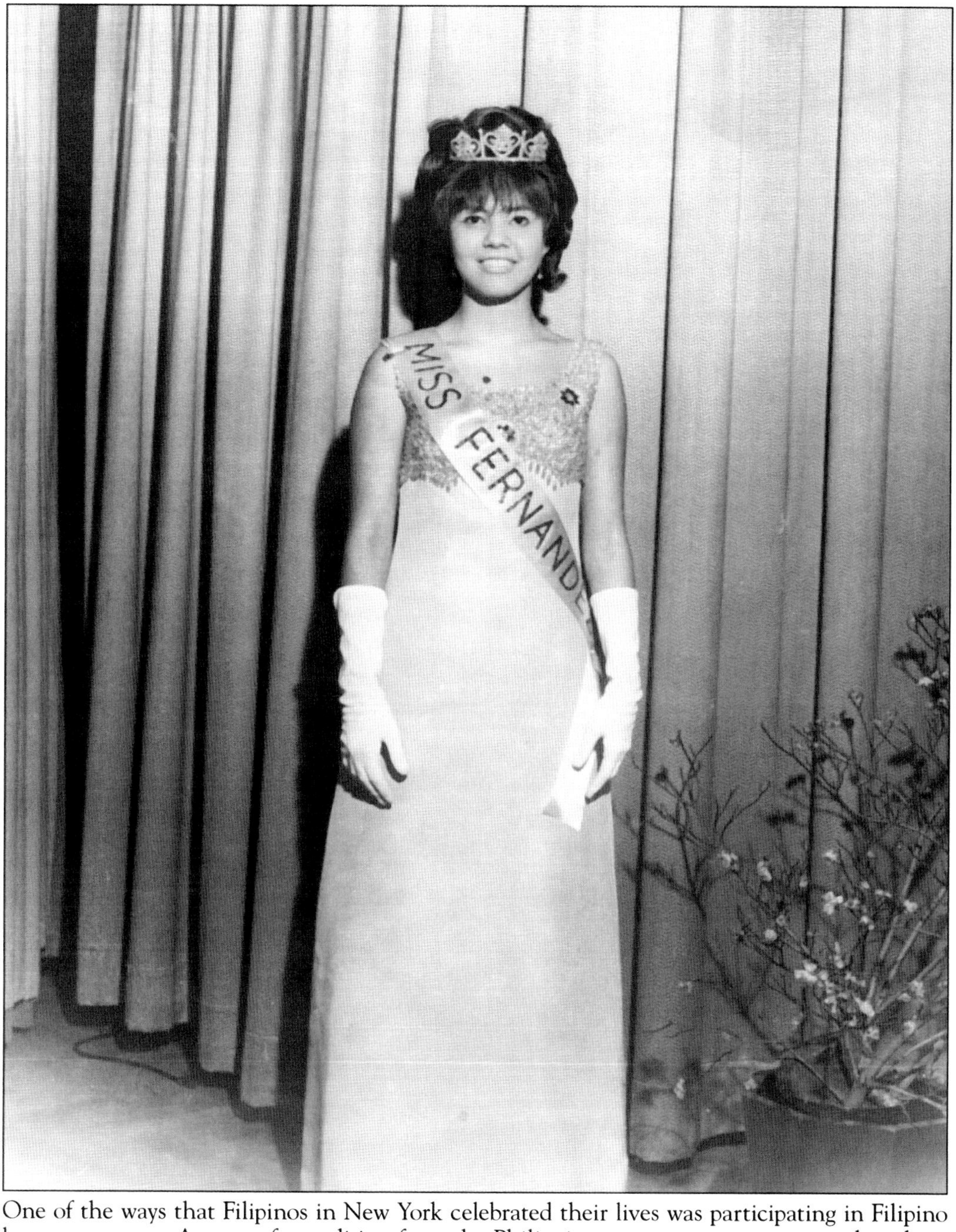

One of the ways that Filipinos in New York celebrated their lives was participating in Filipino beauty pageants. As part of a tradition from the Philippines, young women competed in these contests for the title of Miss Philippines of New York. Pictured here is Dolores Fernandez, who was crowned Miss Philippine America around 1968. (Courtesy of the Alic-Fernandez family.)

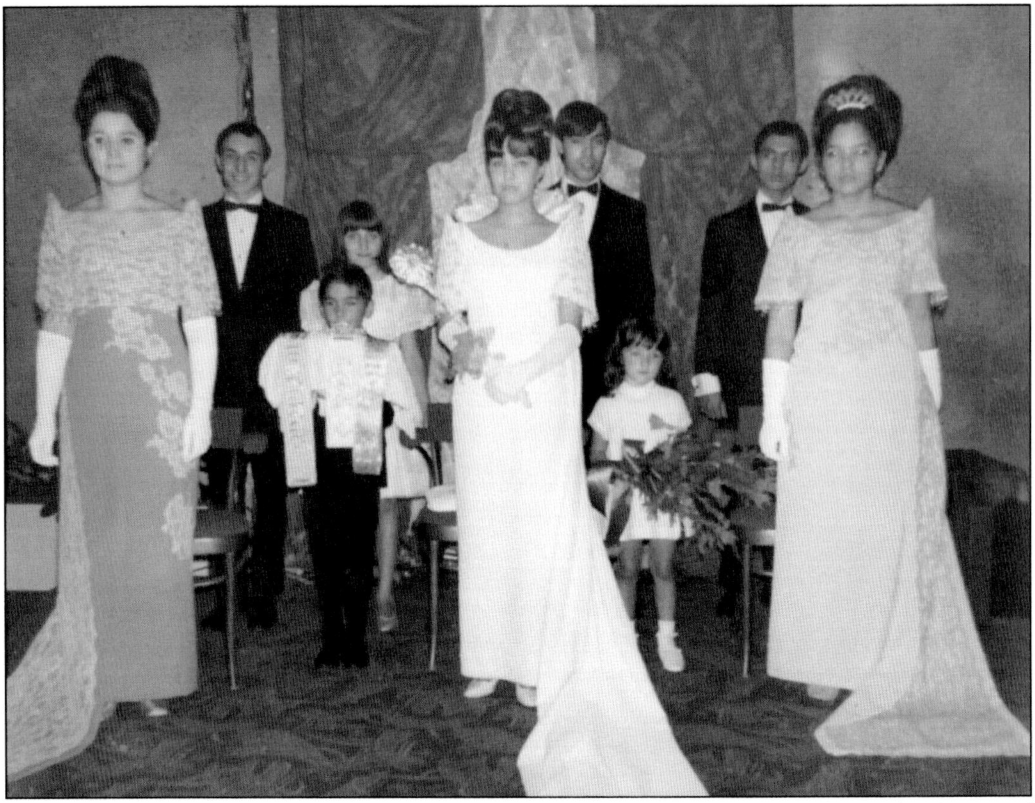

Dolores Fernandez won many beauty pageants as a young woman. Here is she as the Queen of the Philippine Social Club in 1968. She remembers these pageants being held at fancy hotels in Manhattan and that many of her uncles and aunties liked to dress up and dance at these events. This is still a common custom in the present-day Filipino American community of New York City. (Courtesy of the Alic-Fernandez family.)

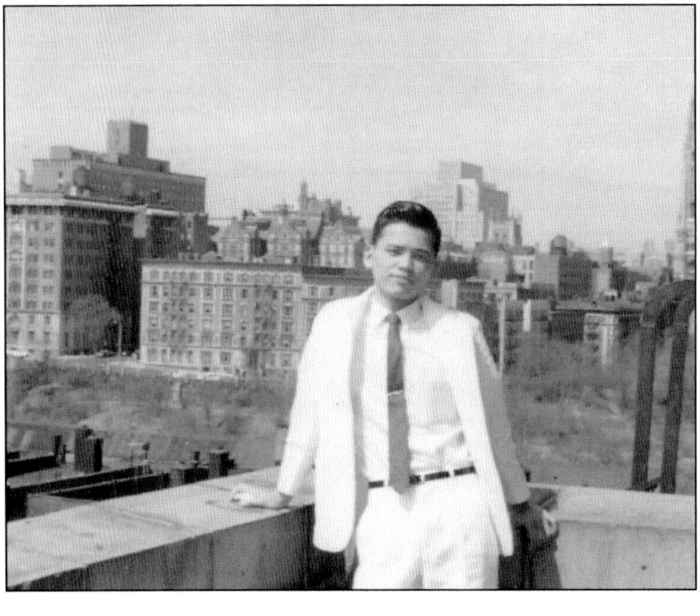

Dr. Dewey Torres was a surgical resident in Harlem at Sydenham Hospital in 1965; he is pictured here on the hospital's rooftop with a view of Harlem. The hospital emergency room was very busy during the mid-1960s as New York City was in the middle of race riots. Dr. Torres told his daughter Grace about how Filipino physicians were the only ones that some people would allow to treat them, and these doctors usually played negotiator, as they were considered neutral parties. (Courtesy of Grace Torres-Hodges.)

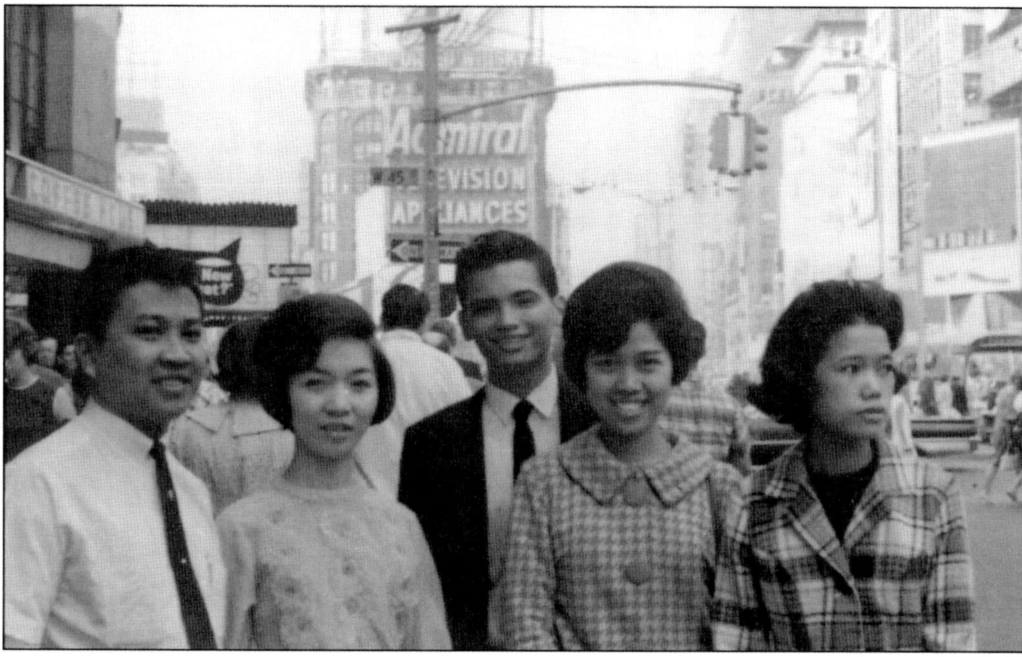

This photograph is of five Filipino twentysomethings in the middle of Times Square in 1965. They all had immigrated to and worked in New York City. From left to right are Tony Go, Severina Castillo (who later married each other), Dewey Torres, Adelaida Layno (who also married each other), and Luz Torres. (Courtesy of Grace Torres-Hodges.)

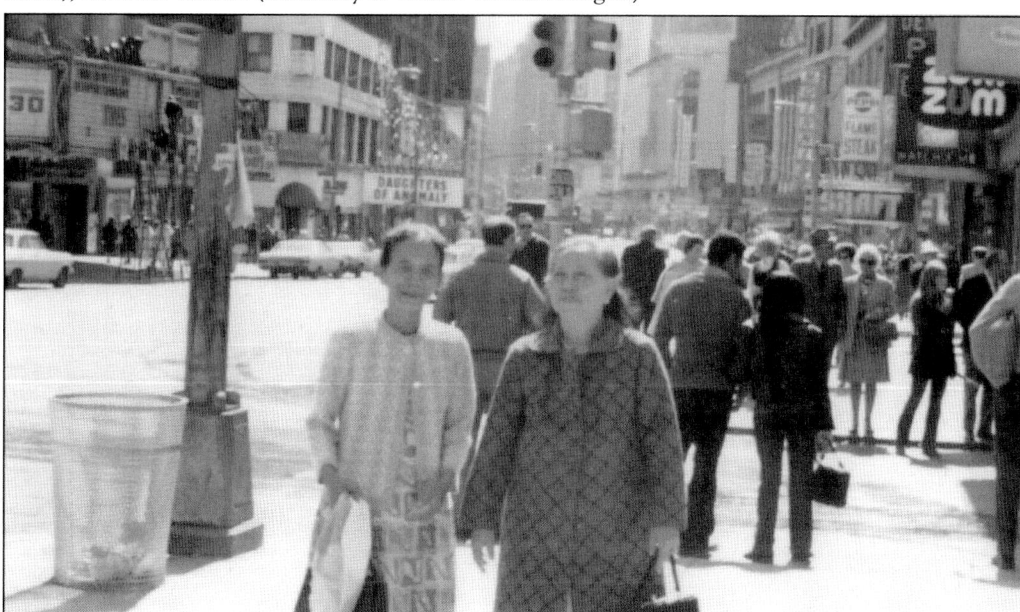

Grace Torres-Hodges writes, "This picture from 1971 is very special to me because it is of both my grandmothers, Aurelia Torres [left] and Gloria Layno. It is amazing to realize that these two ladies from Batangas and Cebu, respectively, ended up at Times Square together. Aurelia had six of her nine children immigrate, and Gloria had five of her six children immigrate to the United States." (Courtesy of Grace Torres-Hodges.)

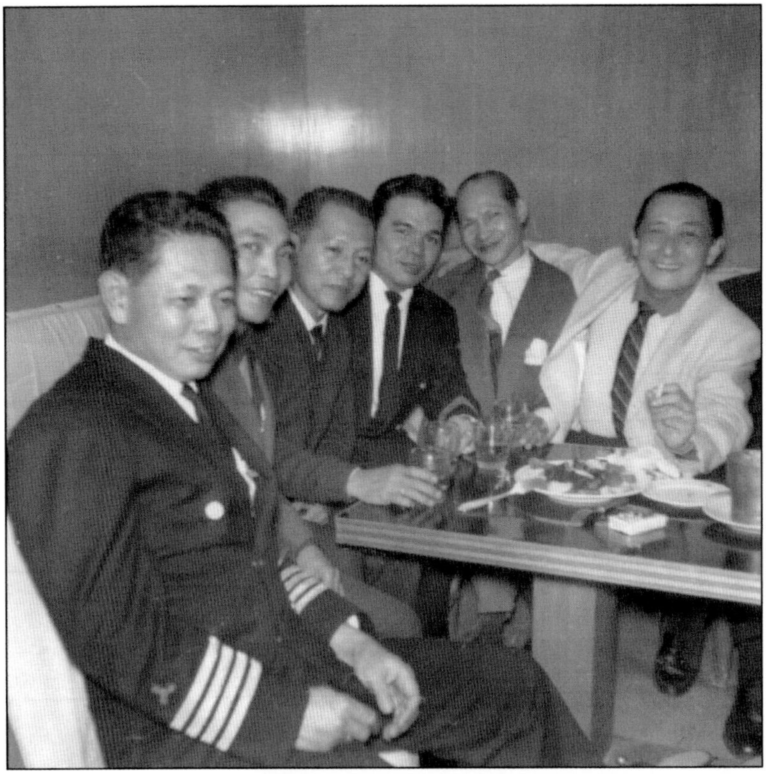

While many Filipinos immigrated after 1965 as doctors, nurses, and engineers, there were still many Filipinos who came to New York as stewards and shipmates. Pictured here in 1965 are seafarers in the Brooklyn Navy Yards. (Courtesy of the Alic-Fernandez family.)

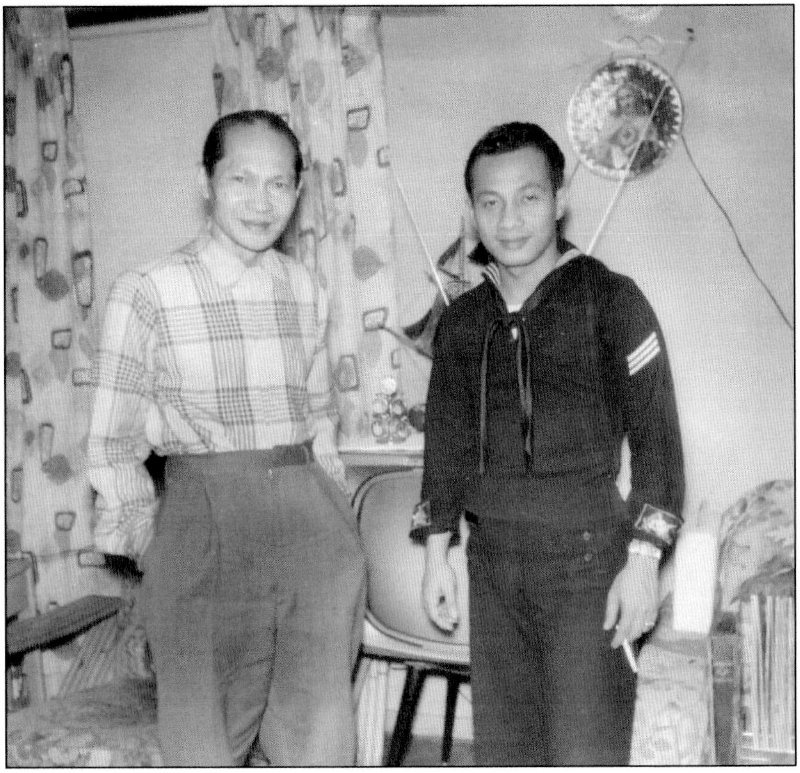

Having served in the US Navy for several years, elderly and retired Navy men served as father figures to many of the young Navy stewards who arrived during this time. (Courtesy of the Alic-Fernandez family.)

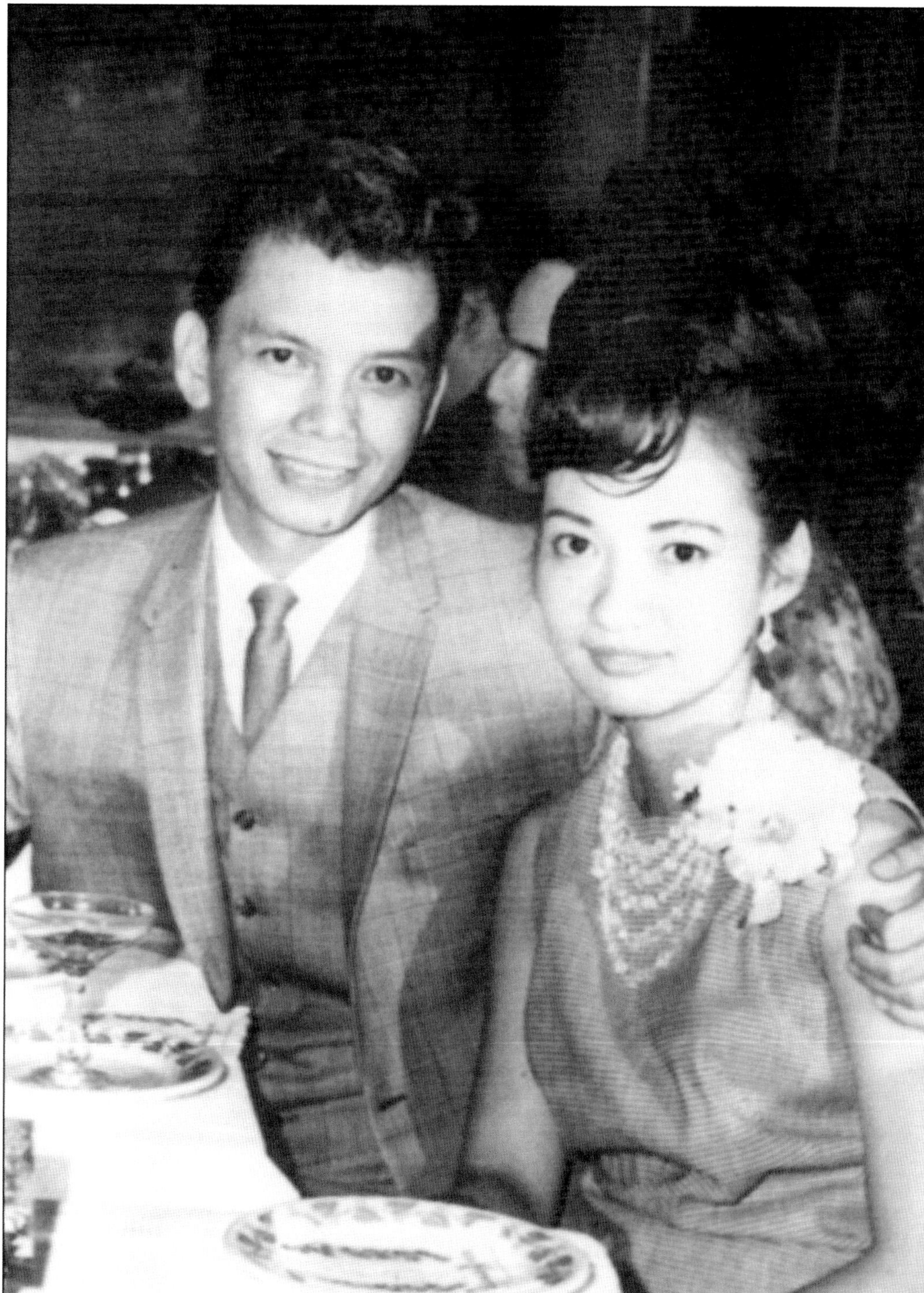

Leonardo Fulgado and Carmencita Menchee Quesada were engaged at the Alameda Room in the Copacabana Restaurant in New York City on August 12, 1967. (Courtesy of Mia Fulgado-Tyler.)

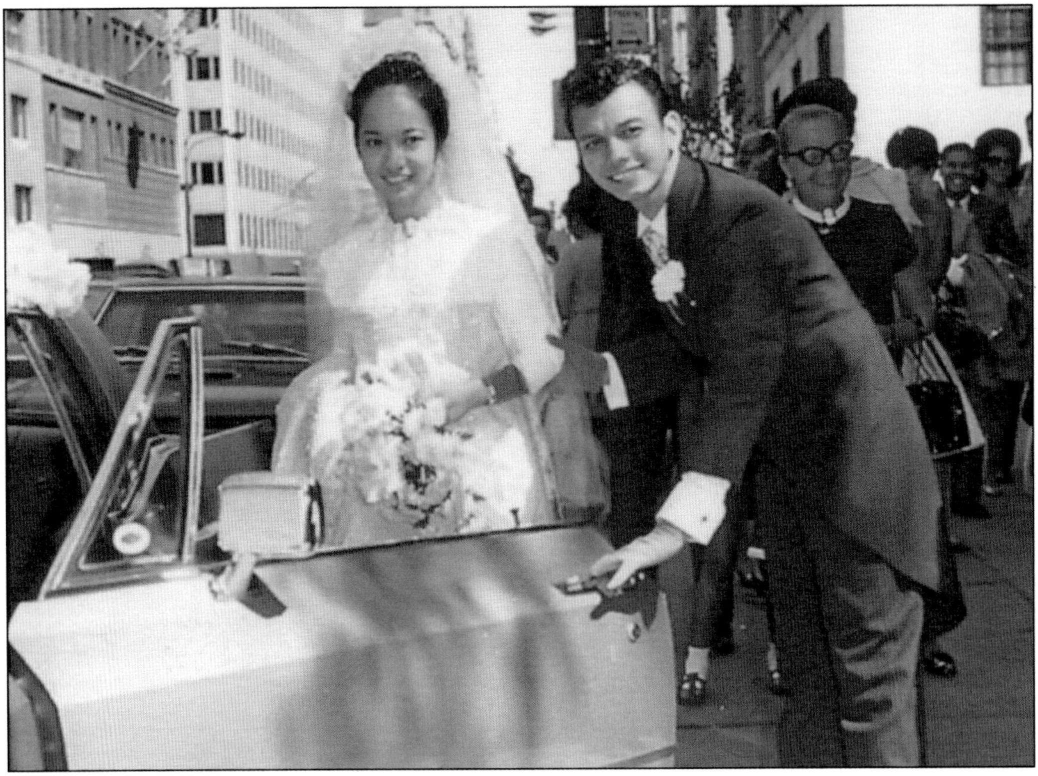

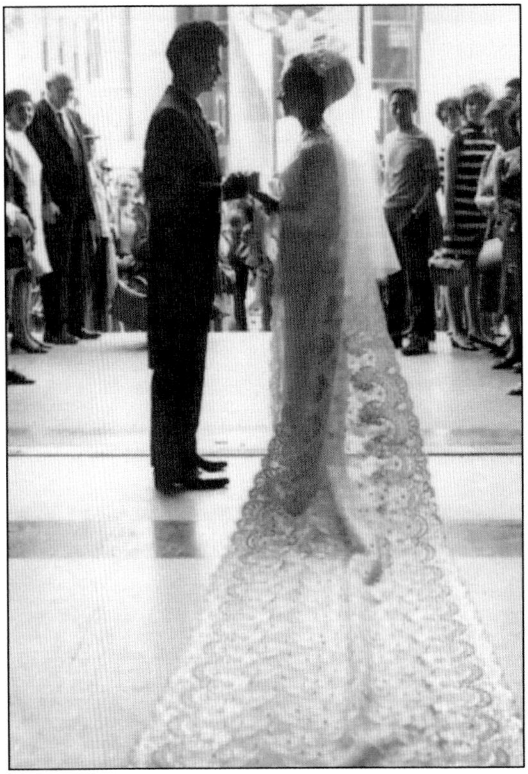

Leonardo and Carmencita Fulgado were married at St. Patrick's Cathedral in Manhattan on September 7, 1968. They raised five beautiful children in Queens. (Both, courtesy of Mia Fulgado-Tyler.)

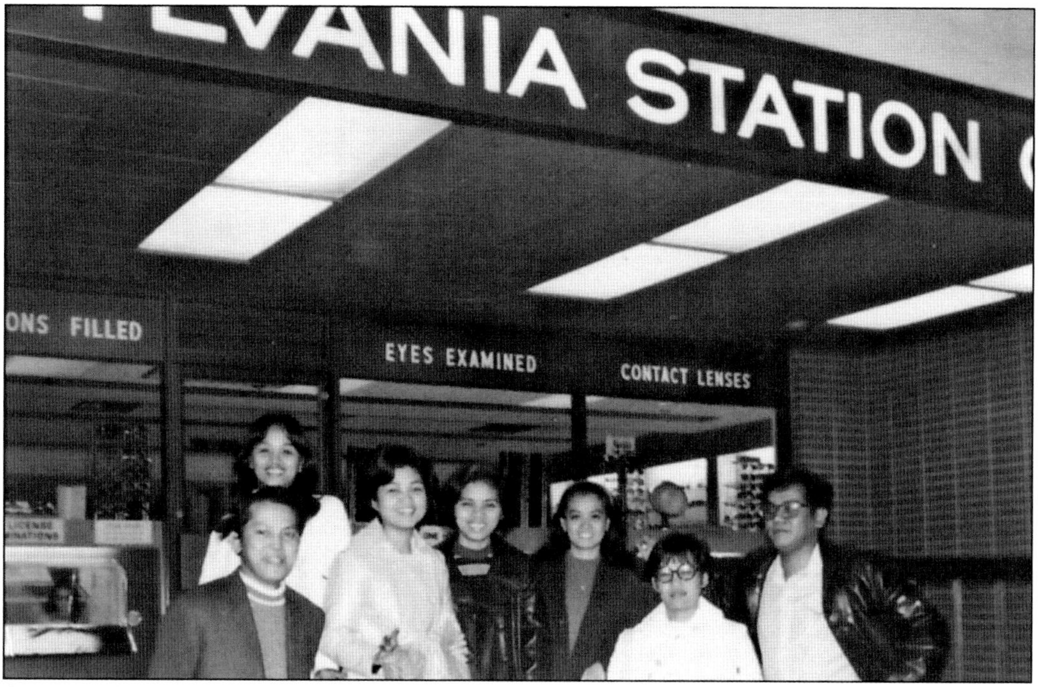

A group of young Filipino American friends stand in front of Penn Station around 1969. From left to right are (first row) Cezar Legasto, Prescilla Oandasan, Divina Gaerlan, and Orlanda Gaerlan; (second row) Dolly Legasto, Rosie San Jose, and Cora Guico. (Courtesy of Glenn Gaerlan.)

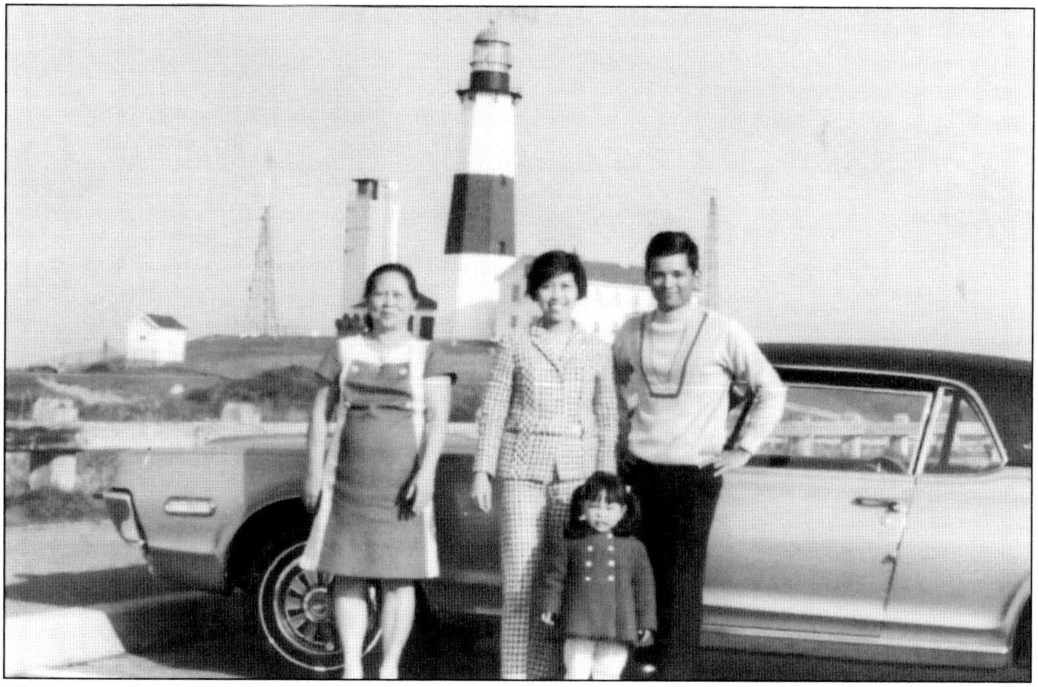

The Torres family lived in Brooklyn in the 1960s. Here is a photograph from 1967 of grandmother Gloria Layno, parents Dewey and Adelaida Torres, and Grace Torres on a weekend visit to Montauk, New York. (Courtesy of Grace Torres-Hodges.)

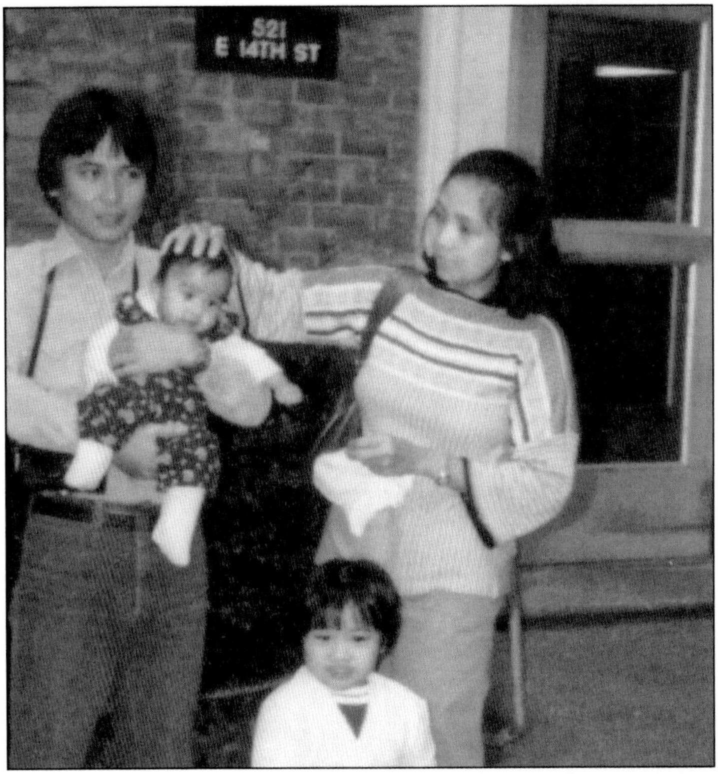

Roengrit Sriken, an immigrant from Thailand, was working for an architectural firm in New York City when his coworker set him up on a date with his wife's Filipina friend Barbara Caluag. The two met and were married a little over a year later. Pictured here are Roengrit and Barbara Sriken in front of their Manhattan apartment on East Fourteenth Street in 1979, along with their daughters Lisa (left) and Julie. (Courtesy of Julie Sriken.)

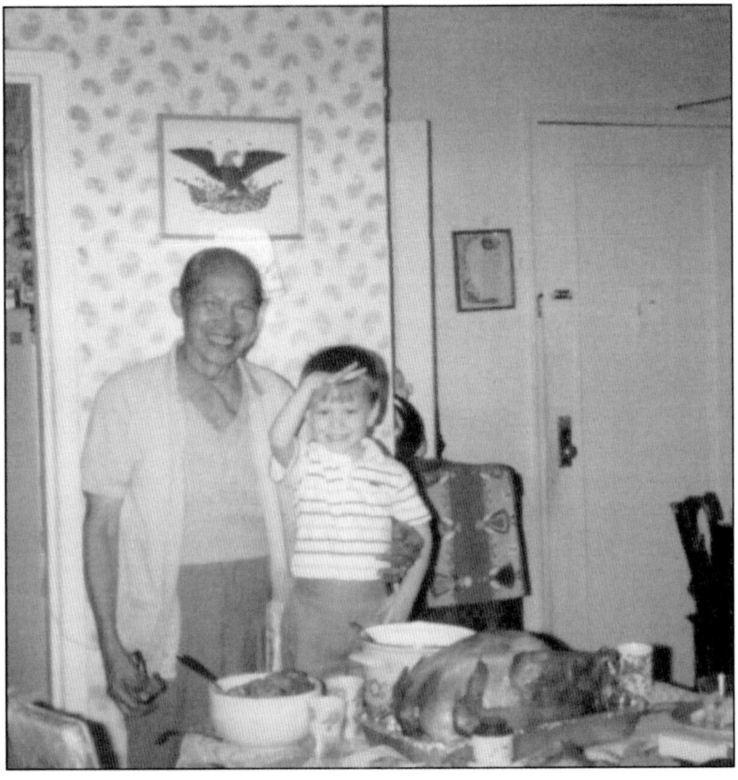

Filipinos in New York kept several of the traditions that were celebrated back home in the Philippines. A *lechon* (roasted pig) was a very common dish that would be served on big occasions. Pio Fernandez brought this treat for his grandson Michael's first birthday, in 1977. (Courtesy of the Alic-Fernandez family.)

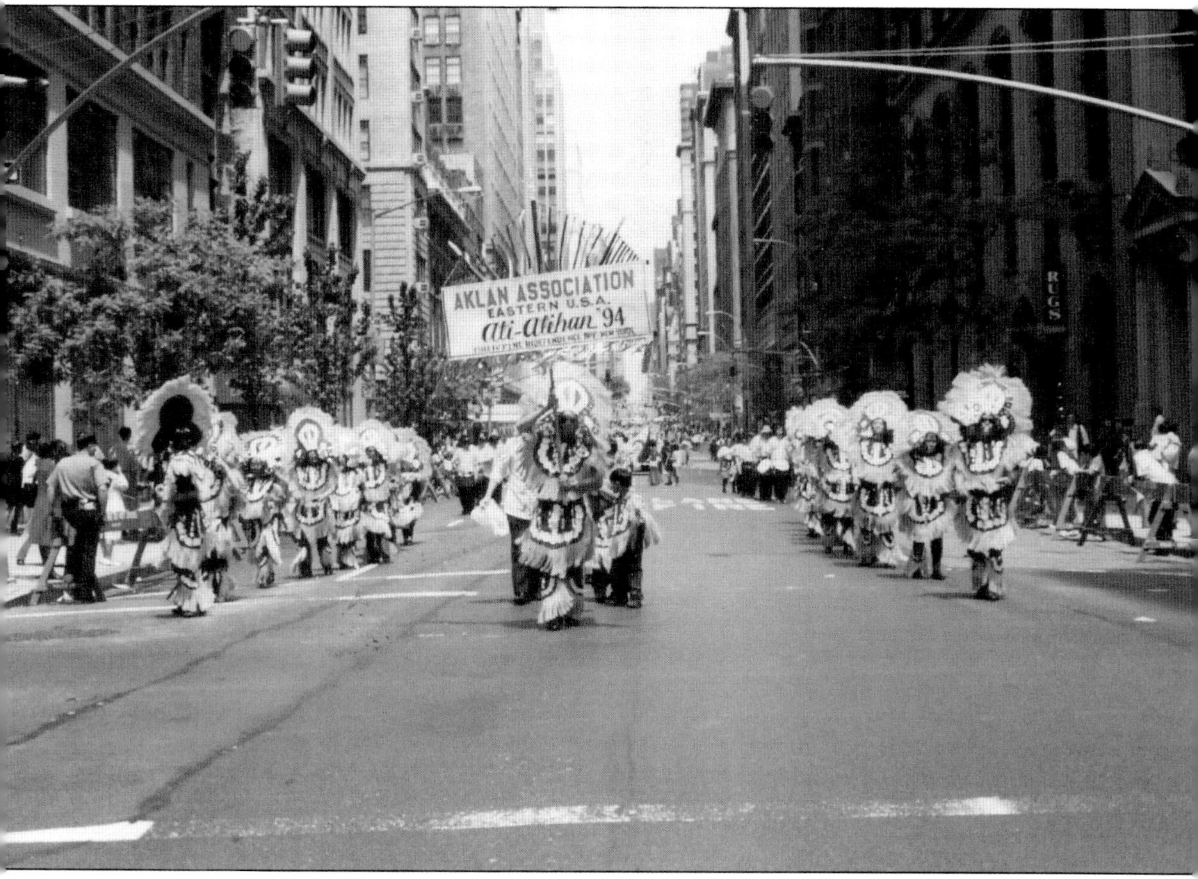

In 1990, the Philippine Consulate General of New York organized the first Philippine Independence Day Parade like the one pictured here in 1994. An annual event on the first Sunday each June, the parade and celebration has annually attracted an estimated 100,000 people, who participate in marching, dancing, singing, and eating native Filipino food. Filipino Americans march down Fifth Avenue representing various sectors of the Filipino American Community, including hometown and regional organizations, professional organizations, cultural artist groups, and more. The parade ends in Madison Square Park, which is the former location of the Fifth Avenue Hotel—the place where Jose Rizal stayed in 1888. (Courtesy of the Tamayo family.)

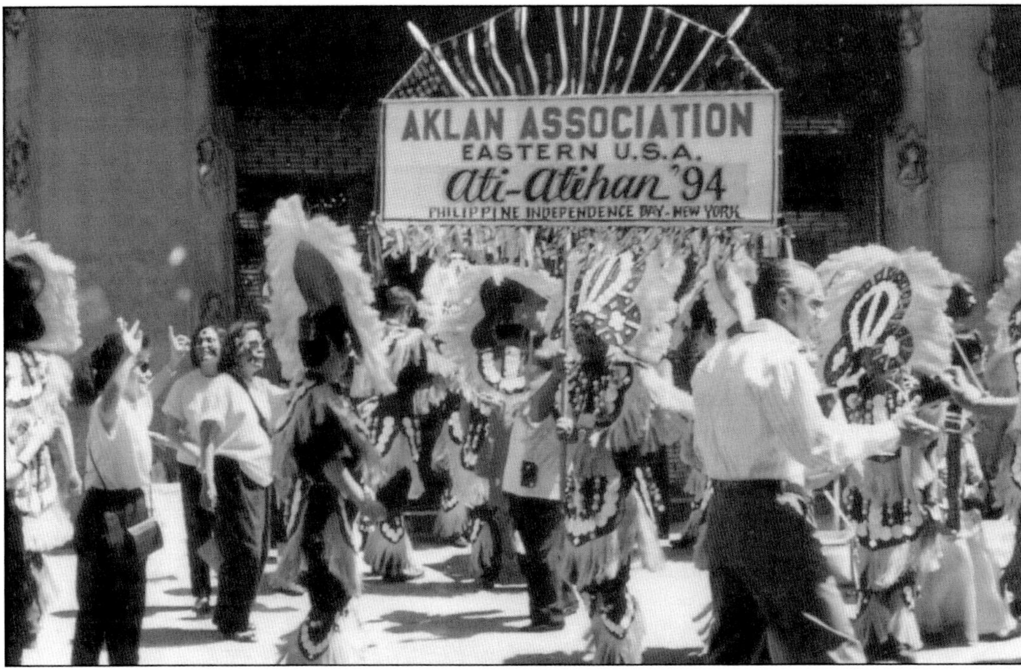

The Aklan Association of the Eastern Seaboard is one of many region-based organizations in the United States. Aklan is a province in the Visayan Islands of the Philippines. In these images are Philippine Independence Day Parade participants dressed in native costumes reflective of the indigenous people of Aklan. (Both, courtesy of the Tamayo family.)

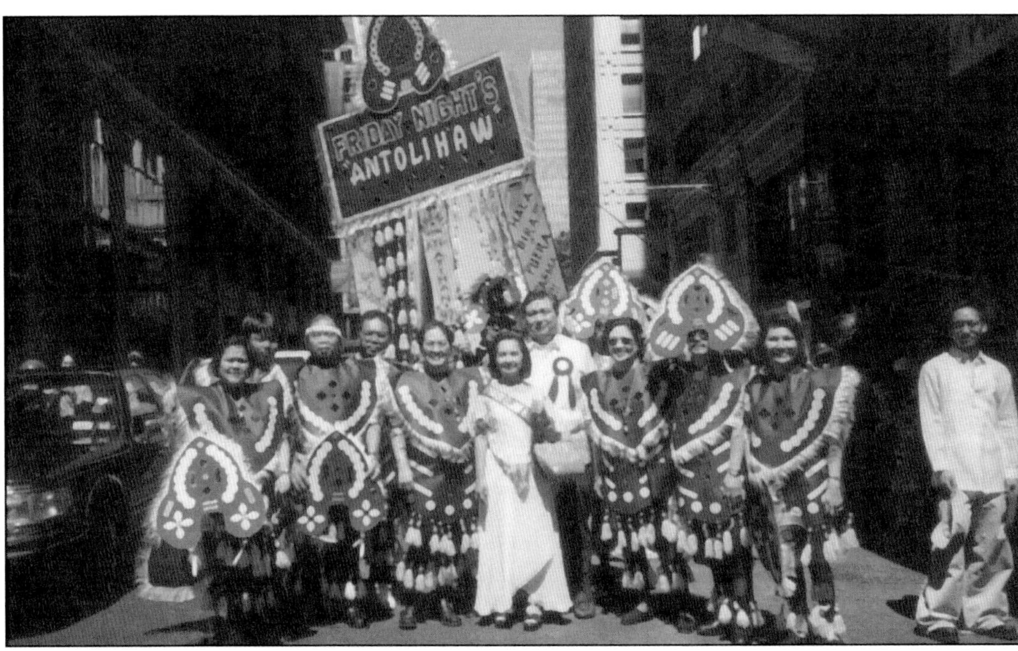

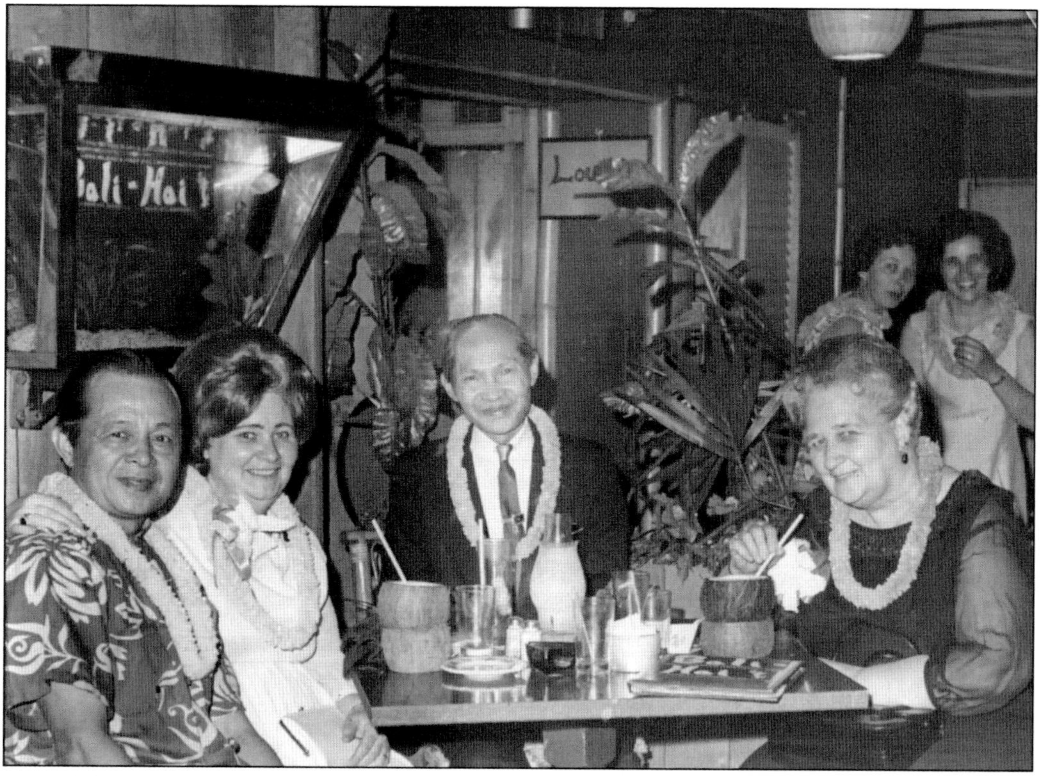

Many Filipinos during this time enjoyed the nightlife that New York City had to offer. This is a group of Filipino immigrants at the Bali Hai in midtown Manhattan—a popular Pacific Islander–themed restaurant in the mid-1970s. Pictured here are, from left to right, John Rayalo, Agnes Fernandez, Pio Fernandez, and Agnes Olsen. (Courtesy of the Alic-Fernandez family.)

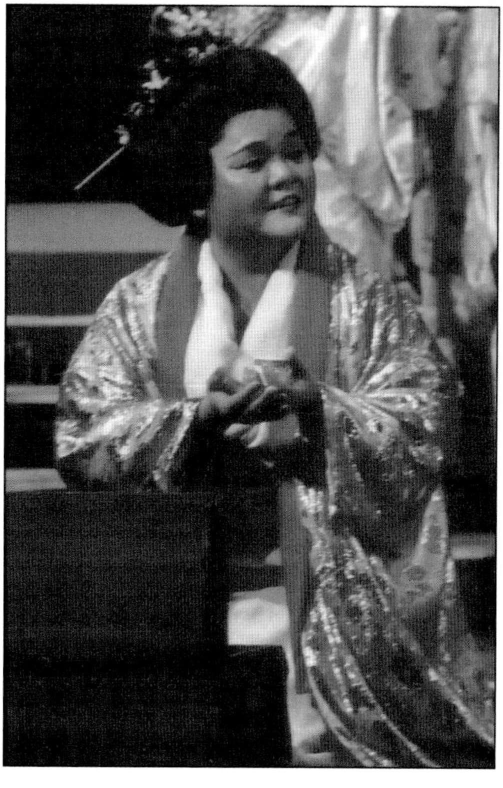

In this photograph is Lani Misenas-Padua, a coloratura soprano from the Philippines in a 1980s production of *Madama Butterfly*. Misenas-Padua continued to perform in New York City in the 1980s and 1990s and is still a New York resident today. (Courtesy of Alexandra Thomas.)

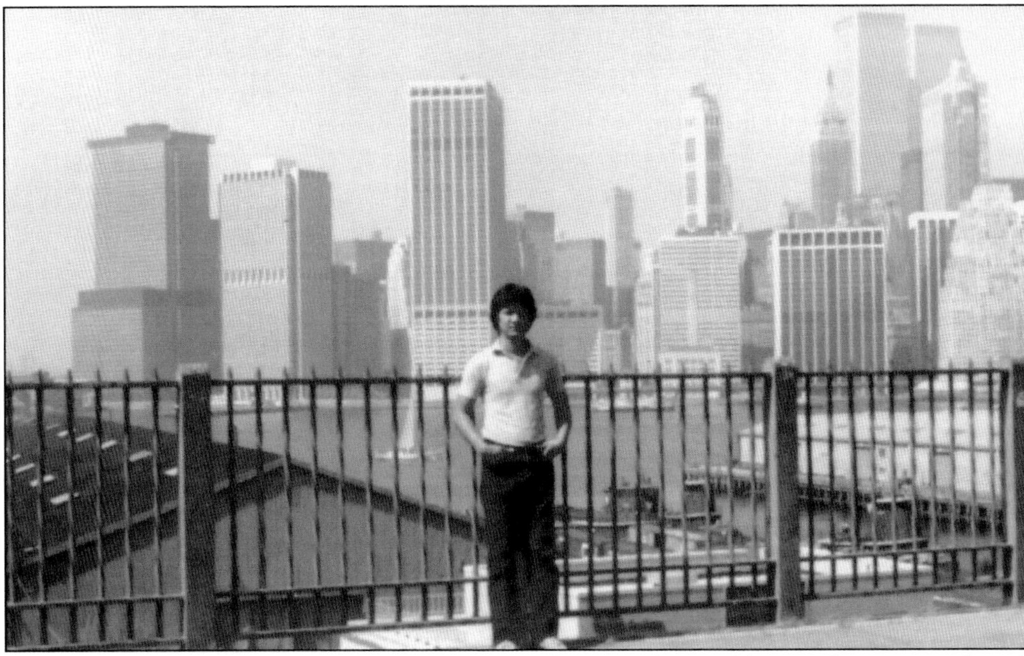

As a young Filipino American immigrant, Victor David poses at the Brooklyn Heights Promenade with a clear view of the downtown Manhattan skyline around 1983. (Courtesy of Nicole David.)

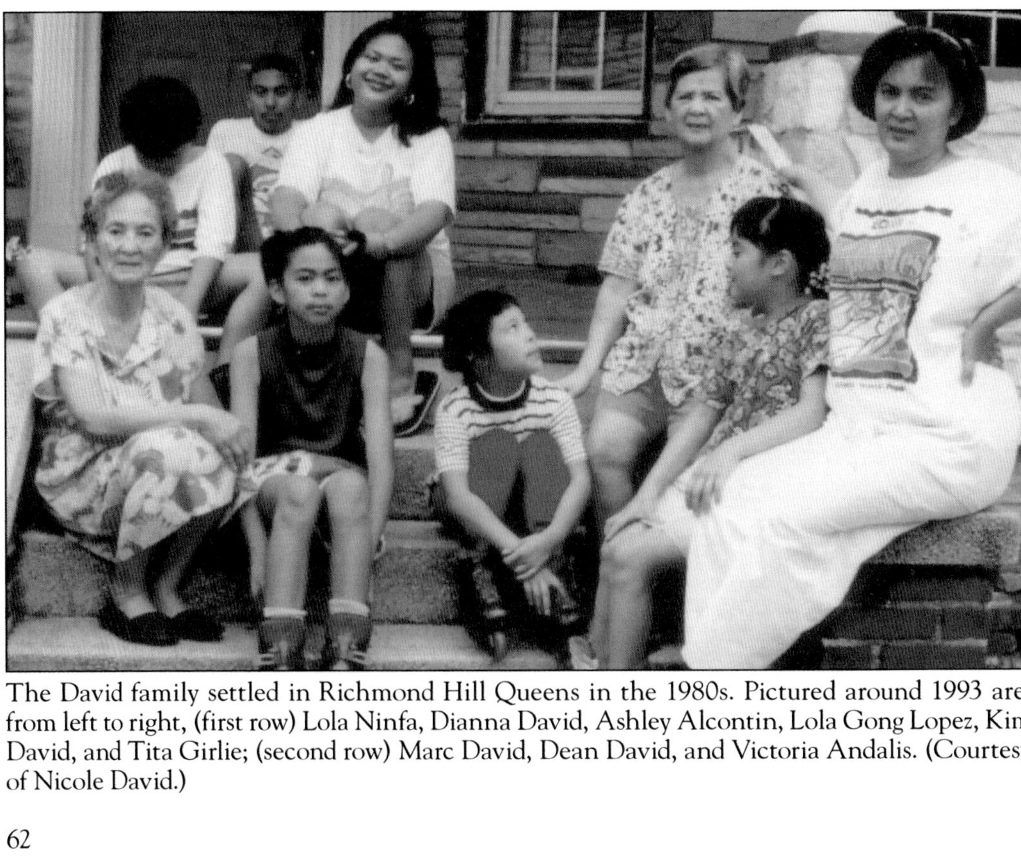

The David family settled in Richmond Hill Queens in the 1980s. Pictured around 1993 are, from left to right, (first row) Lola Ninfa, Dianna David, Ashley Alcontin, Lola Gong Lopez, Kim David, and Tita Girlie; (second row) Marc David, Dean David, and Victoria Andalis. (Courtesy of Nicole David.)

Four

Filipino Enclaves Established in the Five Boroughs

Manhattan, Brooklyn, Queens, Staten Island, & the Bronx

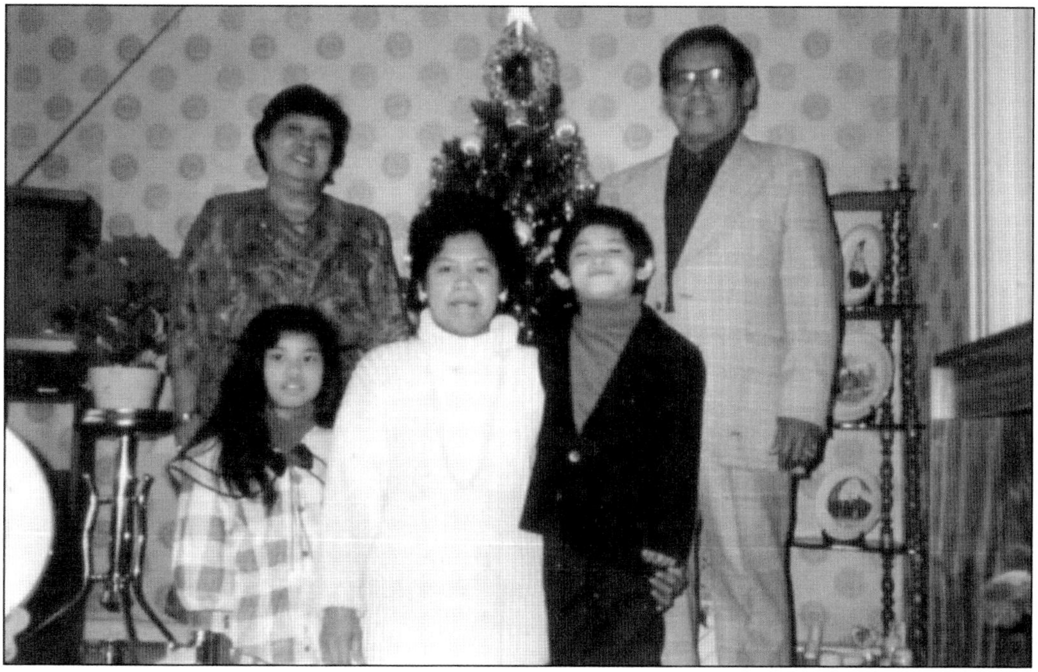

By the 1990s, there was a thriving Filipino American community in each of the five boroughs of New York. While Queens contained the most Filipino Americans by far, there were Filipino Americans that were living in Manhattan, Brooklyn, the Bronx, and Staten Island. Many of these Filipinos were families of the professionals who immigrated beginning in the late 1960s; many were petitioned by their siblings, parents, or children to immigrate to the United States; and many were migrant workers in search of career and financial opportunities. Pictured are members of the Madeja family in Hillside, Queens, about 1990. They are, from left to right, (first row) Terre-Anne Madeja Schneider, Teresita Madeja Cabadin, and Tristan Vizconde; (second row) Filomena Madeja and Andres Madeja. (Courtesy of Tristan Vizconde).

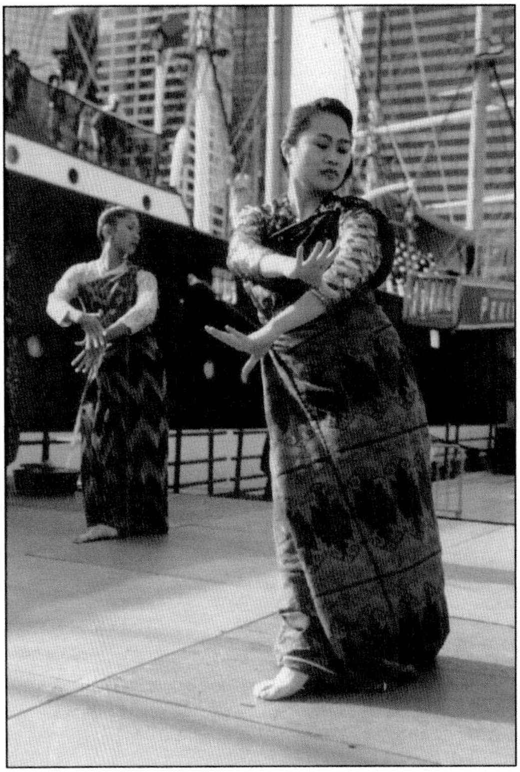

Kinding Sindaw Melayu Heritage is a dance company that has made a Philippine ancestral map in New York City through its mesmerizing performances of Southern Philippines Sultanate's indigenous rituals, court dances, and kulintang music. At two historical landmarks of New York City, the Flatiron Building (below, 1993) and the South Street Seaport (left, 1996), Kinding Sindaw has interwoven the indigenous with the urban, the old with the new, and the ancient with the modern. (Both, courtesy of Corky Lee.)

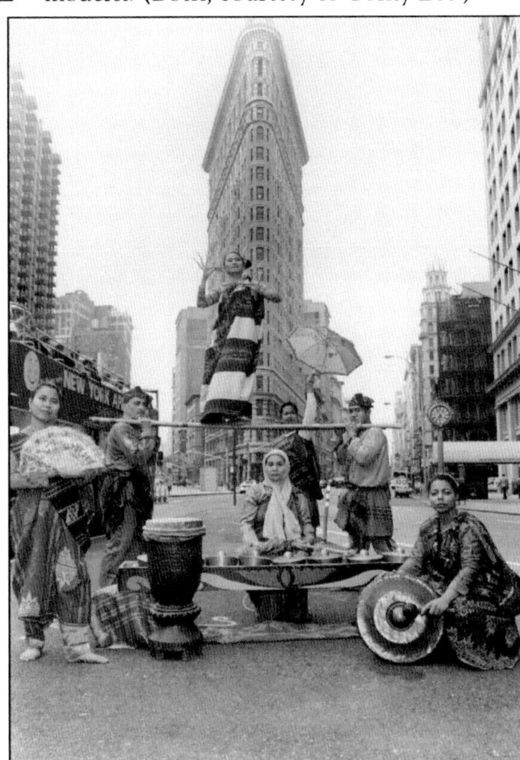

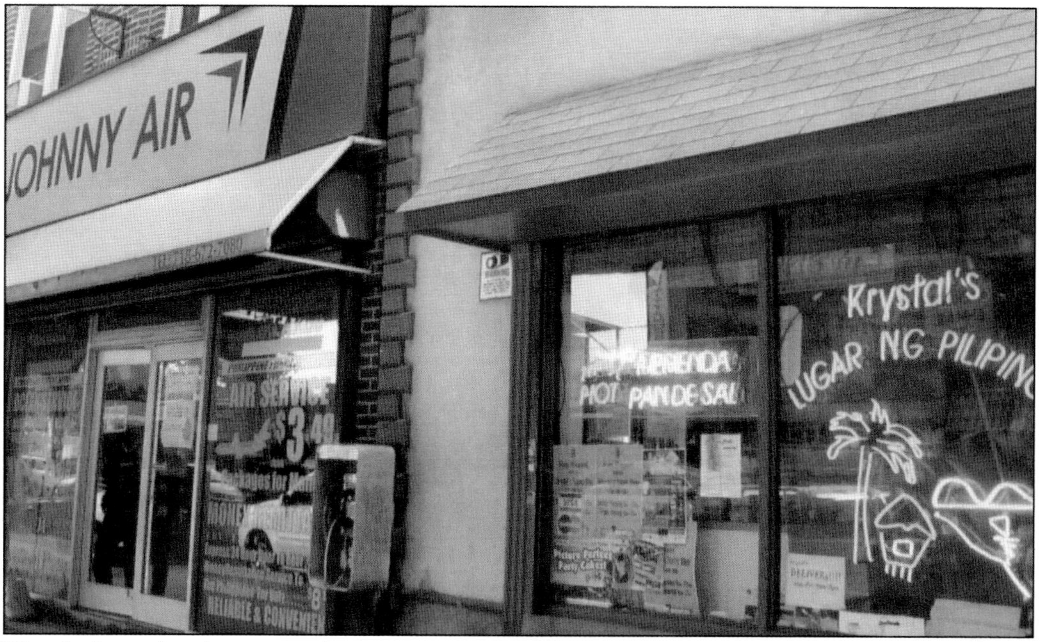

Woodside is often known as the "Little Manila" of New York City, as it houses the largest Filipino American enclave in the five boroughs. There are dozens of Filipino restaurants and shops that serve the needs of Filipino Americans. Pictured above is Roosevelt Avenue, often known as the Main Street of Woodside. Pictured at right is Ted Martinez in front of the Jollibee's in Woodside—the first of the popular Philippine fast-food chain in New York City. (Above, courtesy of FANHS Metro New York Archives; right, courtesy of Ted Martinez.)

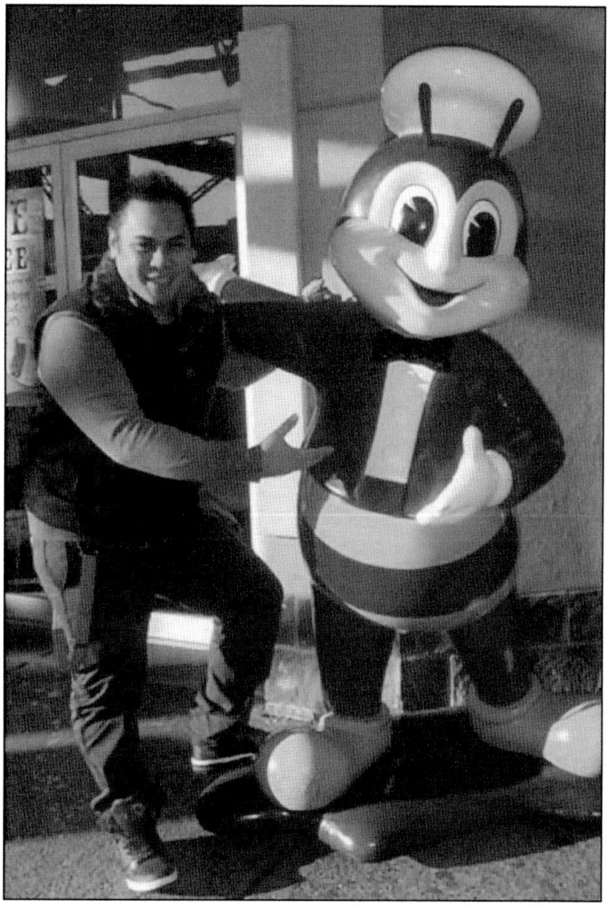

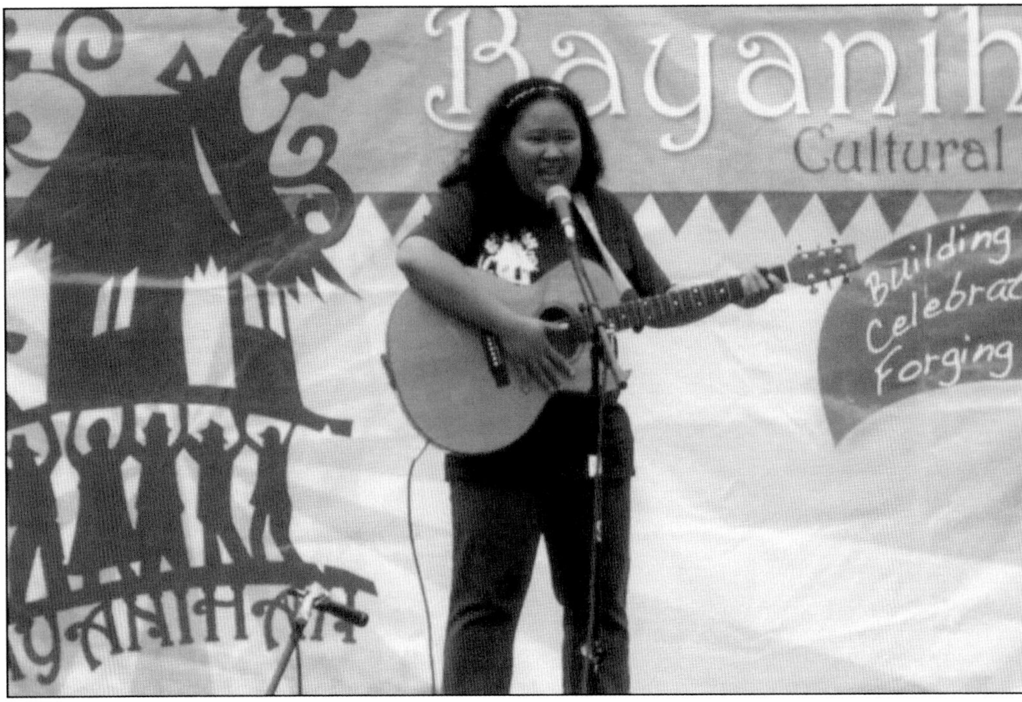

Because of the large Filipino American population, Woodside is where many Filipino American festivals and events take place. Above is Jonna Baldres at the Bayanihan Festival in 2012; below is an Eskrima martial arts demonstration at a street fair in 2013. (Above, courtesy of Philippine Forum; below, courtesy of Kalusugan Coalition, Inc.)

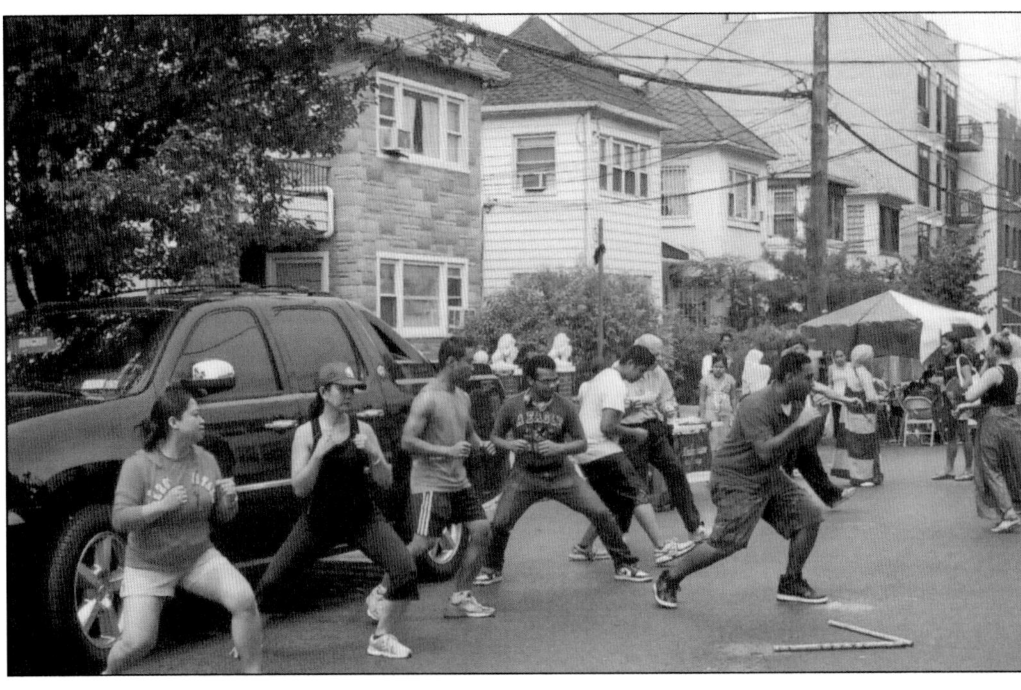

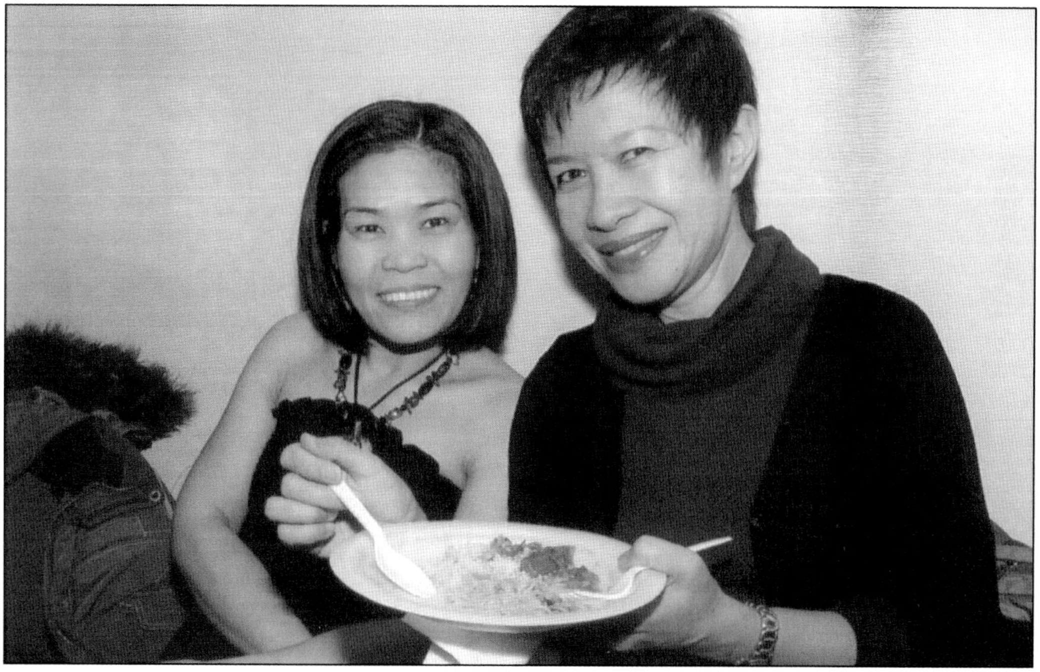

Above are Marilyn Segue (left) and Prof. Agnes "Bing" Magtoto at an event in Woodside, Queens. Professor Magtoto received the FANHS Metro New York Lifetime Achievement Award in 2014. Below is a photograph of Filipino American family members in Hillside, New York, another large Filipino American community in New York. Pictured here are Terre-Anne Madeja Schneider (left), Teresita Madeja Cabadin (center), and Tristan Madeja Vizconde playing in the snow in the early 1990s. (Above, courtesy of Damayan Migrant Workers; below, courtesy of Tristan Vizconde.)

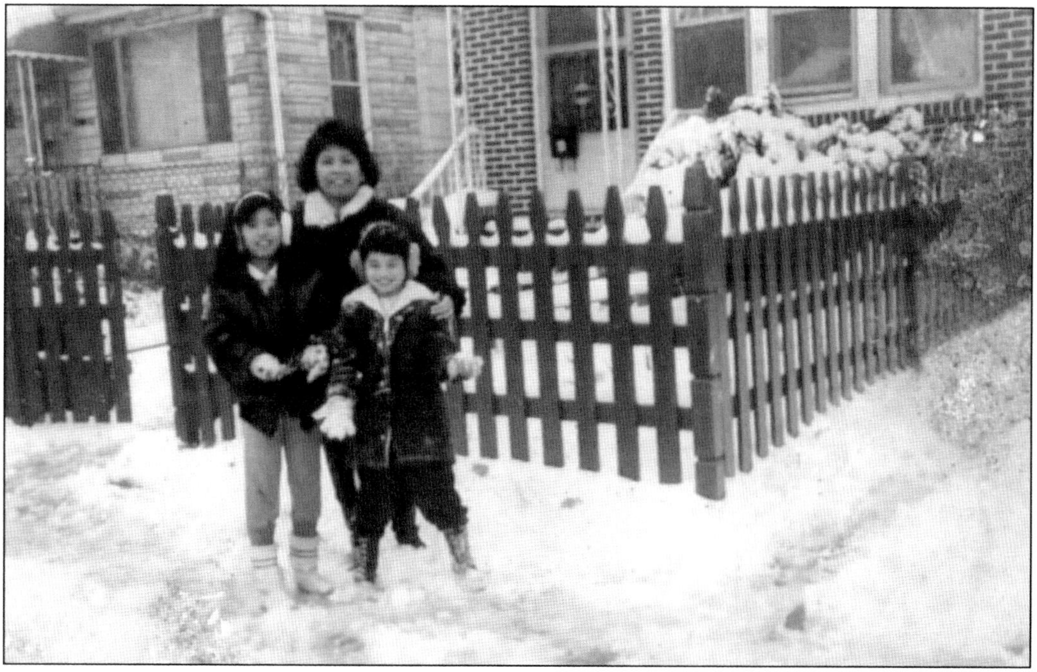

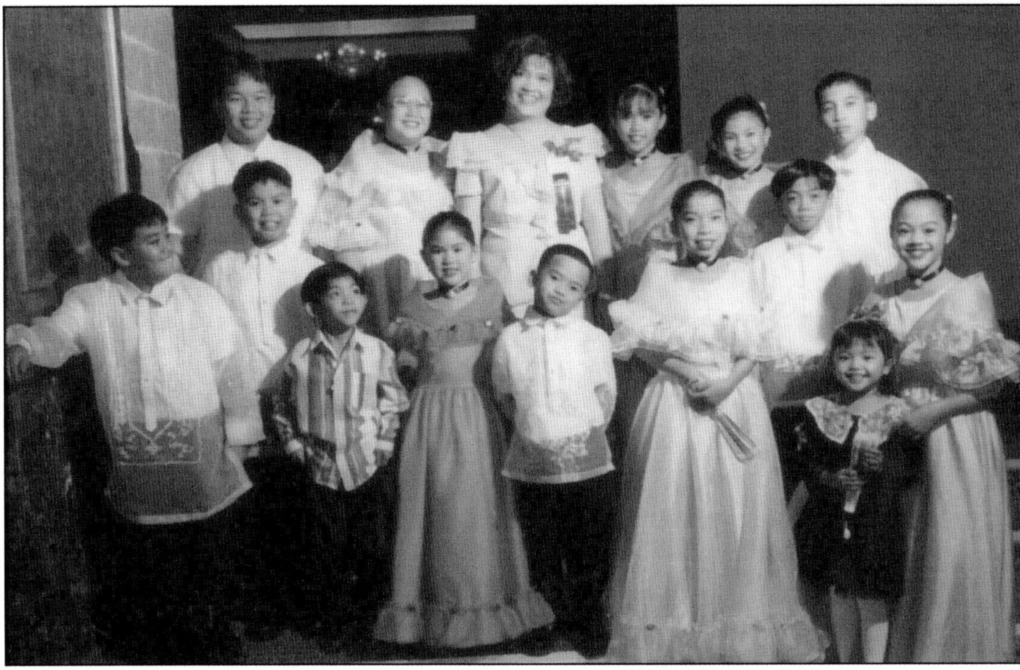

Jamaica, Queens, is also home to a populous Filipino American community in New York. In the image above, there is a group of young Filipino Americans from Jamaica, Queens, in traditional garments at a dinner dance in 1994. In the image below, taken around 2006, there are two generations of Filipino Americans, most of whom have lived in Jamaica, Queens. These include, from left to right, (first row) Father Jake Beltran, Severino Tamayo Jr., Luther Tamayo, Louie Punzalan, Sheila Punzalan, and Rexy Tamayo; (second row) Gail Prado, Joni Yabut, Jed Prado, Julian Tamayo, and Andrei Fajutagana. (Above, courtesy of the Tamayo family; below, courtesy of the author.)

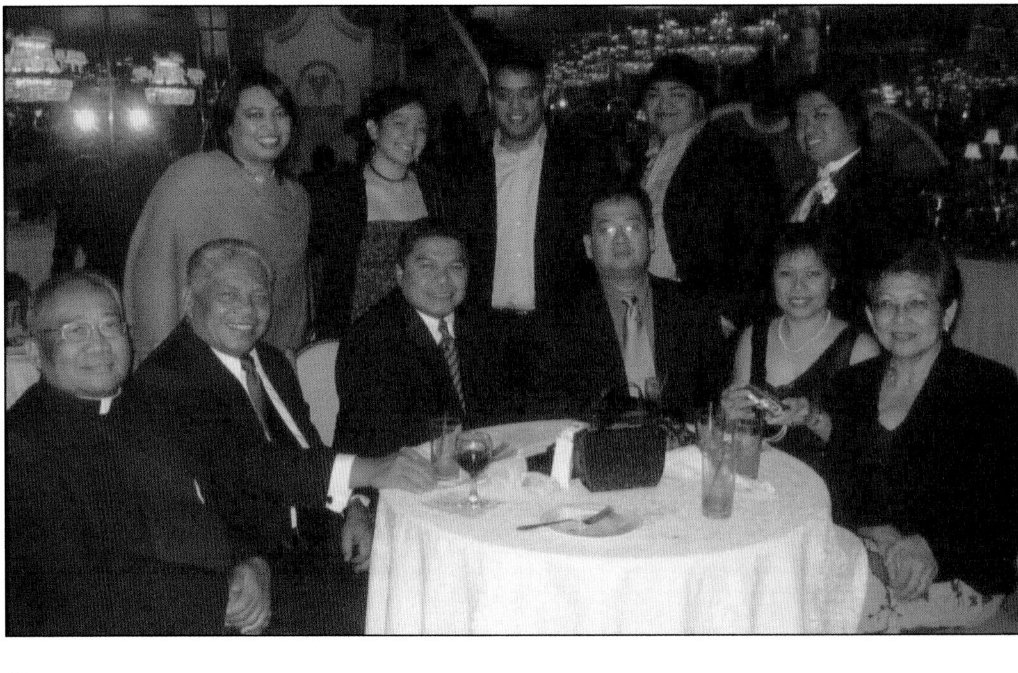

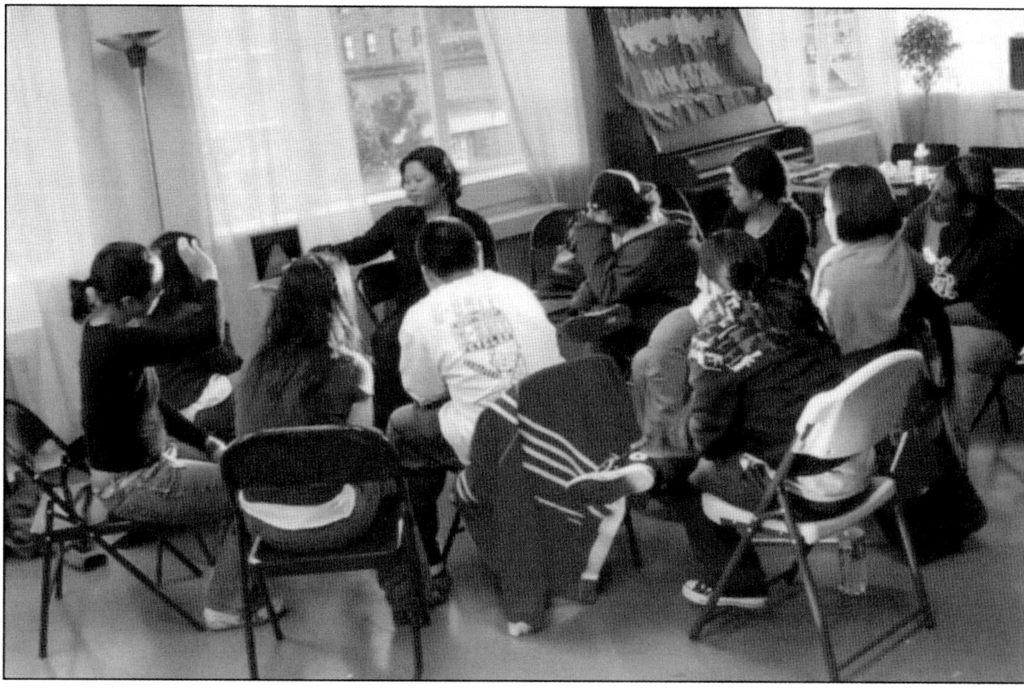

Jackson Heights, Queens, has another large enclave of Filipino Americans in New York City. Above is Ana Liza Caballes, a community organizer, giving an educational workshop to youth around 2004. Below are Riya Ortiz (left) and Allison Joy Faelnar, also community organizers, catching up at a social event in Jackson Heights in 2013. (Above, courtesy of Ana Liza Caballes; below, courtesy of Damayan Migrant Workers.)

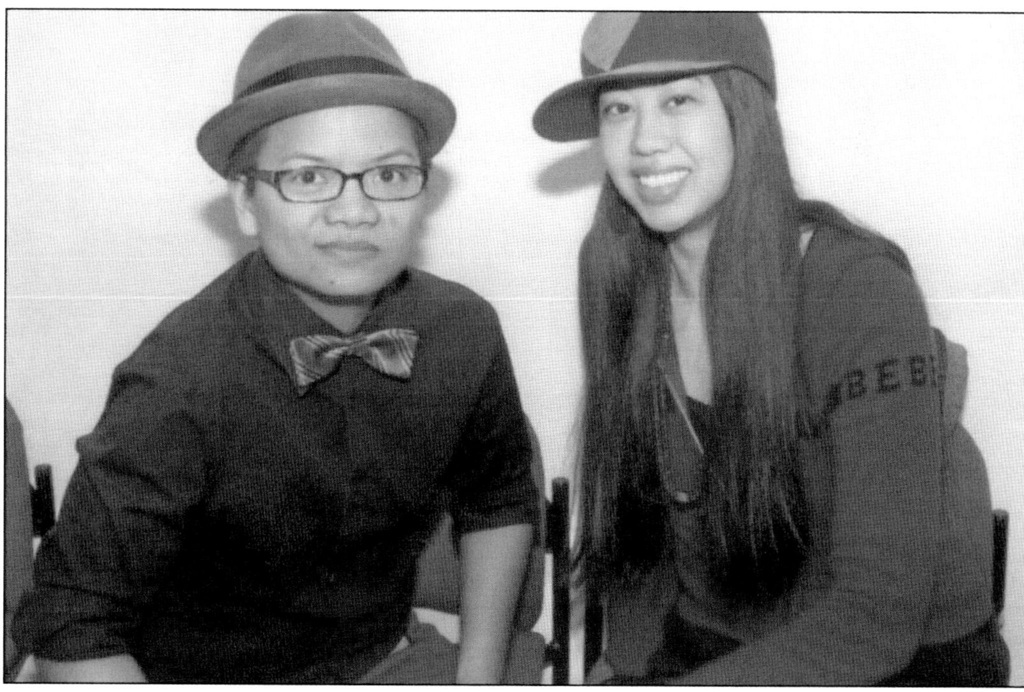

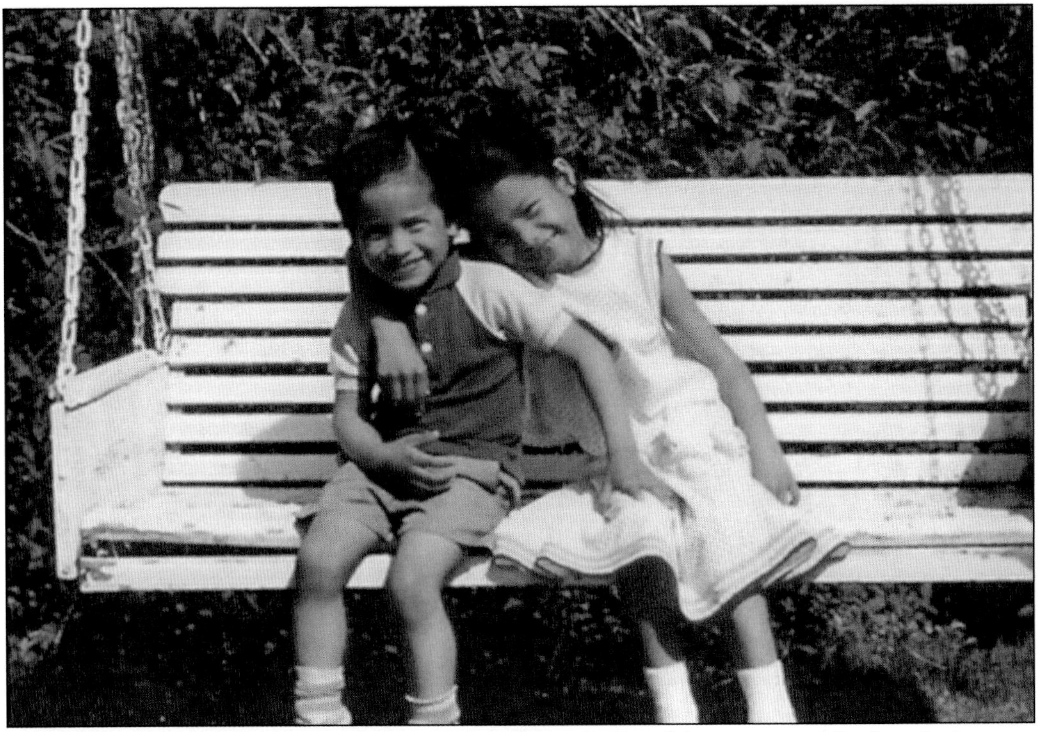

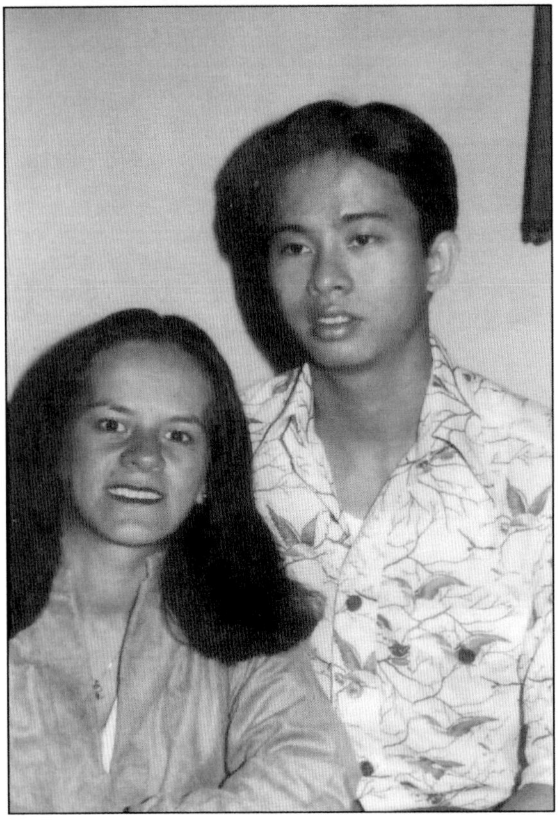

In Brooklyn, one neighborhood where several Filipino Americans settled was Bushwick, with many working at the Wyckoff Heights Medical Center. One of the families that has lived in Bushwick for decades is the Mendoza family. Above are Linda and RJ Mendoza about 1984, and on the left are their parents, Rudy and Stella Mendoza. Rudy immigrated to New York in the 1970s where he met Stella, a New Yorker of Native Hawaiian ancestry. (Both, courtesy of the Mendoza family.)

The Brooklyn Navy Yard continued to be a thriving Filipino American community until the 1980s, when there were fewer Filipino American seafarers that were settling in New York. Pictured here are Pio Fernandez (right) and a friend at the Brooklyn Navy Yard in the late 1970s. (Courtesy of the Alic-Fernandez family.)

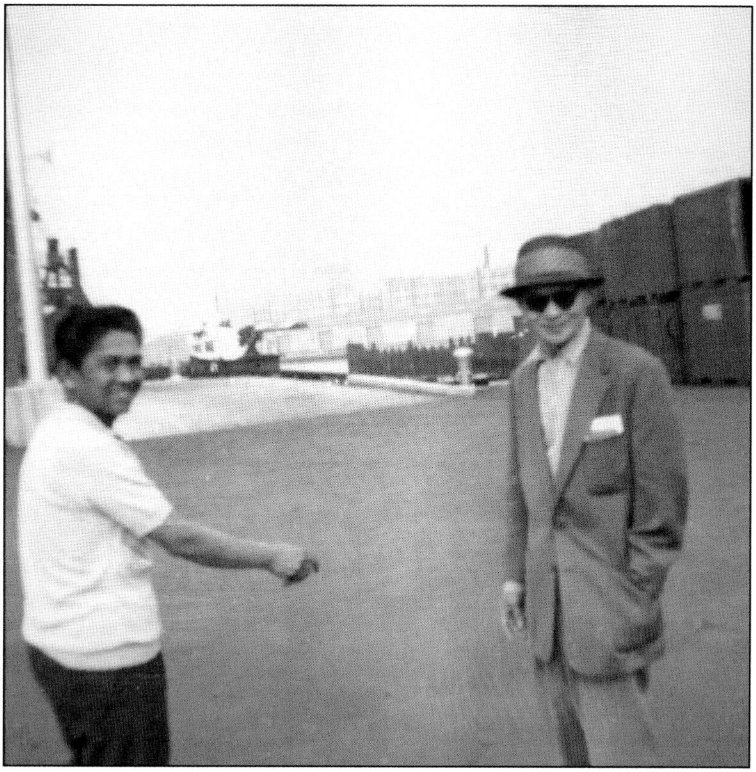

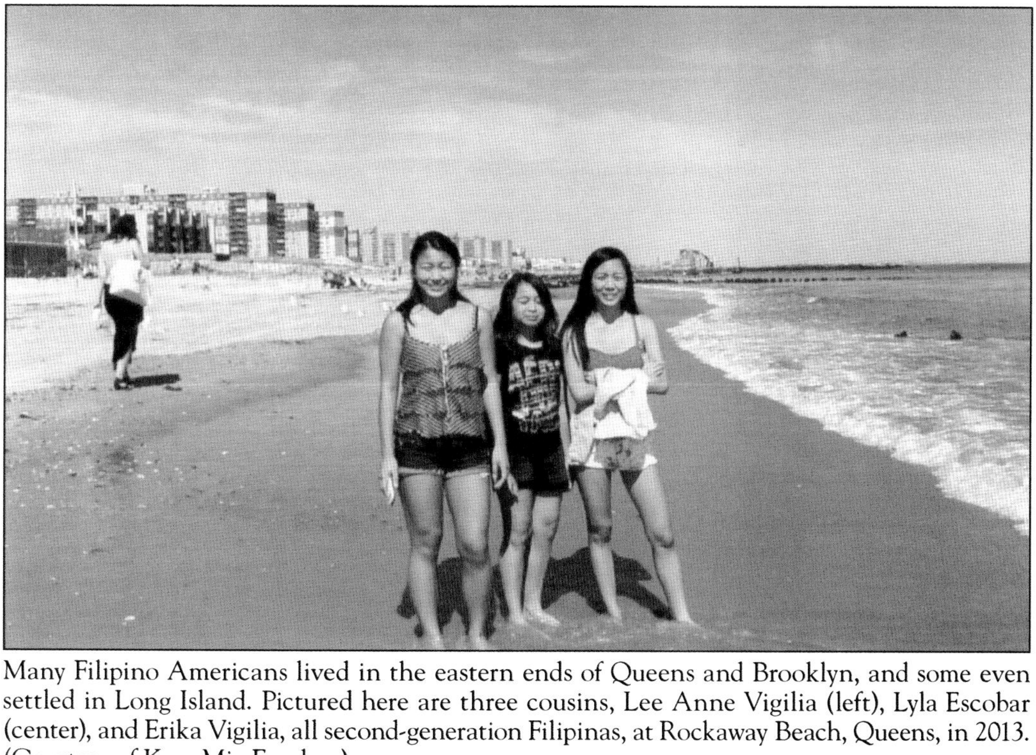

Many Filipino Americans lived in the eastern ends of Queens and Brooklyn, and some even settled in Long Island. Pictured here are three cousins, Lee Anne Vigilia (left), Lyla Escobar (center), and Erika Vigilia, all second-generation Filipinas, at Rockaway Beach, Queens, in 2013. (Courtesy of Kara Mia Escobar.)

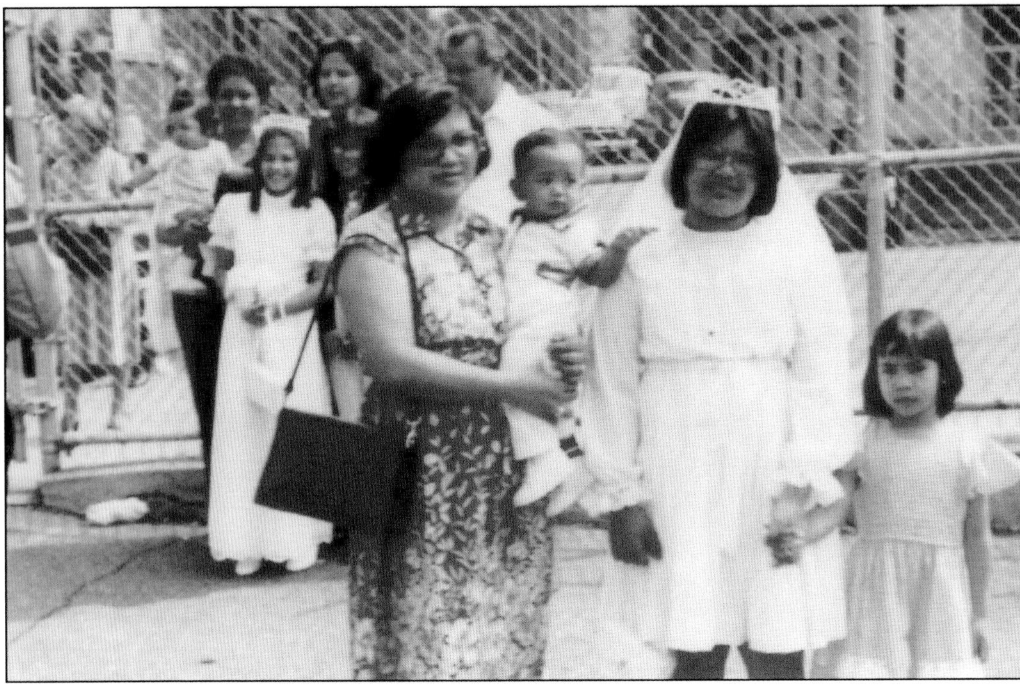

There was a smaller settlement of Filipino Americans who lived in the Bronx. Above is a photograph of a young Filipina with her family at her first communion in the Bronx, in the 1970s. Below is Bernadette Rogan Rynne along with her children Matthew and Thomas, who are of Filipino and Irish descent and were raised in the Bronx around 1994. (Above, courtesy of Rio Guerrero; below, courtesy of Stephanie Rogan Rynne.)

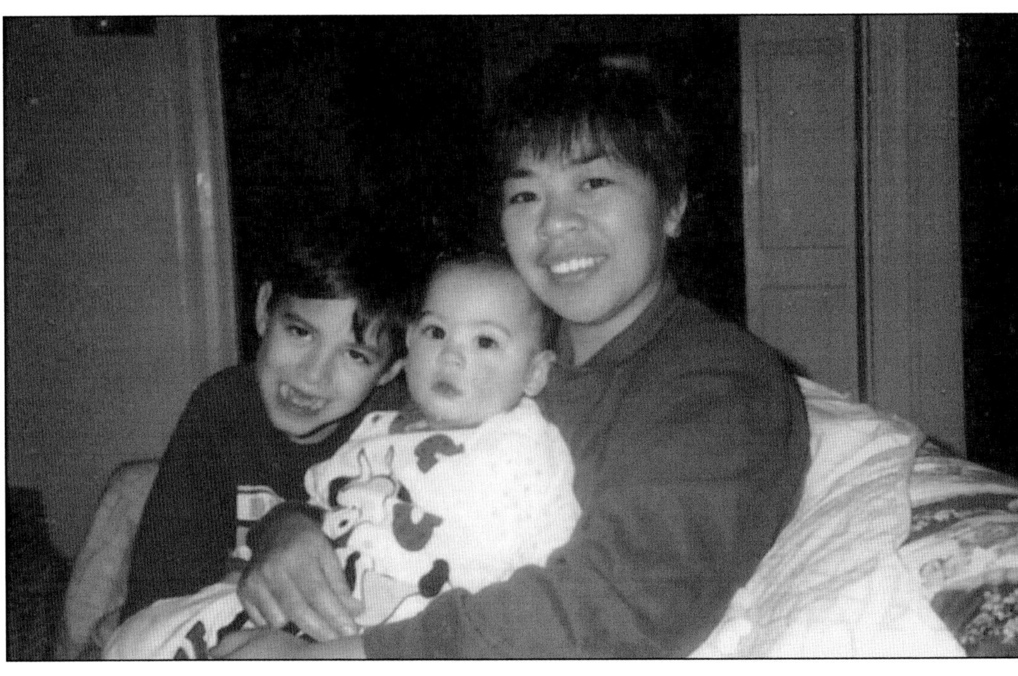

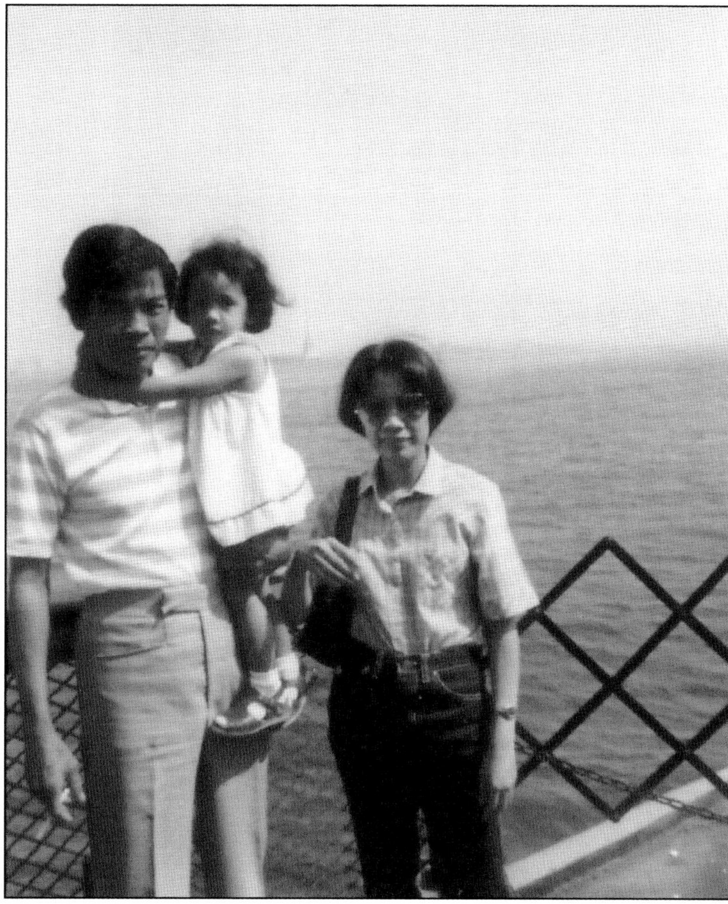

Staten Island is another borough where there is a smaller, but thriving community of Filipino Americans. Agustin Tibo, his granddaughter Cindy Manabat, and his daughter Cora Manabat are pictured here riding the Staten Island Ferry on the Hudson River around 1980. Below is a group of Filipino Americans celebrating Easter in 1987 on Staten Island. (Both, courtesy of Corinne Manabat.)

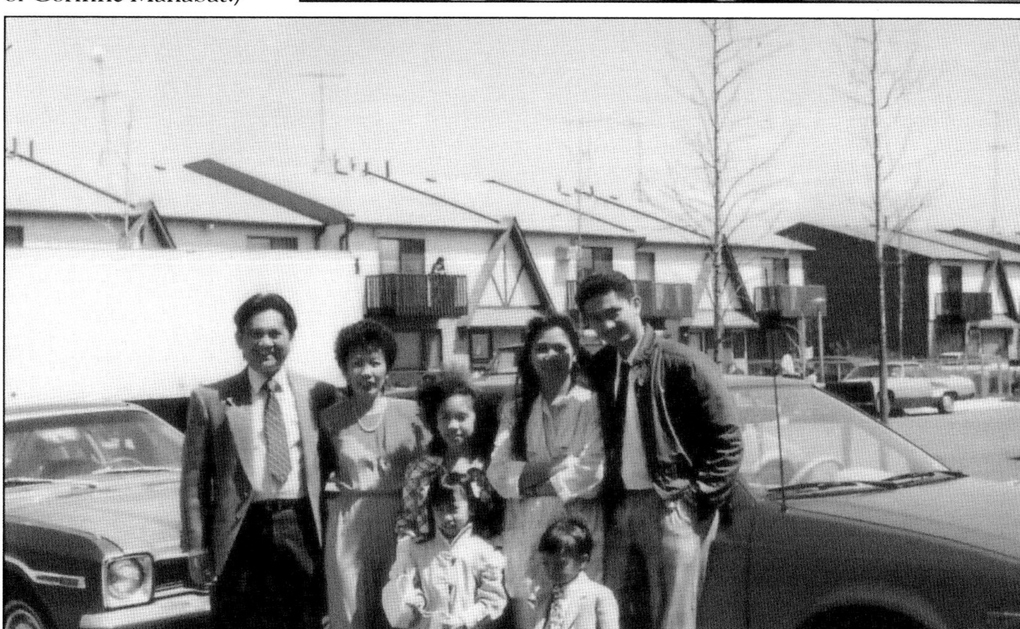

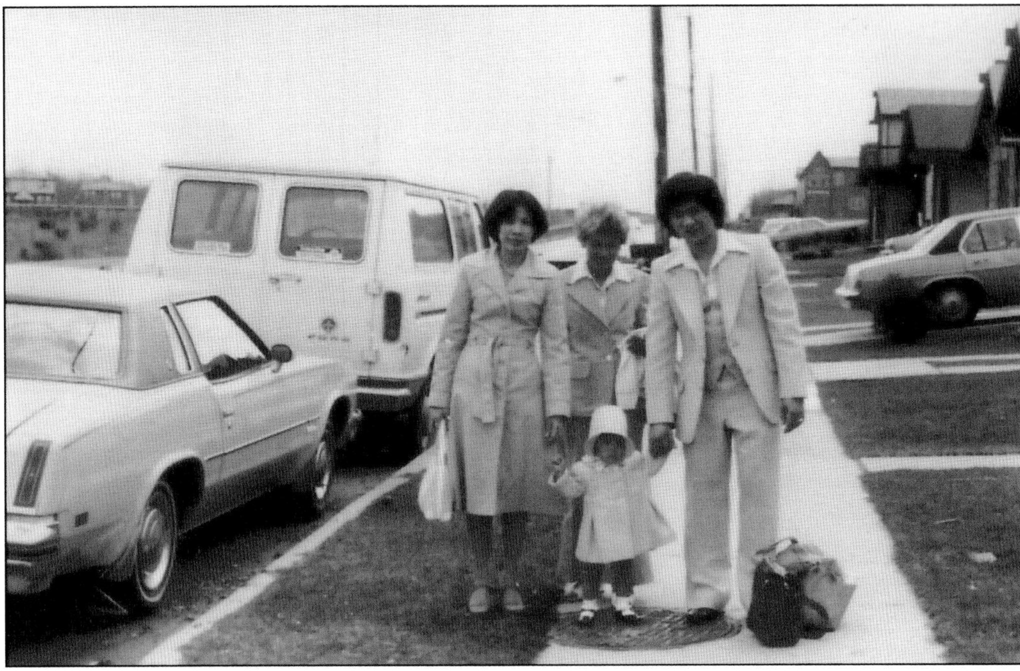

Dressed in their Sunday best are members of the Manabat family on Easter 1979 in Staten Island, New York. Pictured above, from left to right, are Cora Manabat, Cindy Manabat, E. Manabat, and Mariquita P. Tibo. Below is a group of cousins in the Westerleigh area of Staten Island in 1990. From left to right are (first row) Victor Santa Ana, Corinne Manabat, and Anthony David; (second row) Elbert David, Cindy Manabat, and Andrew Santa Ana. (Both, courtesy of Corinne Manabat.)

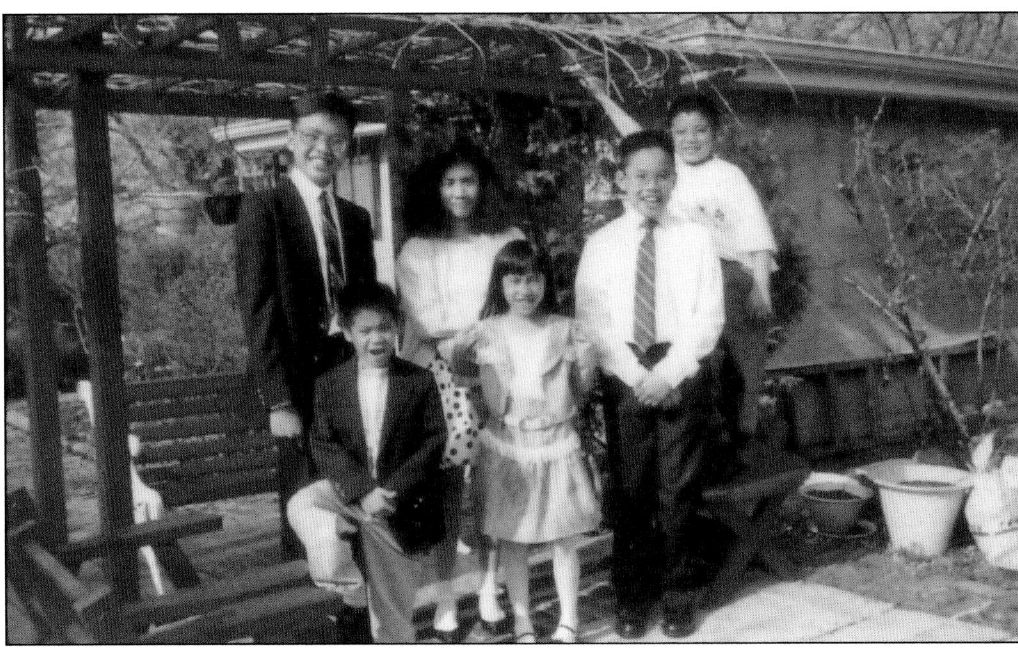

Many Filipino Americans attended public schools in various parts of New York. Pictured are Bryan Andalis and his elementary school principal, Mr. Gold, at his kindergarten graduation from PS 56 in Richmond Hill, Queens, around 1989. (Courtesy of Nicole David.)

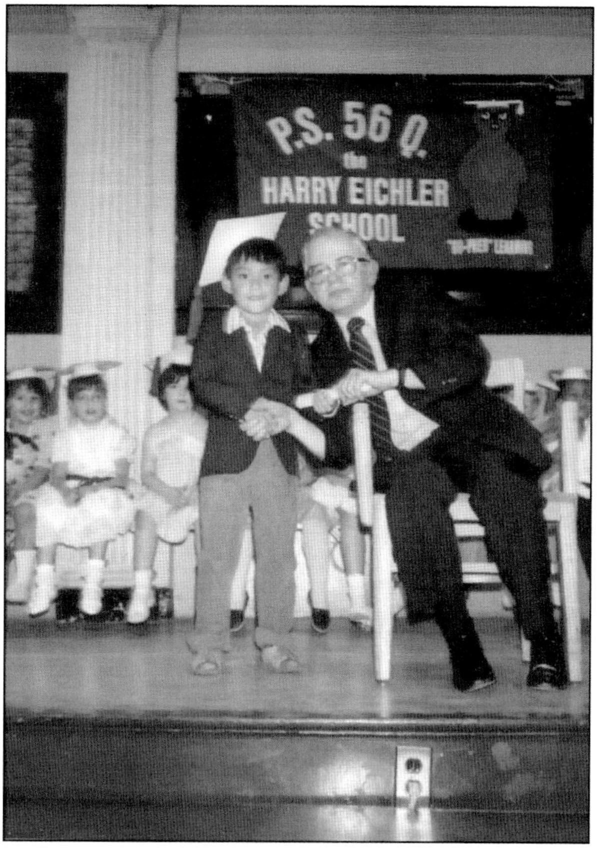

The New York City subway is the most common form of transportation across the five boroughs. Originally costing just five cents per ride from 1904 to 1948, the cost of a subway ride in 2015 is now $2.50. Pictured here are Victoria Andalis (left) and Nadia Palomar riding the subway about 1994. (Courtesy of Nicole David.)

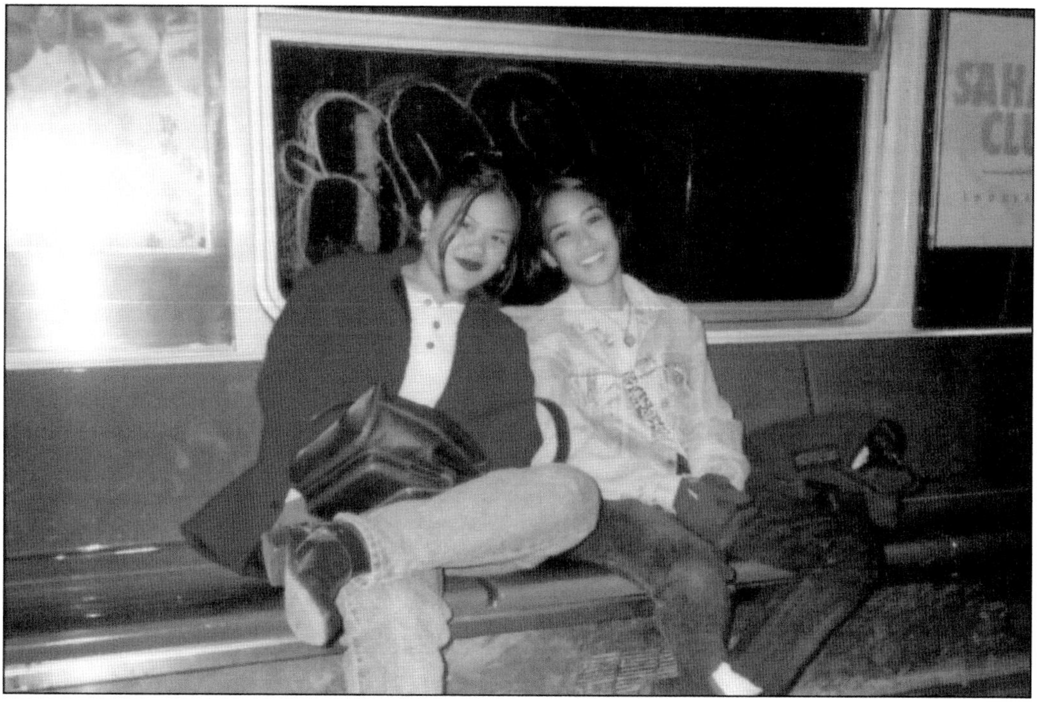

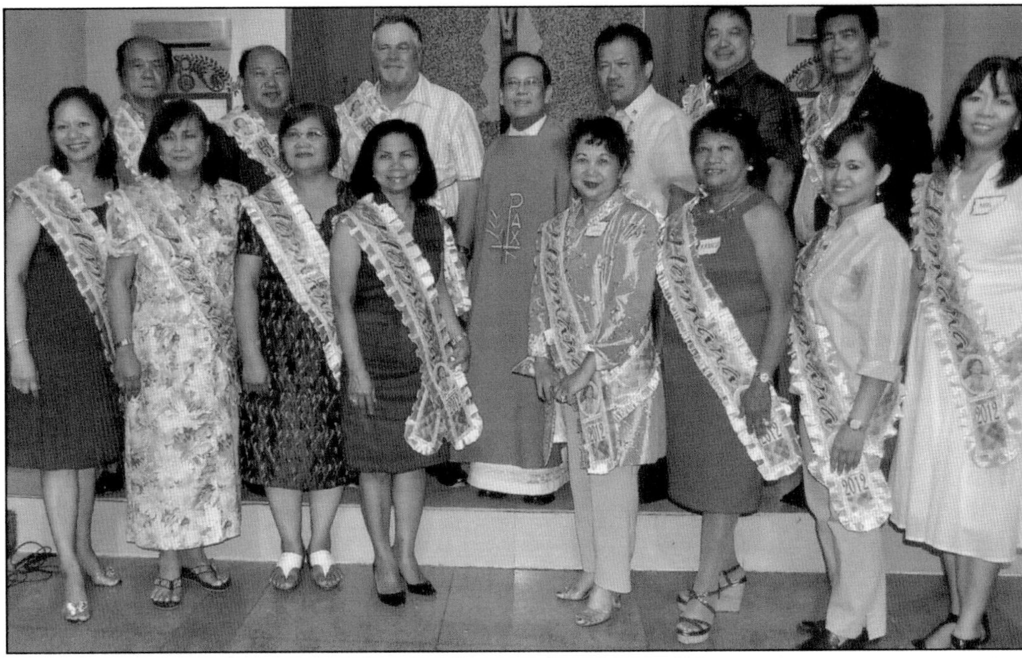

Several Catholic and Christian churches have gathered large Filipino American congregations across New York City. First, the Roman Catholic Chapel of San Lorenzo Ruiz, located on Broome Street in Manhattan, was established in 2005 and named as the official "Church of Filipinos" by Archbishop Edward Cardinal Egan on June 15, 2005. The Filipino Pastoral Ministry of Our Lady of Pompei was established in 1988 and is dedicated to welcome and minister to Filipino immigrants in New York. The church is located within the Greenwich Village neighborhood in Manhattan. Above are members of the Chapel of San Lorenzo Ruiz and below are members of Our Lady of Pompei. (Above, courtesy of San Lorenzo Ruiz; below, courtesy of Filipino Pastoral Ministry of Our Lady of Pompei.)

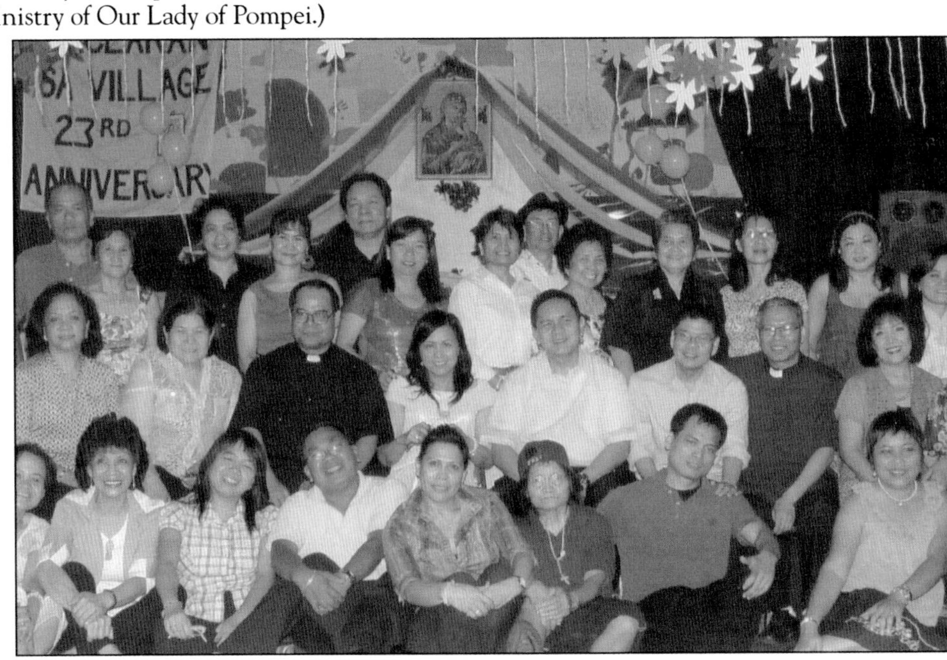

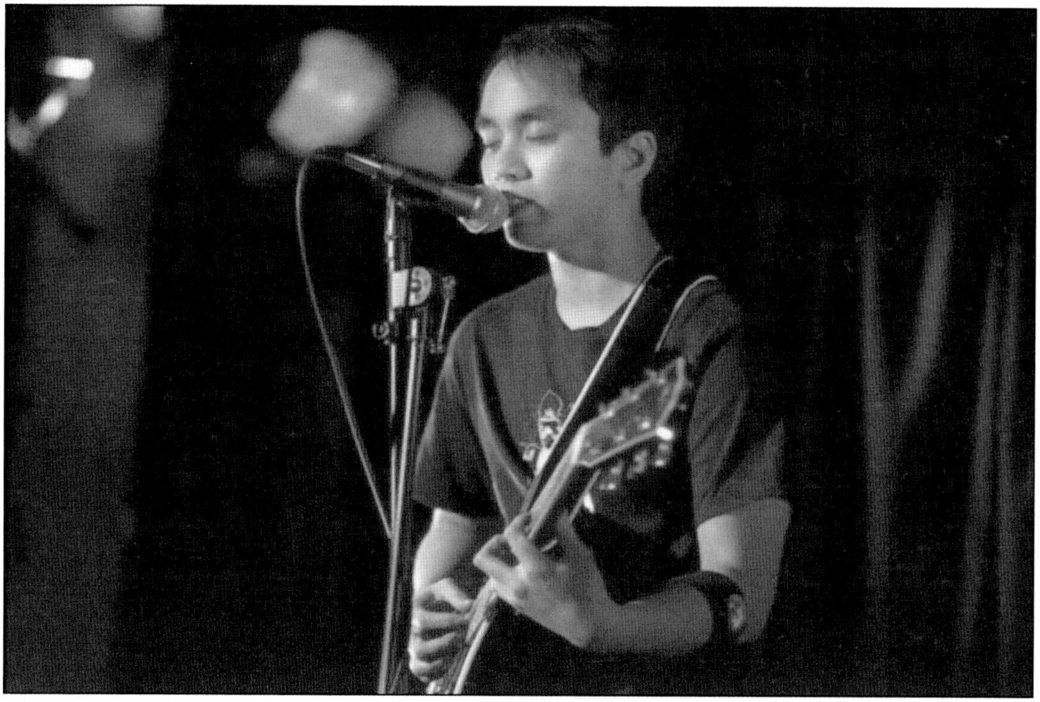

There is a long history of artists that have thrived in New York City. The Sulu Series was a monthly showcase that featured up-and-coming Filipino American and Asian American artists from 2005 until 2010. Pictured here is Jay Legaspi, a singer and songwriter who regularly performed at Sulu Series and other open mic nights across New York City. (Courtesy of Sulu Series.)

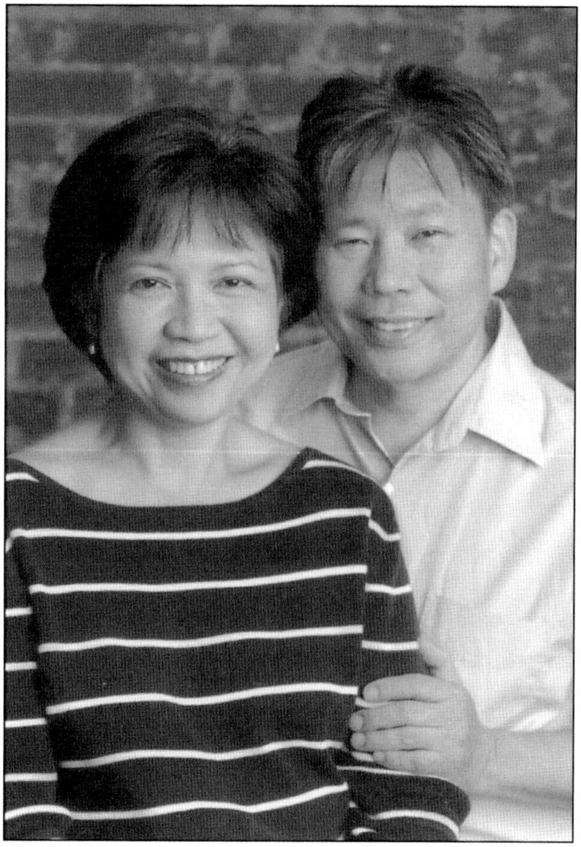

The Filipino restaurant scene has been alive as long as Filipinos have been present in New York; many have flourished, while others eventually went out of business. Pictured here are Amy Besa and Romy Dorotan, owners and chefs at the Purple Yam restaurant in Brooklyn, one of the most revered Filipino restaurants in New York City. (Courtesy of Amy Besa.)

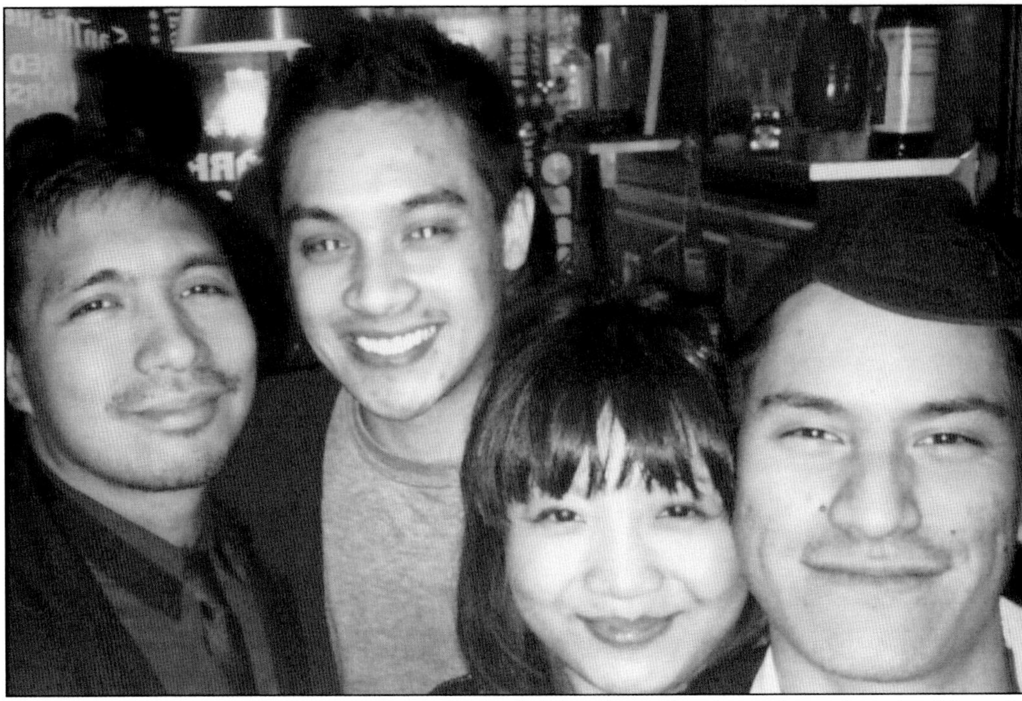

New York City is known for its spectacular nightlife—from the disco days of Studio 54 to the contemporary bar scenes in Manhattan's Greenwich Village or Lower East Side, Brooklyn's Williamsburg or Bushwick, or Queens's Long Island City or Astoria, there is always something for Filipino Americans to do in New York. Pictured here, from left to right, are Larry Tantay, Andrew Zarate, Fronthy Nguyen, and RJ Mendoza-Nadal at Jeepney—a Filipino restaurant in the East Village of Manhattan. (Courtesy of the author.)

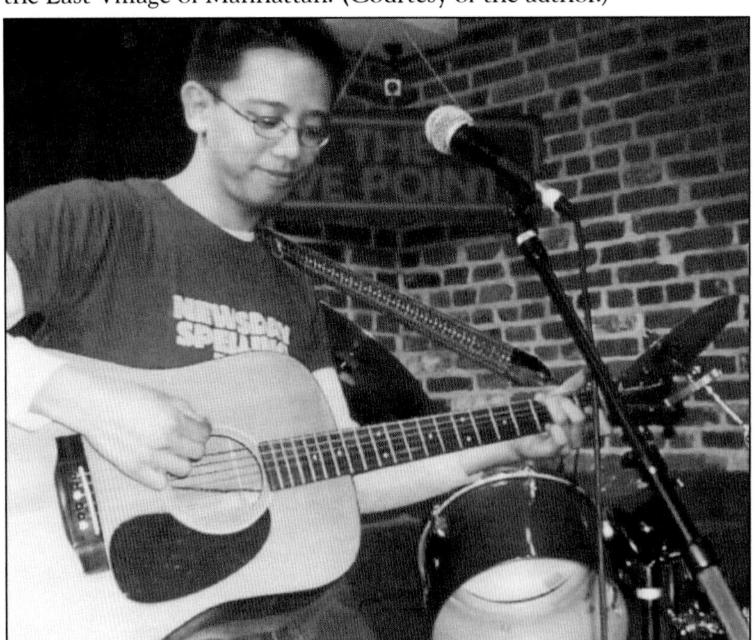

Open microphone (or open mic) nights were a place for Filipino American artists to perform in front of live audiences, particularly in debuting their new material. Actors, poets, writers, musicians, singers, and comedians have graced various open mics, in hopes of captivating audiences and sharing their art forms. Pictured here is singer-songwriter John-Flor Sisante performing at the Five Points Variety Hour in 2007. (Courtesy of Five Points Variety Show.)

Over the past decades, there have been many successful Filipino restaurants that have emerged as staples of New York City cuisine. In Manhattan, there is Maharlika, Grill 21, Ugly Kitchen, Jeepney, and Cafe 81. In Brooklyn, there is Umi Nom, Lumpia Shack, and Purple Yam. In Queens, there is Papa's Kitchen, Tito Rad's Grill, Krystal's, Engeline's, Payag, Ihawan, and more. And in the past, people may have enjoyed the food of Kuma Inn, Dragonfly, Cendrillon, and Elvie's—all notable restaurants that had successful runs in New York. Pictured on the right are Nicole Ponseca (the owner and founder of Maharlika and Jeepney) and journalist Jose Antonio Vargas. Pictured below are two Filipina Americans, Lee Anne Vigilia (left) and Kara Mia Escobar, enjoying a *kamayan*-style (hand eaten) lunch at the Ihawan Restaurant in Queens. (Right, courtesy of Nicole Ponseca; below, courtesy of Kara Mia Escobar.)

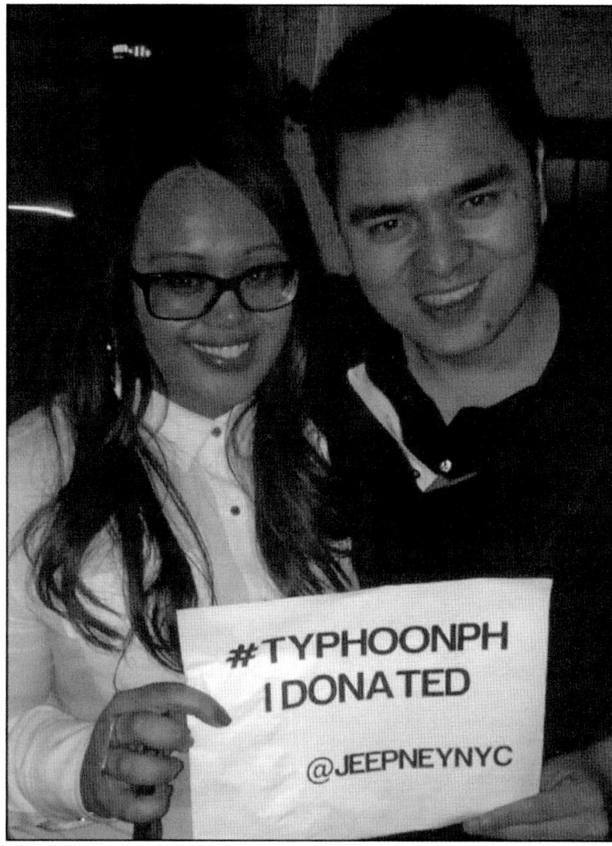

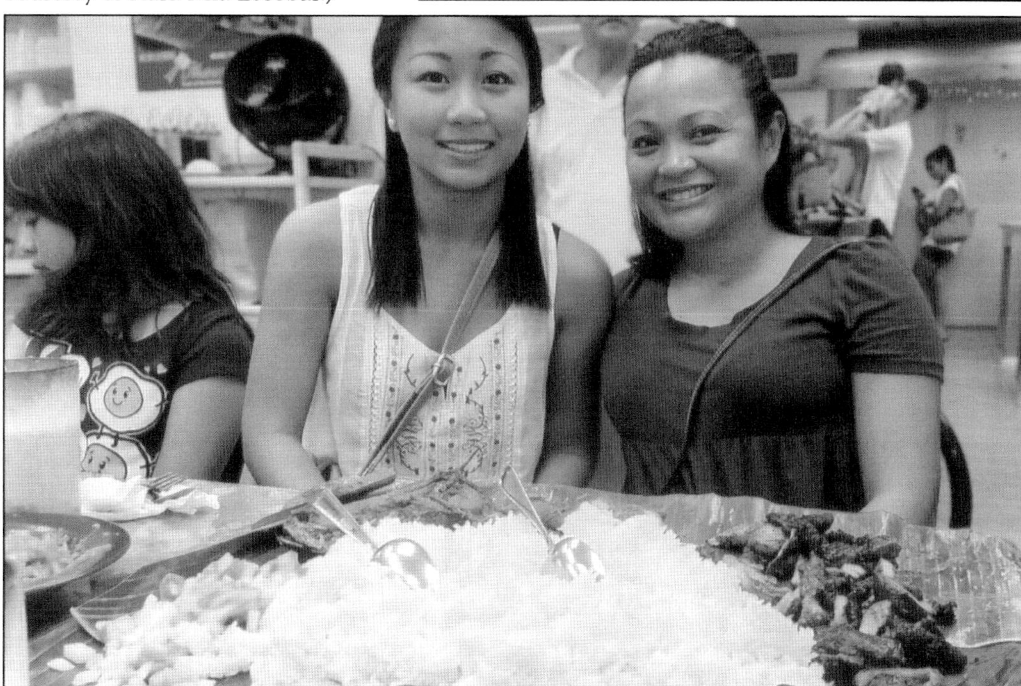

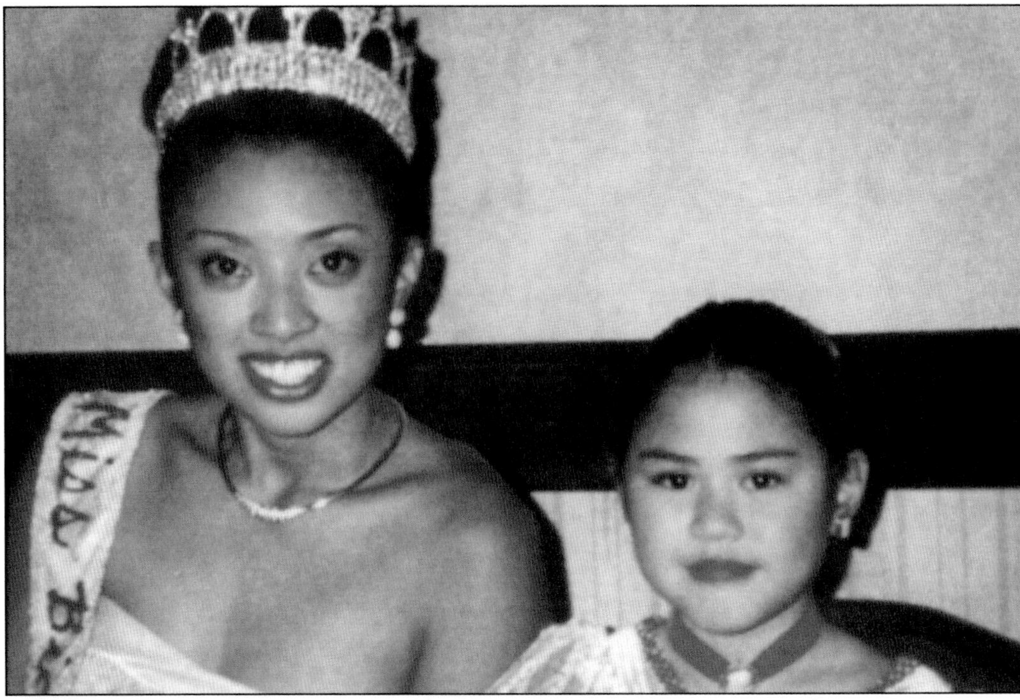

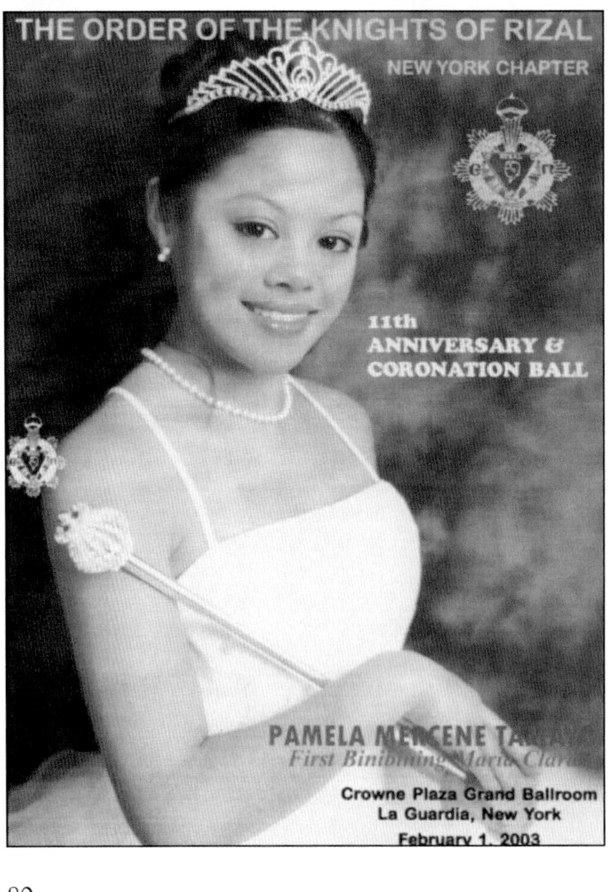

Like in many Filipino American communities across the United States, beauty pageants have always been present among Filipino Americans in New York. Many of these beauty pageants are accompanied by extravagant galas that celebrate various hometowns and regions of the Philippines. Pictured above is Jaclyn Reburiano (left), who was Miss Bicolandia USA in 1999, along with her cousin Kathleen Siapno. Pictured on the left is Pamela Tamayo who was the "First Binibining Maria Clara" of the Order of the Knights of Rizal New York Chapter in 2003. (Above, courtesy of Jaclyn Reburiano Chan; left, courtesy of Julian Tamayo.)

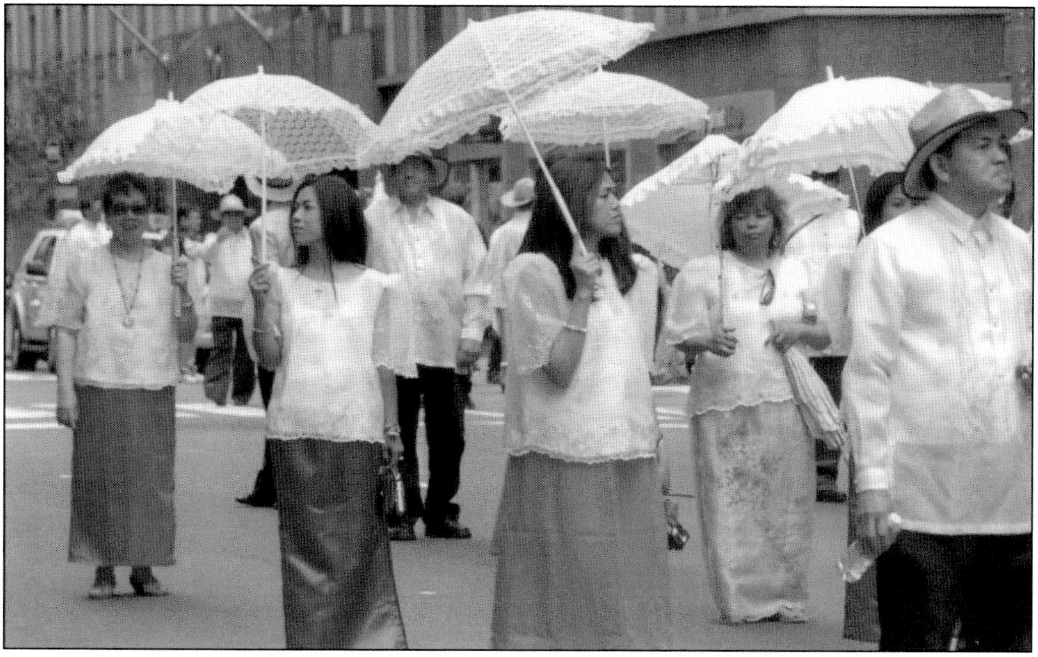

The Philippine Independence Day Parade has been a staple in New York City since 1990. Pictured here are parade marchers in traditional Filipino formal wear in 2011. (Both, courtesy of Daniel Ballesteros.)

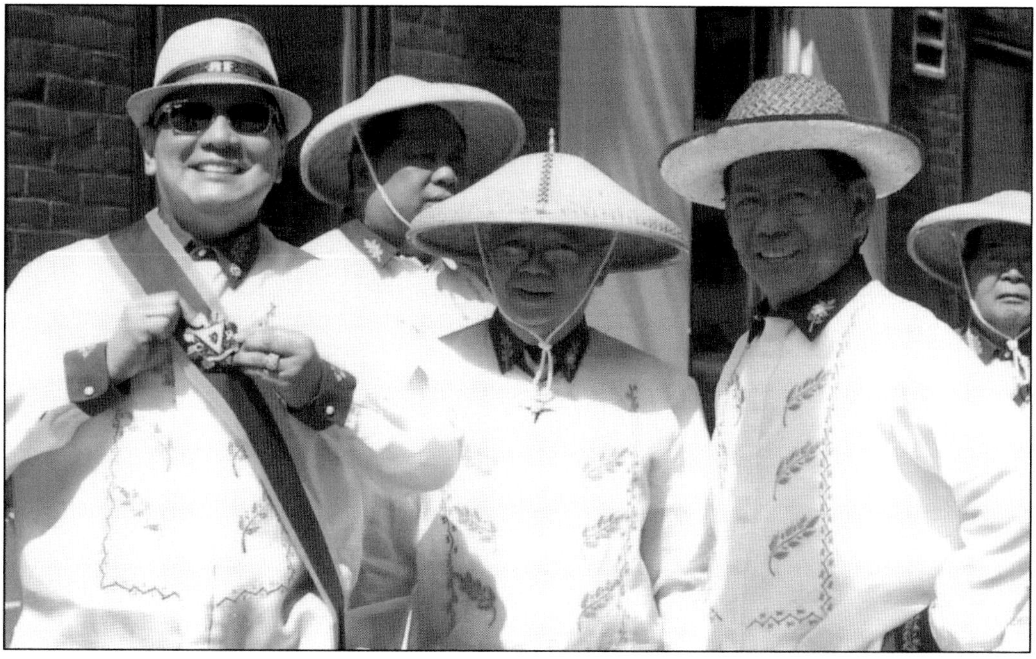

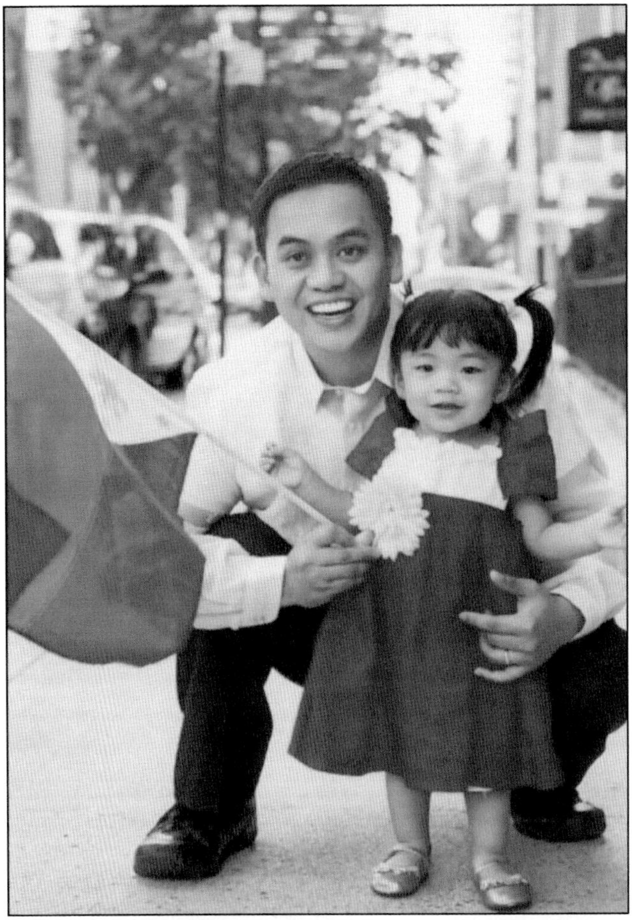

Joe Valdez and one-year-old daughter Isabelle Celine enjoyed the Philippine Independence Day Parade in New York City on June 2, 2013. Pictured below is the Jaycees organization at the parade on that same day. (Right, courtesy of Joe Valdez and Bel Molina; below, courtesy of Mia Fulgado.)

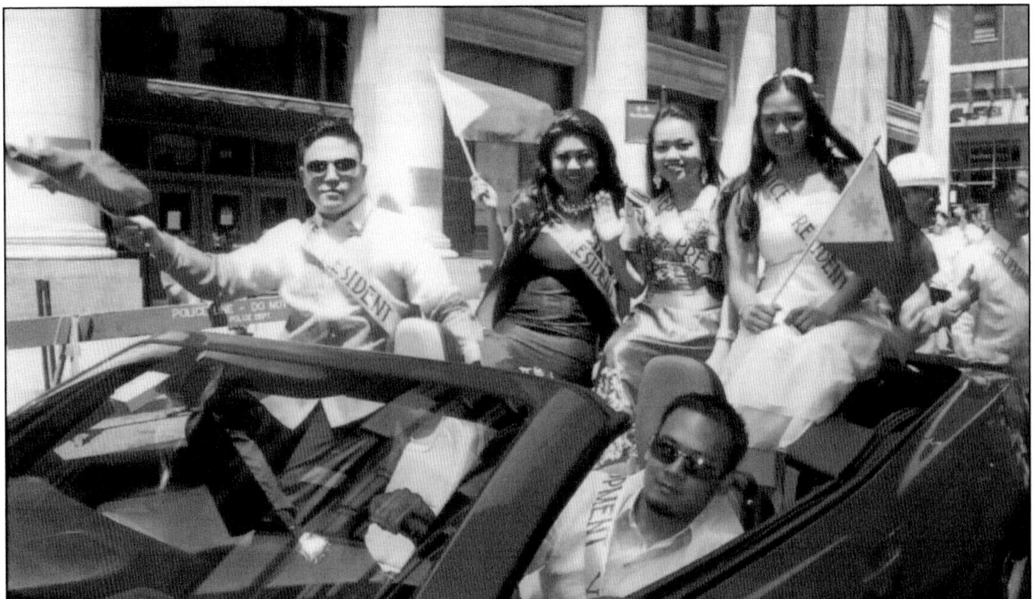

Five

Filipino American Organizations
Past and Present

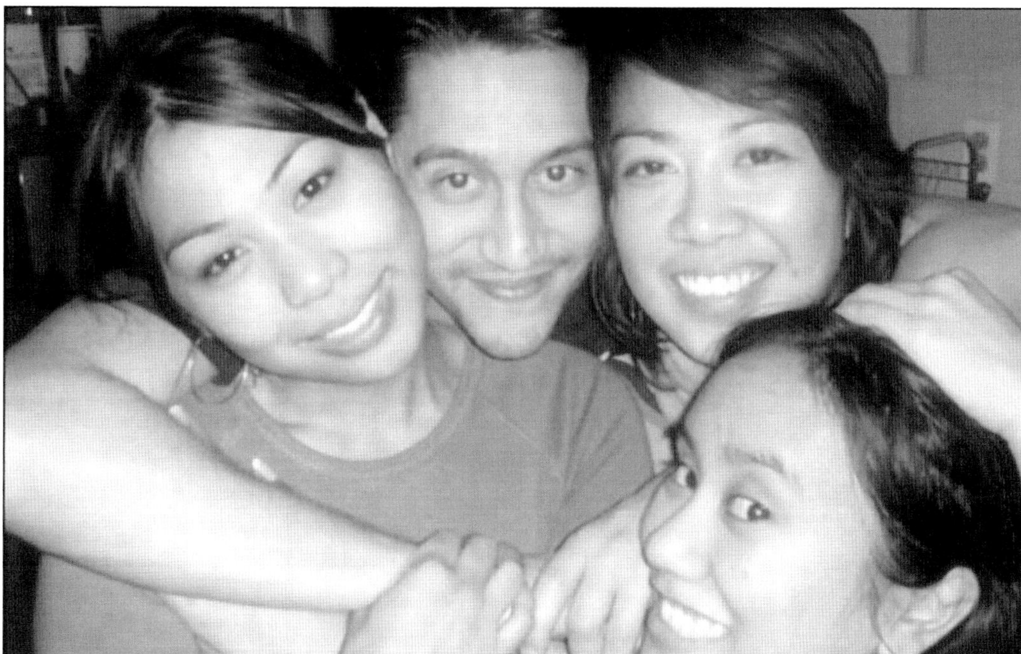

There have been hundreds of Filipino American organizations in New York City since the first Filipino Students' Association formed in the early 1900s. Some of these organizations have been regional or hometown organizations for immigrants wanting to stay connected with people from their same region or hometown in the Philippines. For example, the San Esteban Circle in the 1930s consisted of young students with roots in San Esteban in Ilocos Sur in the Philippines, while the Pampanga Foundation is a current organization that aims to promote the province of Pampanga to those in the American Northeast. Other organizations are interest-based groups focusing on civic issues, social justice activism, and arts. For instance, Topaz Arts is an organization that promotes contemporary performance and visual arts, while AF3IRM is a transnational feminist organization that advocates for women's rights. Finally, some organizations are career-based, gathering Filipinos of similar professions and fields. Examples include the Philippine Nurses Association and the Association of Fil-Am Teachers of America. Pictured are, clockwise from left, Marie Obaña, John Miller, Leah Obias, and Corinne Manabat—young Filipino American community leaders in 2004. (Courtesy of the author.)

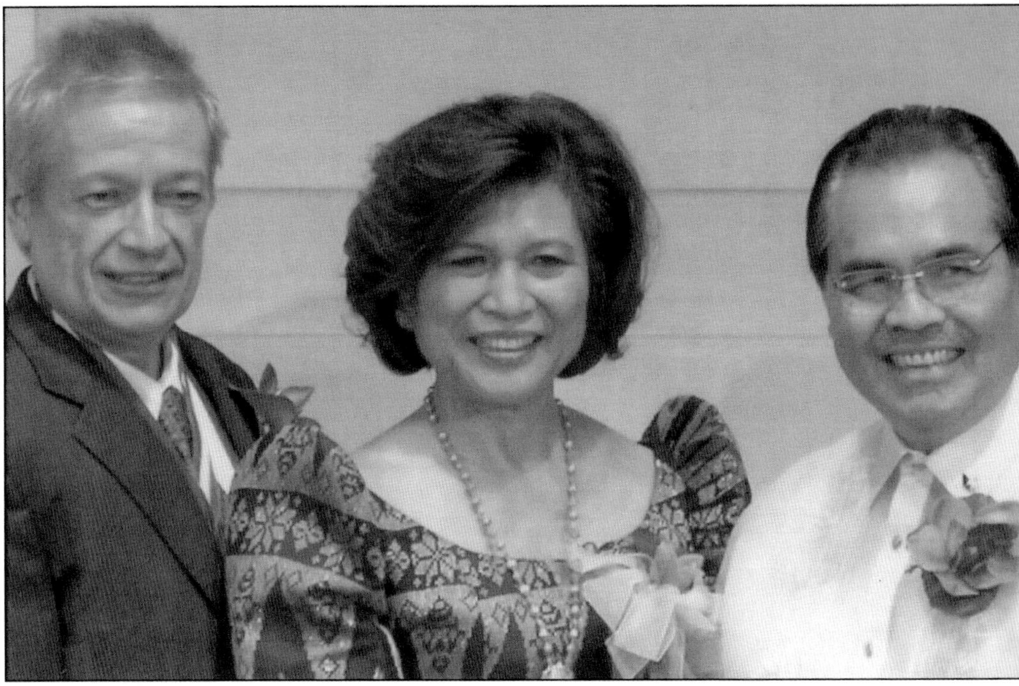

The Philippine Consulate General in New York (PCGNY) provides services and assistance to Filipino nationals residing in the states of Connecticut, Delaware, Maine, Massachusetts, New Hampshire, New Jersey, New York, Pennsylvania, Rhode Island, and Vermont. Pictured above are the current Philippine consul general, Mario de Leon Jr. (right), along with Jorge Ortoll (executive director of Ma-Yi Theater), and entrepreneur Loida Nicolas-Lewis at the annual Outstanding Filipino Americans of New York (TOFA) Awards in 2012. Pictured below is the *Panunuluyan-A Filipino Christmas Tradition* at the Kalayaan Hall Philippine Center in New York City, cosponsored by the PCGNY, the Philippine Center Management Board (PCMB), JCI Philippine-New York (Jaycees), and the Catholic Fellowship of Young Filipino Professionals (CFYFP). Consul general Mario de Leon Jr. plays the shepherd. (Above, courtesy of Troi Santos and Elton Lugay; below, courtesy of Dominic Senador and Bel Molina.)

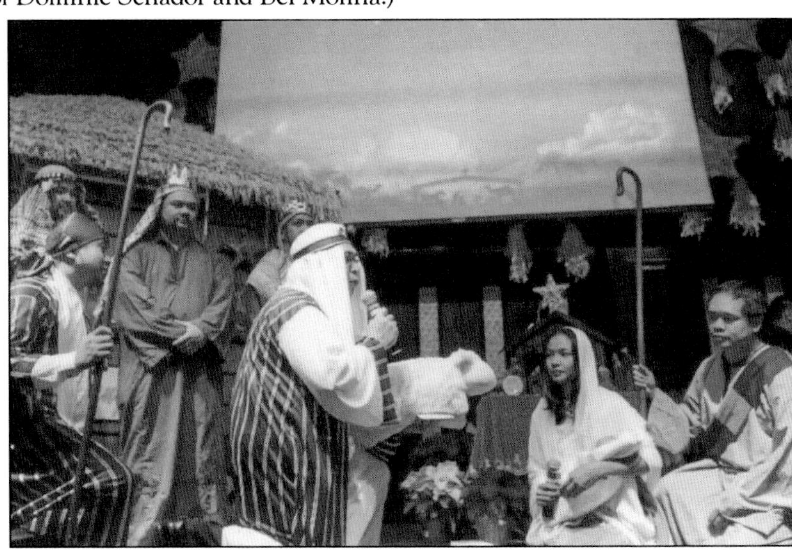

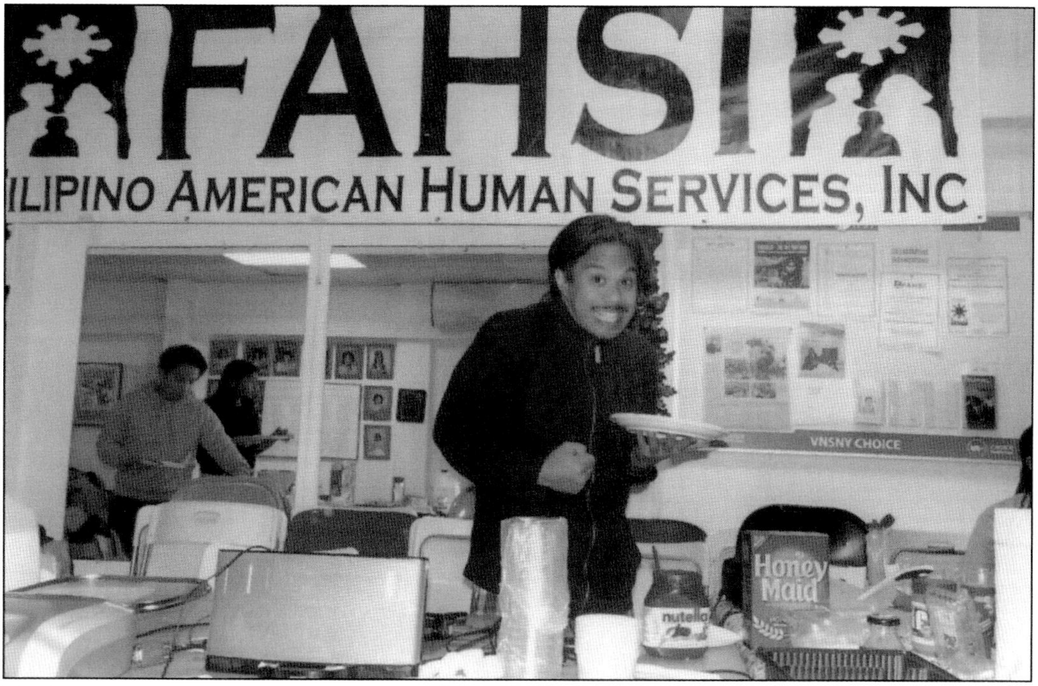

Established in 1993, Filipino American Human Services, Inc. (FAHSI) is a community-based nonprofit organization dedicated to improving the social conditions and enhancing the self-reliance of the Filipino and Filipino American communities of New York City. FAHSI's vision is an empowered Filipino American community with a strong sense of identity and commitment to civic participation. Pictured above is Andre Dimapilis, a former youth director of FAHSI in 2012; below are participants at a Youth Day at FAHSI in 2012. (Both, courtesy of FAHSI.)

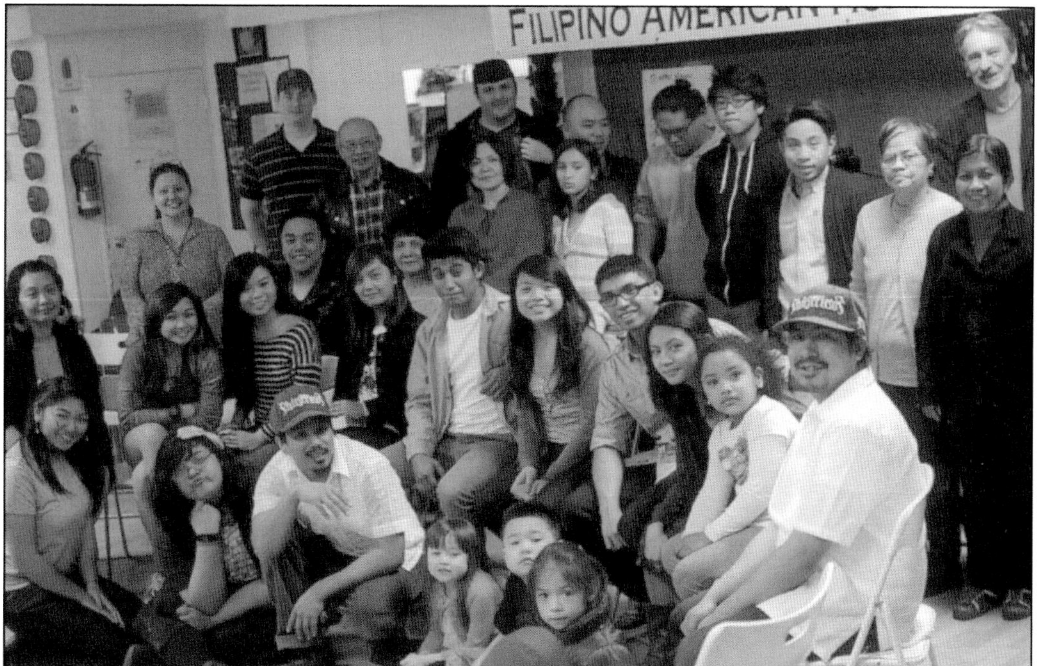

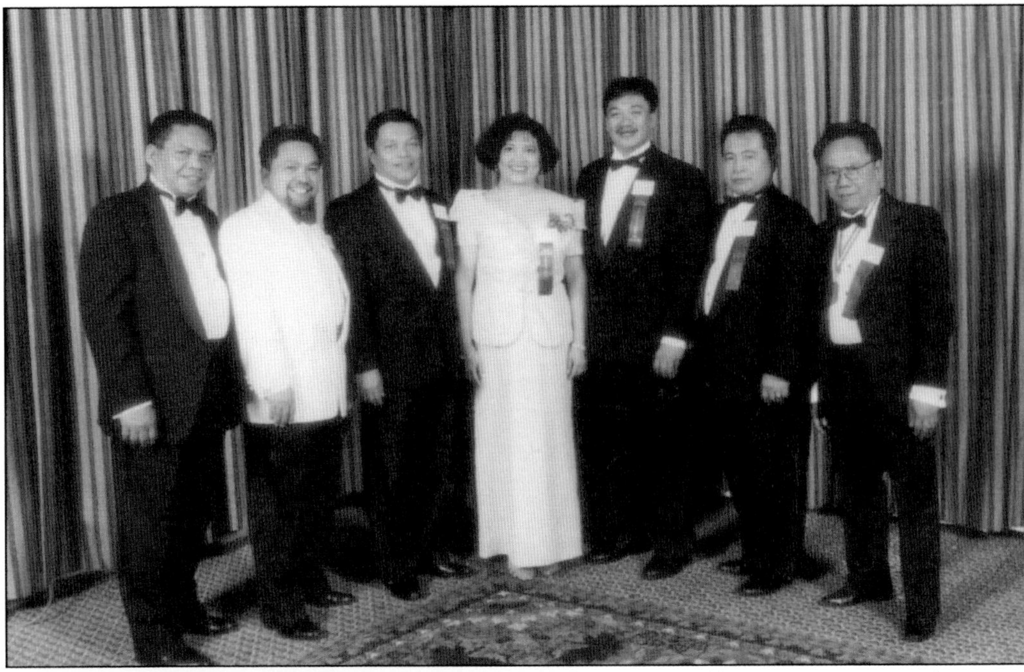

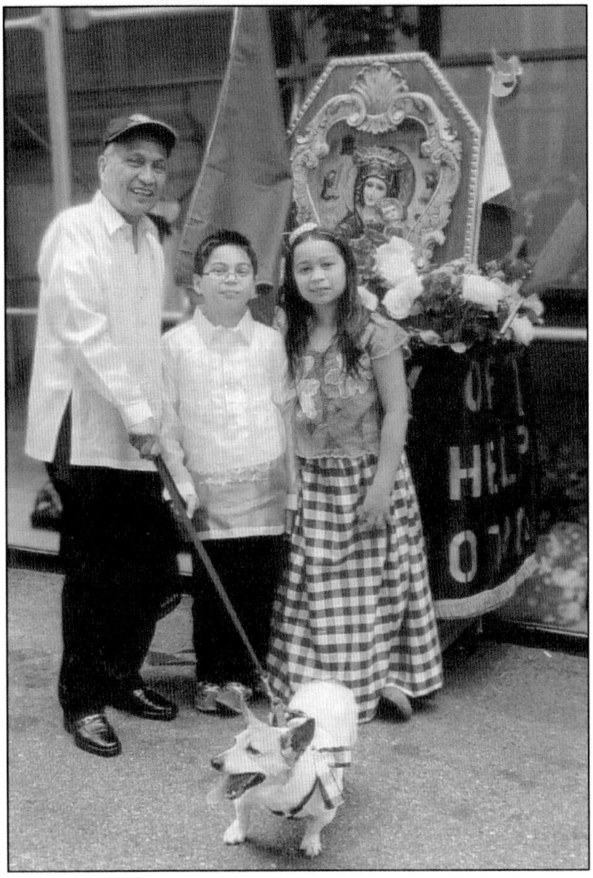

Pictured here are two examples of regional Filipino American organizations in New York City. Above are members of the Aklan Association of the Eastern Seaboard from 1999. On the left is Ben Q. Vigilia, president of the Ilocano-American Association, Inc. for 2013–2014, with grandchildren Jaden Castillo and Lyla Escobar. (Above, courtesy of Julian Tamayo; left, courtesy of Kara Mia Escobar.)

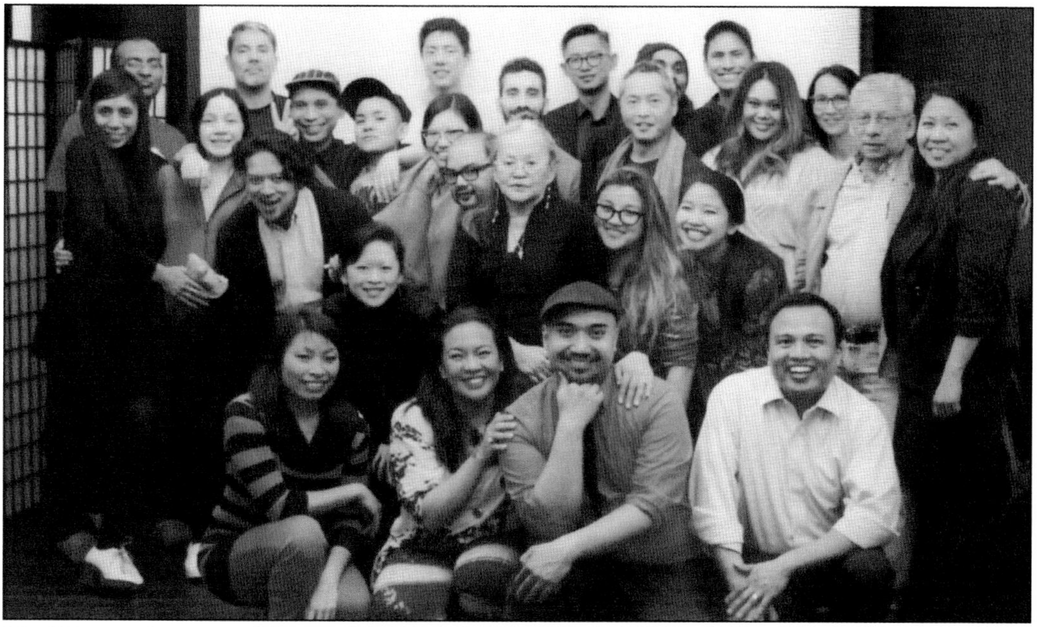

The Filipino American Museum (FAM) is the first museum focused on examining the connection between contemporary Filipino American arts and the roots and traditions of the Filipino diaspora. FAM presents its findings through live performances, exhibits, installations, community forums, online content and otherwise. Pictured are FAM staff and board members in 2014. (Courtesy of Nancy Bulalacao-Leung.)

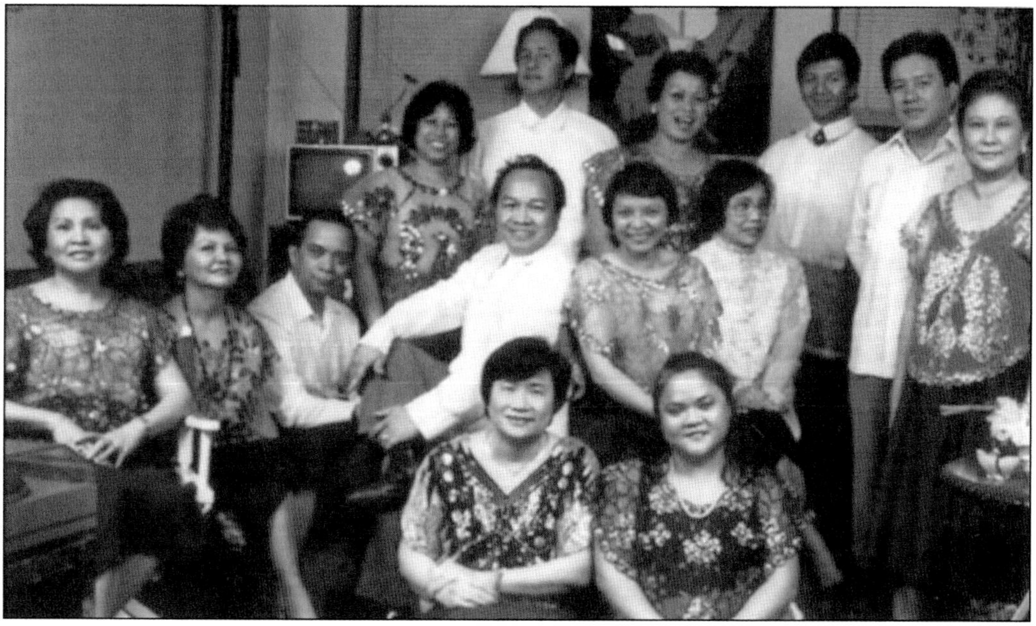

The Foundation for Filipino Artists, Inc. (FFAI) is a nonprofit organization whose mission is to help artists promote and develop human awareness and cultivate the utmost potential of people to be able to take on leadership roles in training and human development towards global responsibility for the betterment of the global community and New York. Pictured here are members in the early 2000s. (Courtesy of Foundation for Filipino Artists, Inc.)

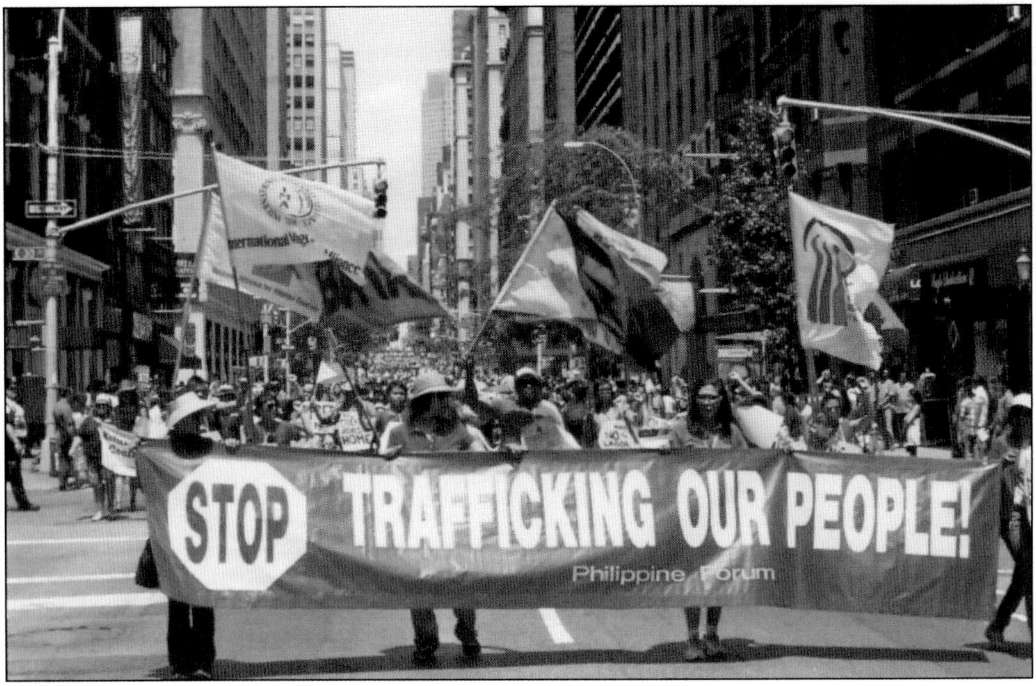

Philippine Forum is a nonprofit community grassroots organization offering direct services to the Filipino and the larger immigrant communities in New York. It was founded on December 10, 1996, and recently formed its New Jersey chapter in 2008. Pictured above are Philippine Forum members marching in the Philippine Independence Day Parade in 2013; pictured below are members in front of the Bayanihan Center in Woodside, Queens. (Both, courtesy of Philippine Forum.)

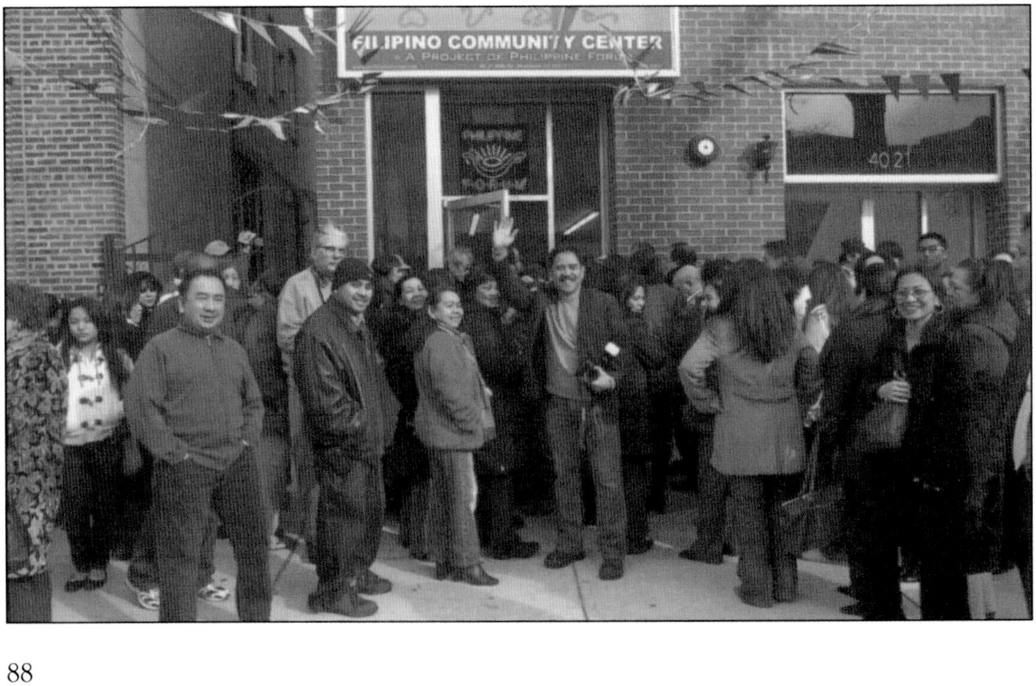

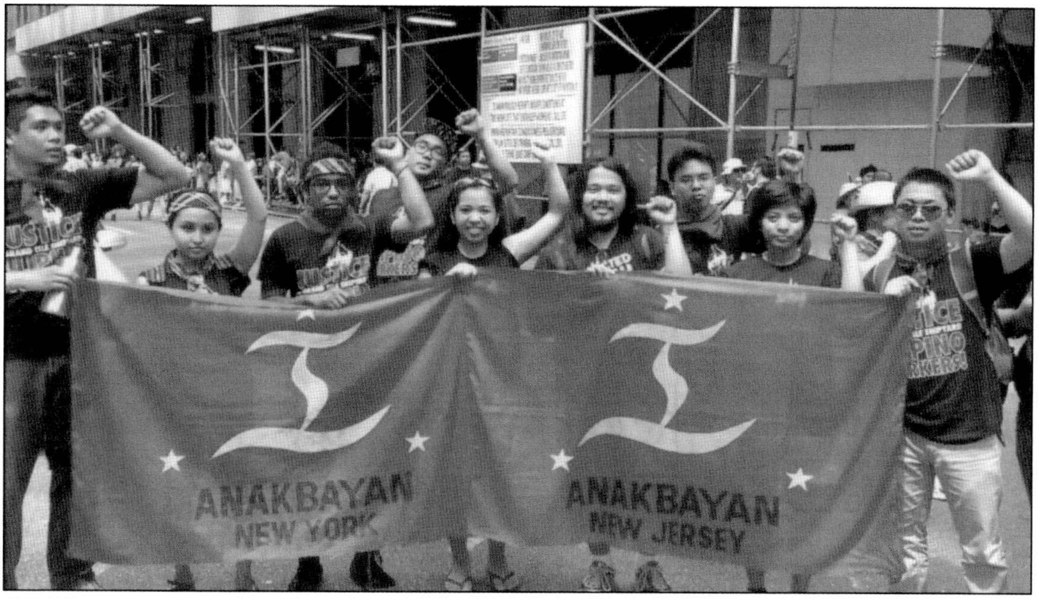

Anakbayan is a youth and student organization working to educate, organize, and mobilize the community to address important issues that affect Filipinos in the United States and the Philippines. The organization's aim is to unite Filipino youth of all backgrounds in order to achieve genuine freedom and democracy in the Philippines. Pictured here are members in 2013. (Courtesy of Anakbayan.)

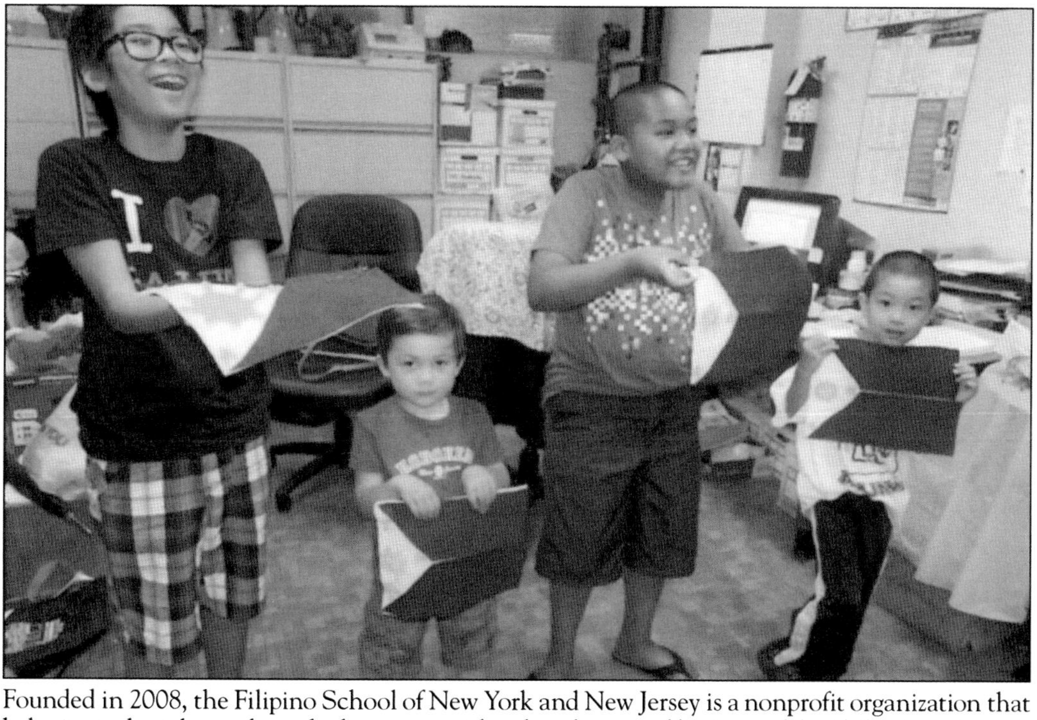

Founded in 2008, the Filipino School of New York and New Jersey is a nonprofit organization that helps its students learn about the languages, rich cultural arts, and heritage of the Philippines through its programs, workshops, special events, and other educational activities. These youth participants are excited to be learning about the Philippine flag. (Courtesy of Venessa Manzano.)

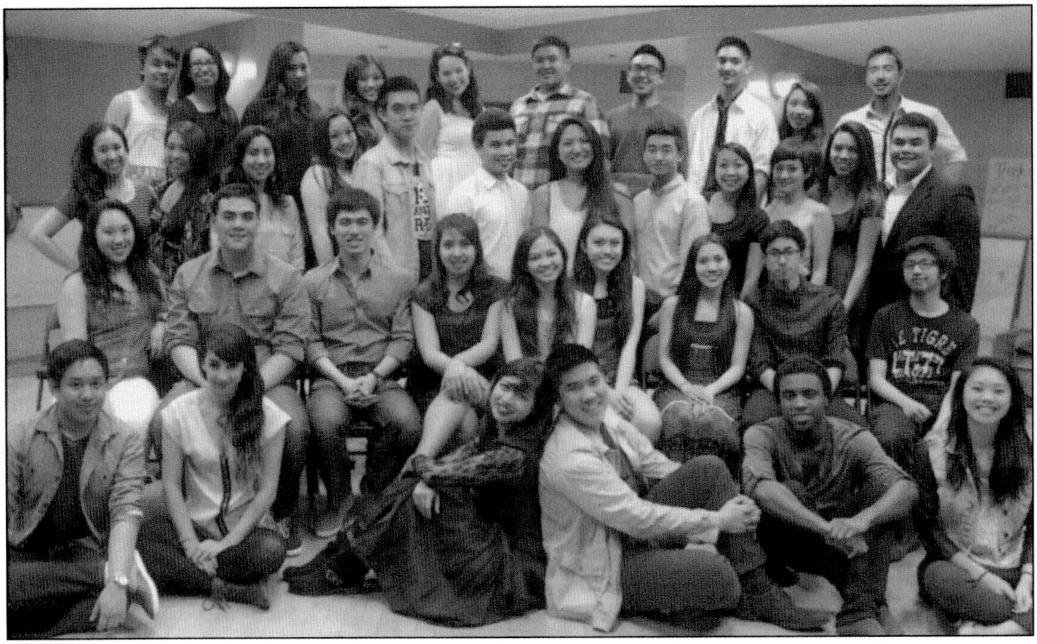

The International Filipino Association (IFA) at New York University has served the local community for 28 years. IFA was the brainchild of seven students, and originally started as an intramural basketball team in 1985. The club has since grown into a platform for connecting students with similar backgrounds, educating others about rich Filipino culture, and creating a forum for deconstructing Filipino issues and current events. Pictured here are members in 2013. (Courtesy of Kristina Rodulfo.)

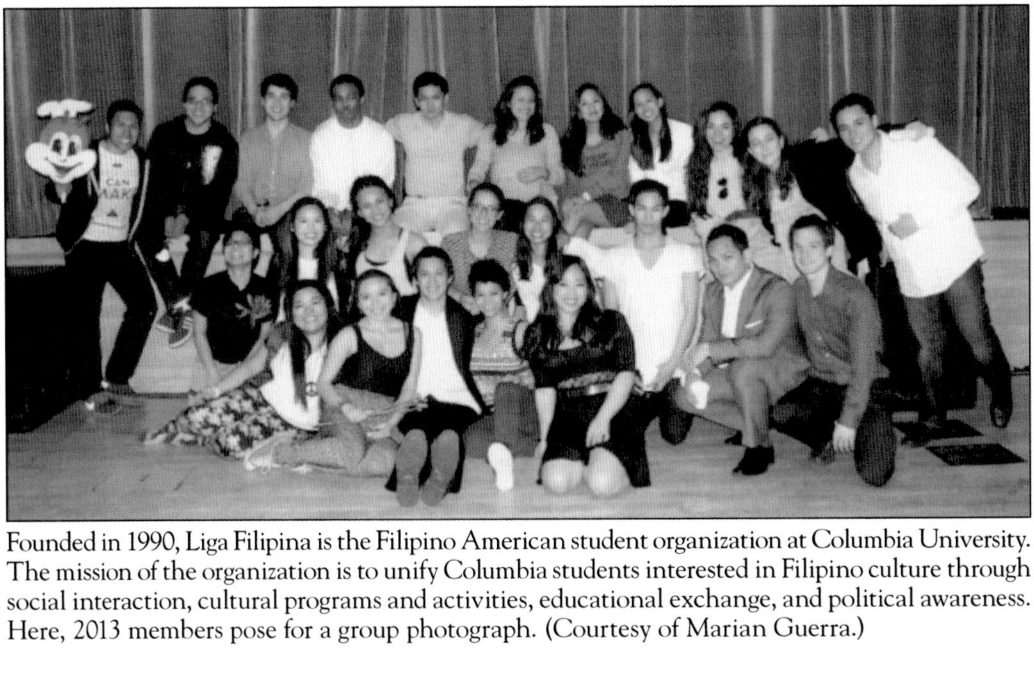

Founded in 1990, Liga Filipina is the Filipino American student organization at Columbia University. The mission of the organization is to unify Columbia students interested in Filipino culture through social interaction, cultural programs and activities, educational exchange, and political awareness. Here, 2013 members pose for a group photograph. (Courtesy of Marian Guerra.)

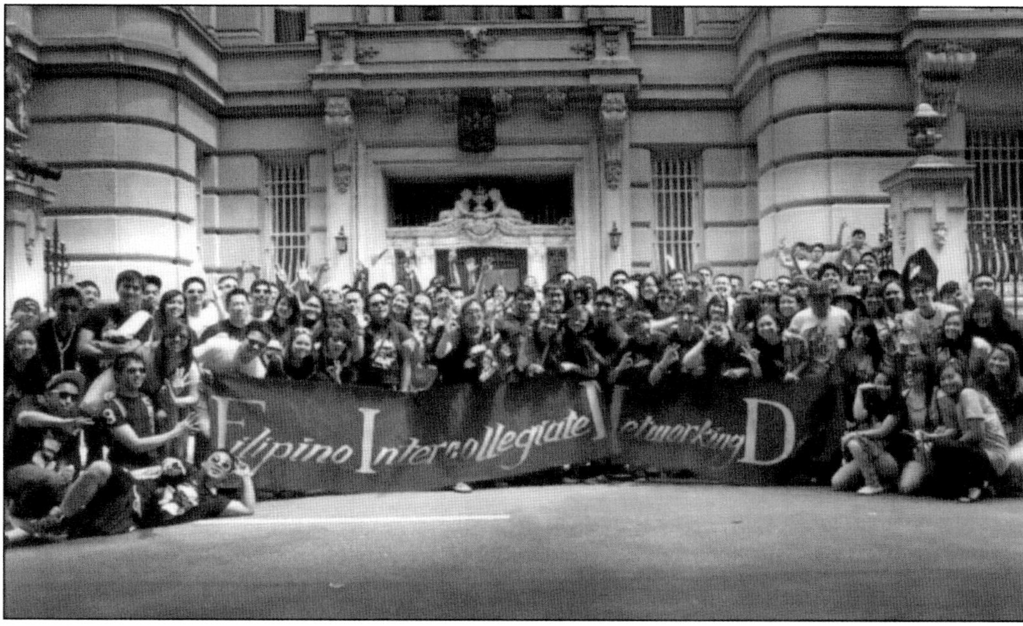

Founded on April 11, 1992, the Filipino Intercollegiate Networking Dialogue (FIND, Inc.) stands as a symbol to the ethnic consciousness presently seen on university campuses. Currently, its network actively links over 90 East Coast colleges, universities, vocational, and technical schools. Pictured here are members at the Philippine Independence Day Parade in 2013. (Courtesy of FIND, Inc.)

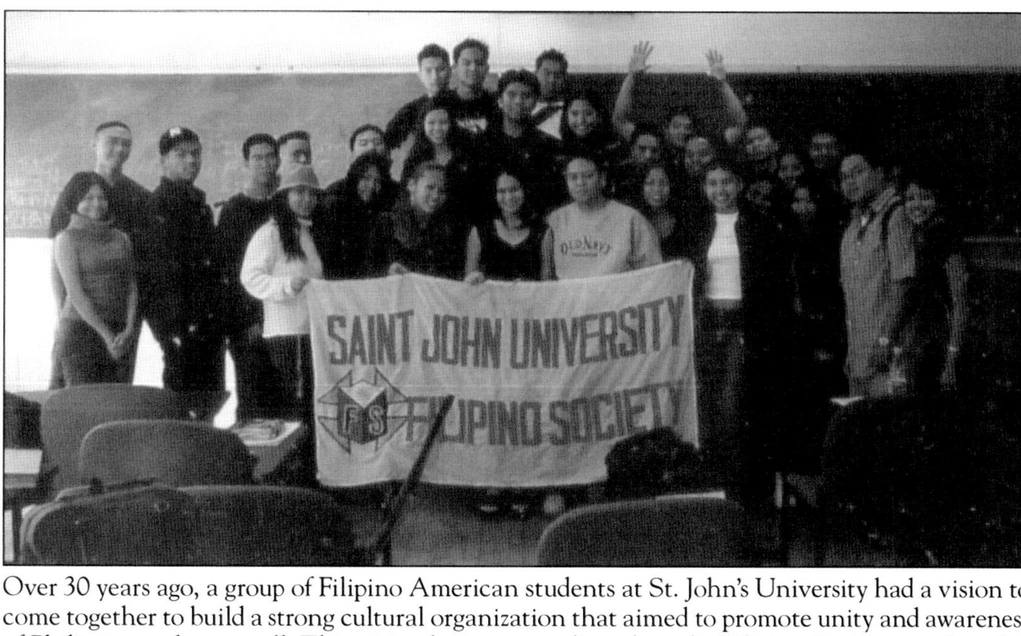

Over 30 years ago, a group of Filipino American students at St. John's University had a vision to come together to build a strong cultural organization that aimed to promote unity and awareness of Philippine culture to all. This vision became a reality when the Filipino Society was founded in 1985. These young men and women came together wishing to learn more about their history, background, and origins. In 2004, the Filipino Society's name was officially changed to PARE, Philippine Americans Reaching Everyone. Members of the 1997 St. John's University chapter are pictured here. (Courtesy of Mia Fulgado-Tyler.)

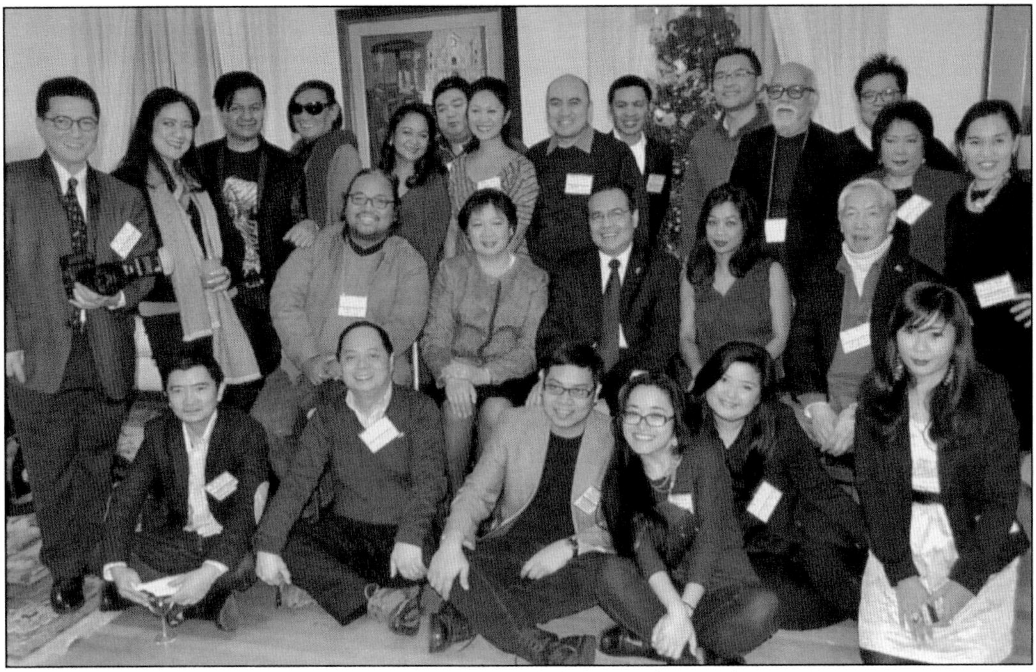

The Fil-Am Press Club of New York is a private club for working Filipino American journalists and communication professionals in the New York tristate area. Members took a break from the festivities at their annual holiday party in 2013 to pose for a photograph. (Courtesy of Momar Visaya.)

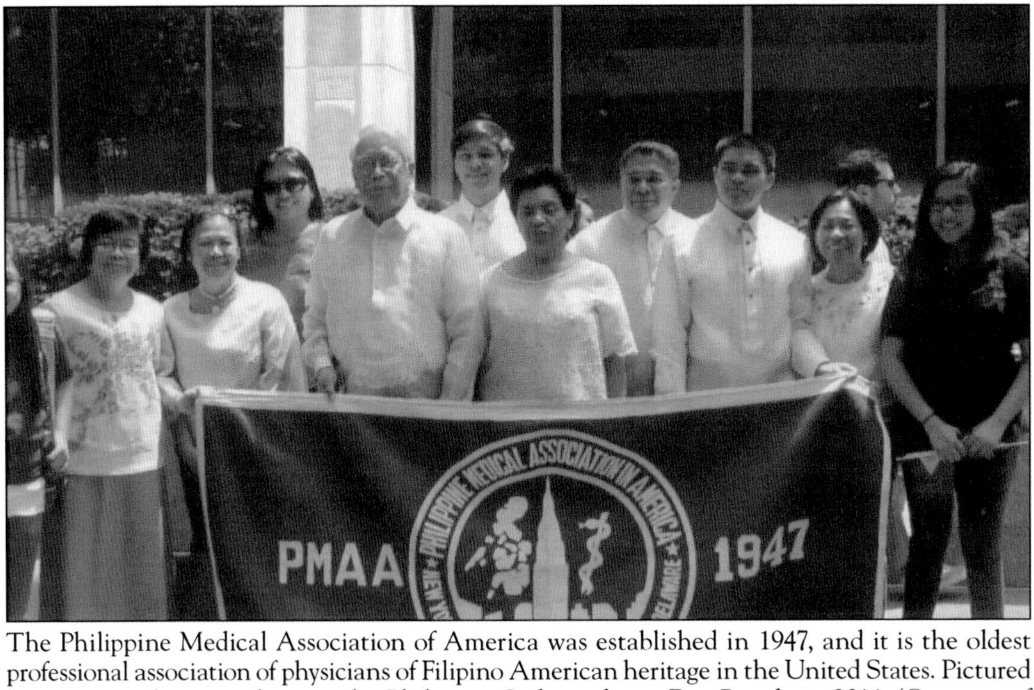

The Philippine Medical Association of America was established in 1947, and it is the oldest professional association of physicians of Filipino American heritage in the United States. Pictured here are members marching at the Philippine Independence Day Parade in 2014. (Courtesy of Bernadette Rogan Rynne.)

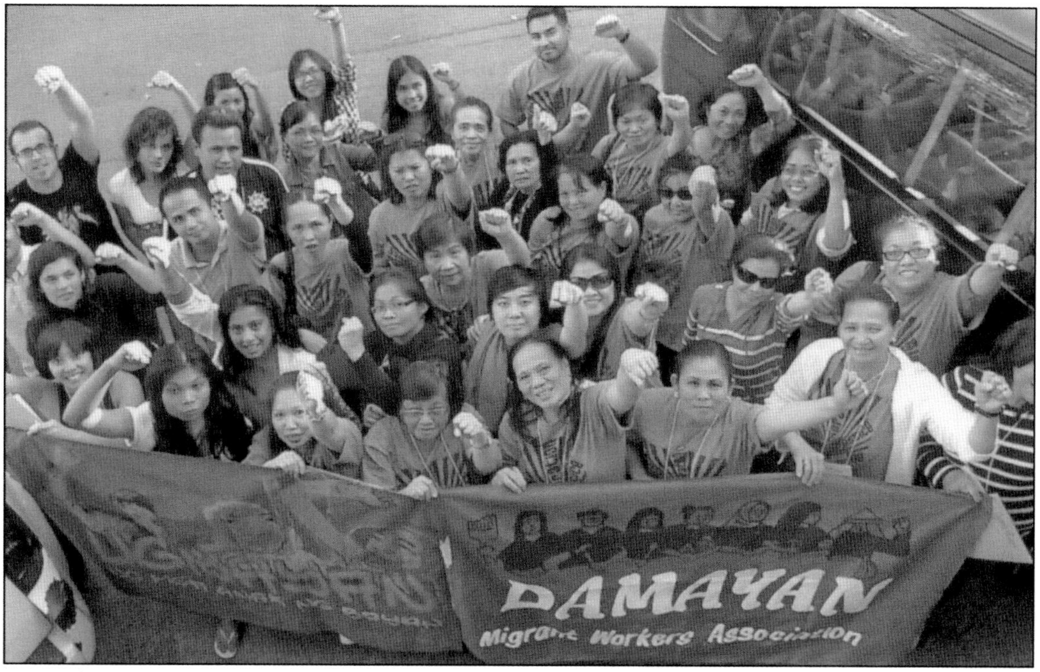

Formed in 2004, Ugnayan Youth for Justice and Social Change is a comprehensive grassroots organization of Filipino and Filipino American youth based in New York and New Jersey. Through collective leadership, progressive culture, and community engagement, Ugnayan strives to reclaim the true history of the Filipino and Filipino-American people to better understand how local and personal issues and struggles are interconnected. It contributes to various movements for justice, peace, and genuine liberation of the Filipino people (Courtesy of Ana Liza Caballes.)

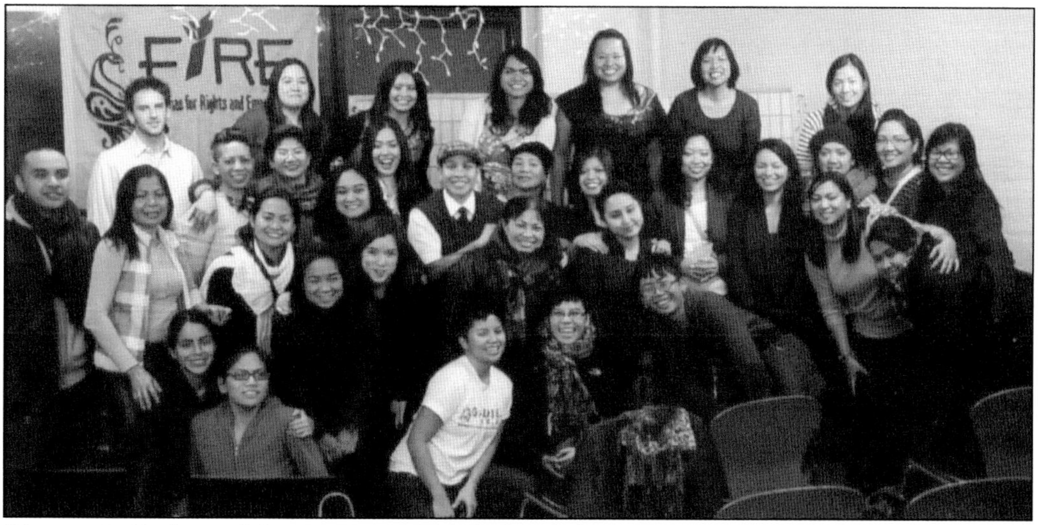

Filipinas for Rights and Empowerment (FiRE), founded on April 14, 2007, is a mass-based women's organization serving New York City and its surrounding areas. It is dedicated to global and local Filipina and Filipina American issues and connects the Filipino diaspora to the women's struggle in the Philippines by organizing across class, gender, sexual identity, and age lines. Bringing female and female-identified people together, FiRE challenges pervading stereotypes by creating self-defined Filipina identities. (Courtesy of FiRE.)

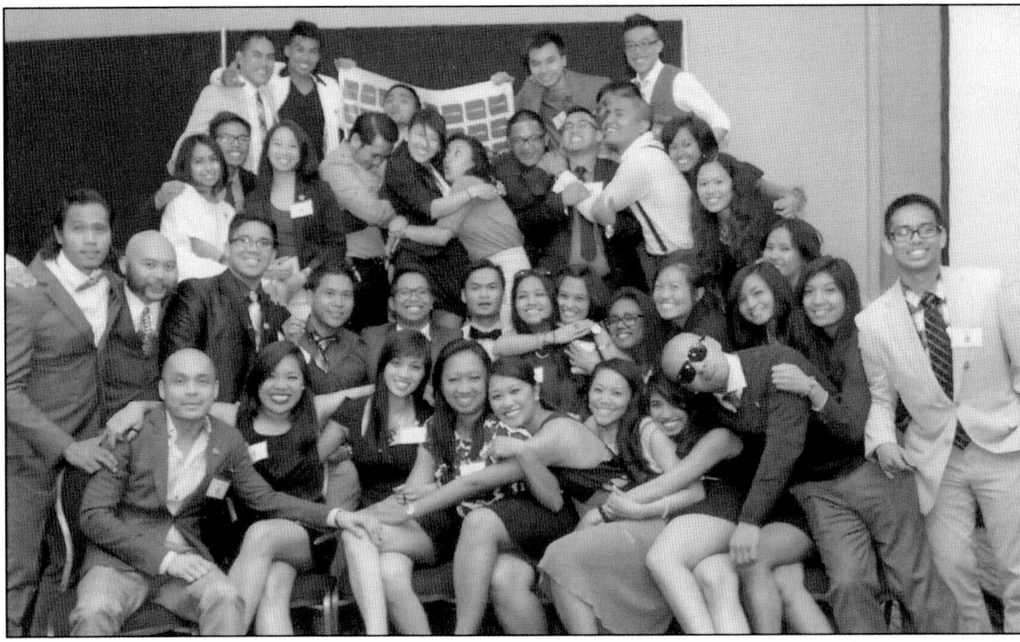

Comprised of young professionals and students, Pilipino American Unity for Progress, Inc. (UniPro) is a New York City–based nonprofit organization that was established in 2009. Bonded by the common vision of promoting unity within the community, UniPro seeks to educate, collaborate, and stimulate dialogue among Pilipino American organizations, programs, and institutions. UniPro also engages in various projects that promote the Pilipino community in American society. (Courtesy of Iris Zalun.)

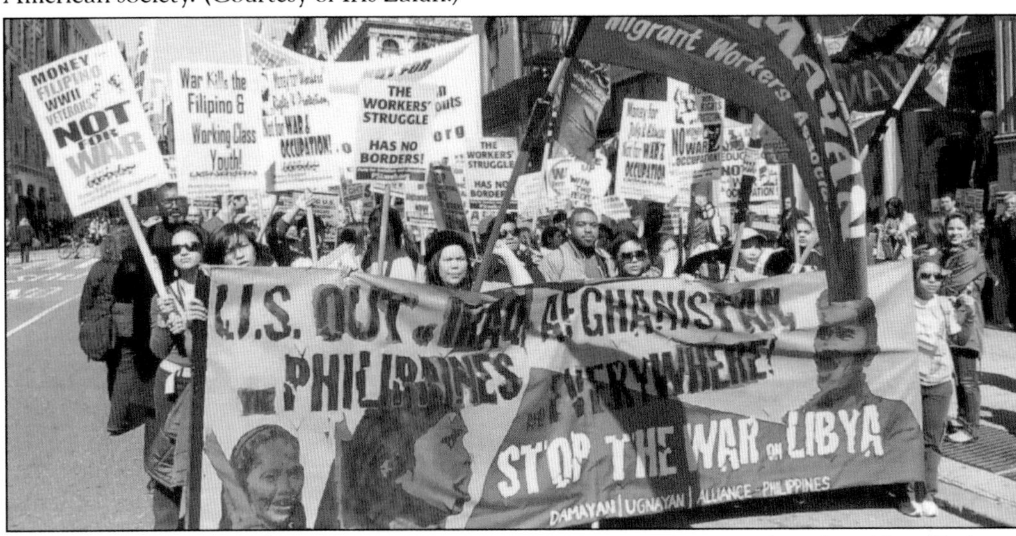

Damayan Migrant Workers Association is a grassroots organization based in New York and New Jersey of and for Filipino immigrant workers and led by Filipino female domestic workers. Damayan was officially founded in 2002 and became a 501(c)(3) nonprofit in 2003. Its mission is to educate, organize, and mobilize low-wage Filipino workers to fight for their labor, health, gender, and immigration rights; contribute to the building of the domestic workers movement for fair labor standards, dignity, and justice; and to build workers' power and solidarity towards justice and liberation. (Courtesy of Riya Ortiz.)

Kinding Sindaw is a dance theater ensemble resident of La MaMa Experimental Theatre. Since 2000, Kinding Sindaw has served as a resource for history, culture, dance, and music of the indigenous people of the Philippines. Pictured is Amira Aziza, one of the company's artists. (Courtesy of Ellen Anisha Goro.)

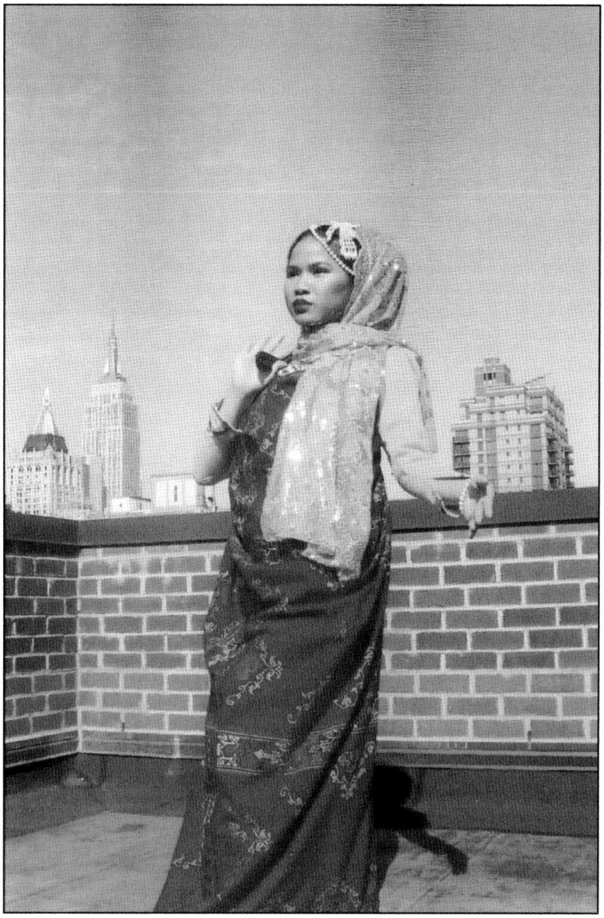

Created by Leslie Espinosa, Kilusan Bautista, and Precious Sipin, Tagalogue is an annual show that provides a platform for artists to educate and inspire. Performers from 2012 pose for a group photograph. (Courtesy of Precious Sipin.)

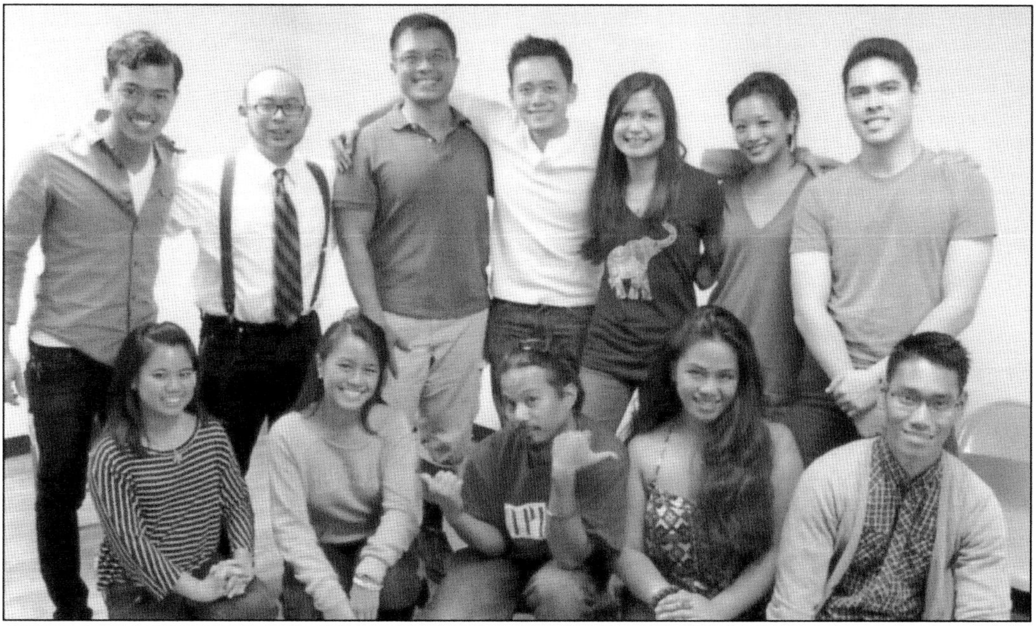

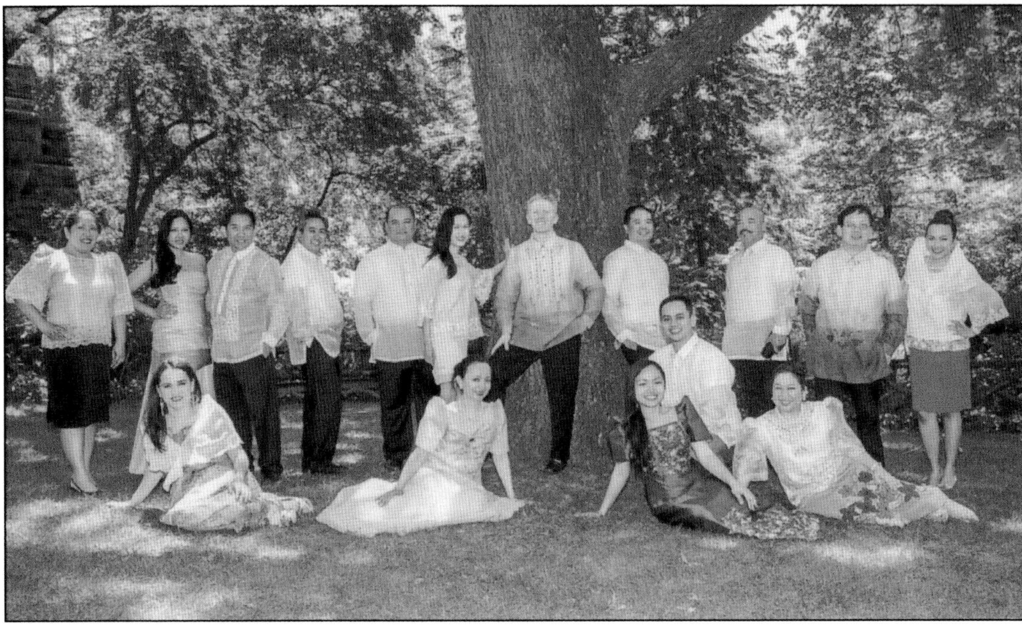

JCI Philippine-New York, Inc. (Jaycees) is group of young men and women whose mission is to develop leaders who will create positive change in the local and global community and their own lives through training and networking opportunities. Its mission is to offer quality projects, balanced programs, opportunities to network with other organizations, serve the community, and further the ideas of Junior Chamber International. (Courtesy of Mia Fulgado-Tyler.)

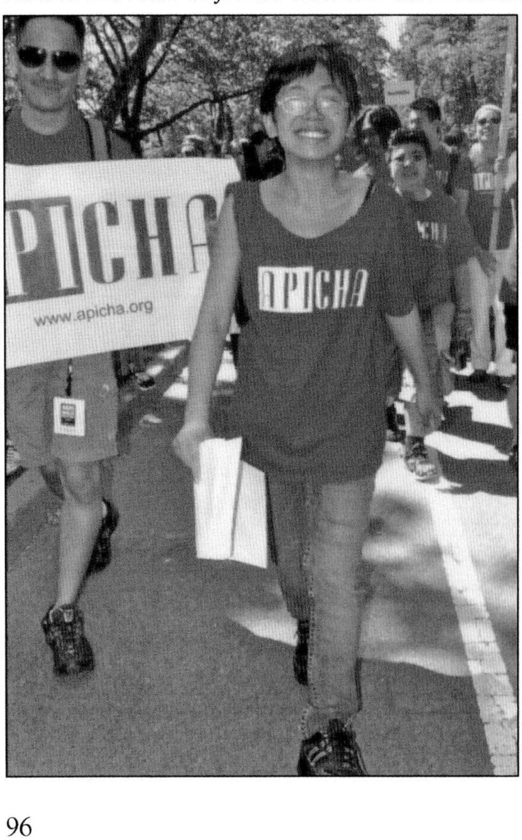

APICHA Community Health Center, formerly known as the Asian/Pacific Islander Coalition on HIV/AIDS, aims to provide affordable health care for underserved and vulnerable people living in the New York City boroughs and on the Lower East Side of Manhattan. APICHA has been serving the Filipino American community since its inception in 1989. APICHA staff member Melanie Dulfo marches in the annual AIDS Walk in 2012, with RJ Mendoza-Nadal holding the sign. (Courtesy of RJ Mendoza-Nadal).

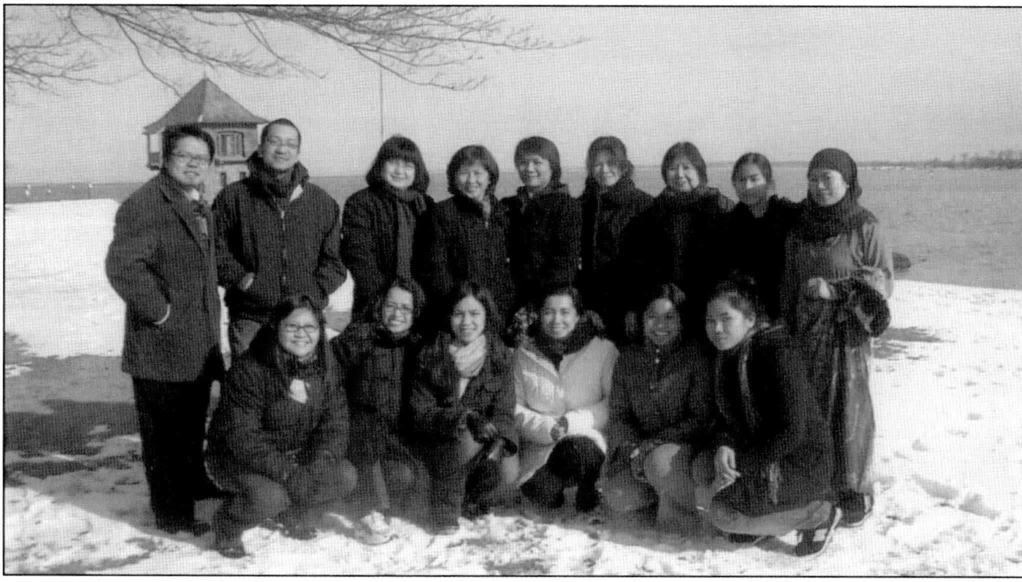

Kalusugan Coalition, Inc. (KC) was formed in 2004 when a handful of community members and health workers came together to respond to the fact that there were few wide-scale initiatives that specifically address the Filipino American community's health needs, despite the growing population. Founding members organized a community health forum and conducted a community health needs assessment to begin the dialogue and documentation of Filipino New Yorkers' priority health concerns. Pictured here are founding members of Kalusugan in 2004. (Courtesy of Noilyn Abesamis-Mendoza.)

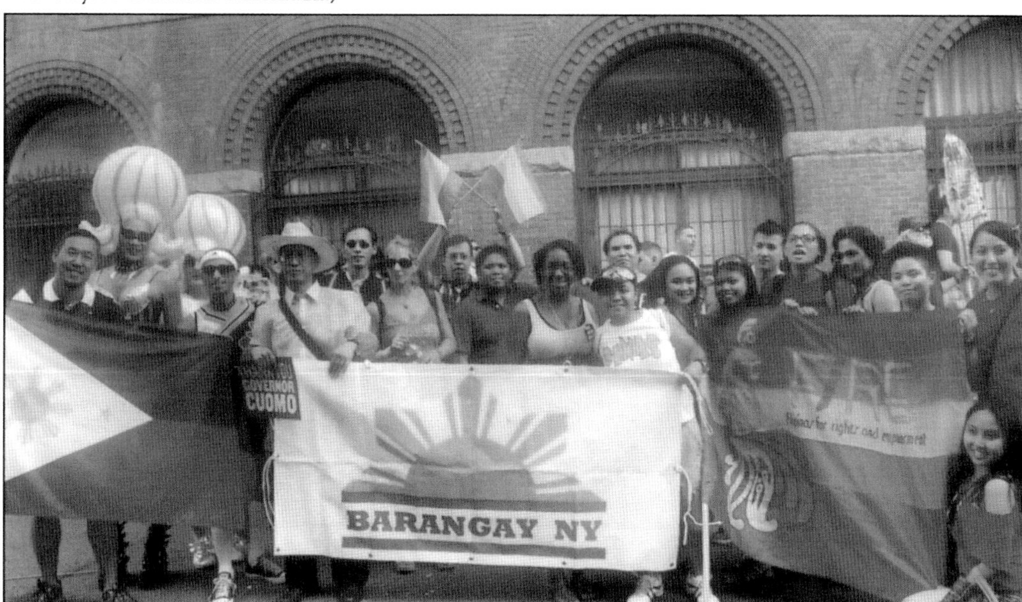

Barangay NY is an organization serving the needs and interests of all segments of the Philippine LGBTQ community in the Greater New York area. It is committed to providing a supportive safe space to discuss issues relevant to lesbian, gay, bisexual, transgender, queer, or questioning people of Philippine descent through cultural, social, and advocacy events. Pictured here are Barangay Members at the 2011 LGBTQ Pride Parade in New York City. (Courtesy of Eric Montesa.)

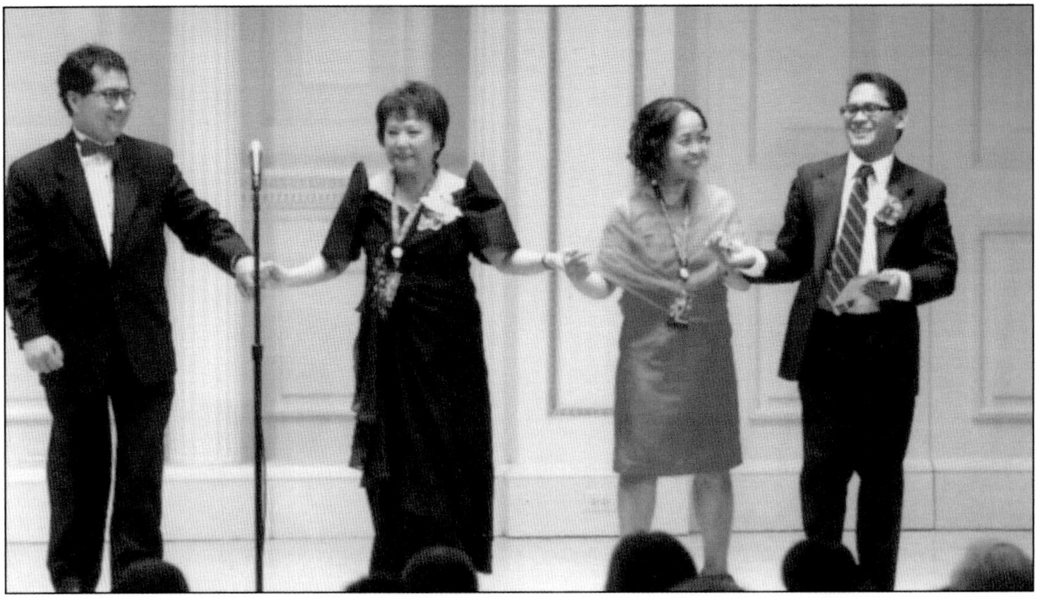

The Outstanding Filipino Americans (TOFA) is an awards event held annually at Carnegie Hall in New York during the Filipino American History Month celebration in October. It was created to recognize and celebrate the achievements of individuals and organizations that have raised the profile of the Filipino American community in a unique way. Here, the 2012 coordinators of TOFA take the stage. Pictured are, from left to right, Rolan Gutierrez, Myrna de Guia Gutierrez, Cristina Pastor, and Elton Lugay. (Courtesy of Elton Lugay.)

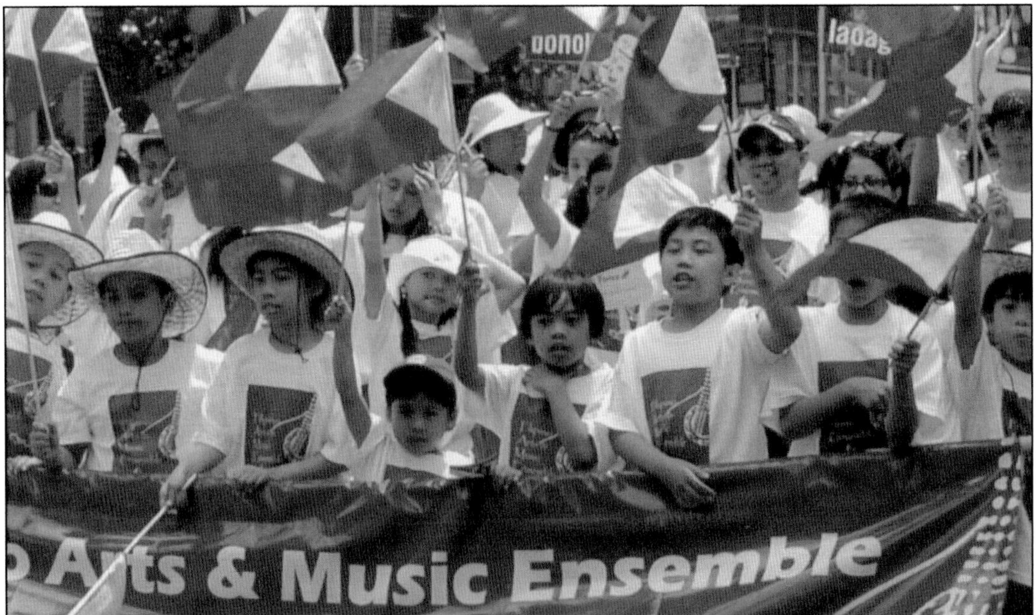

Established in 1993, the Filipino Arts and Music Ensemble (FAME) is a nonprofit organization located in Brooklyn, New York, whose mission is to preserve, present, and promote the art and musical heritage of people of Filipino descent and cultivate the vanishing music of the Filipino heritage. (Courtesy of FAME.)

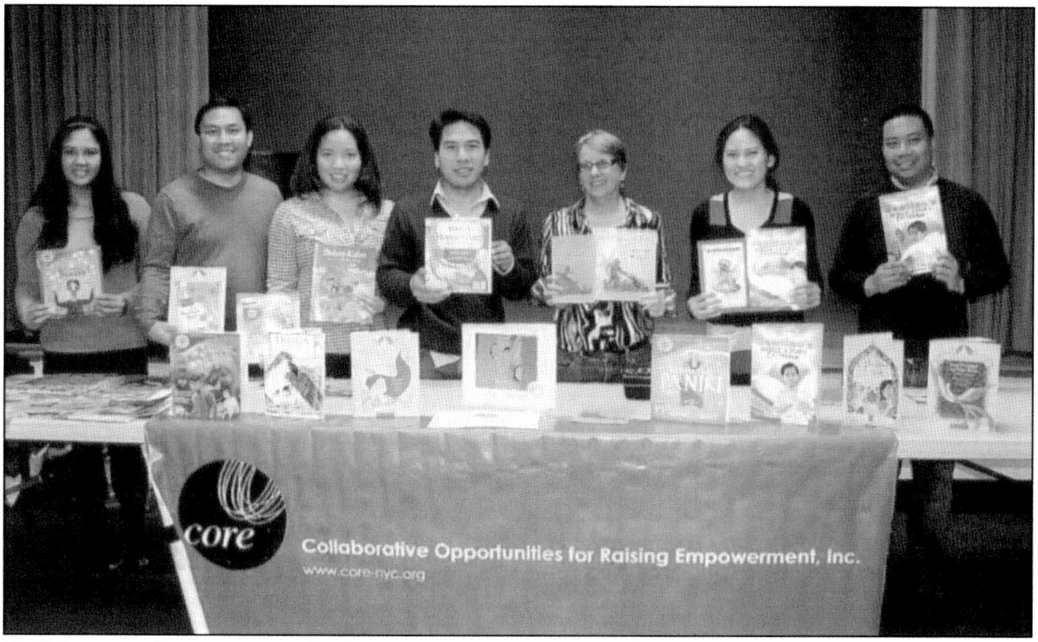

Collaborative Opportunities for Raising Empowerment, Inc. (CORE) is a not-for-profit organization whose primary vision is to empower Filipino professionals in the United States as a collective body. Founded in 2003, it also seeks to provide an avenue for socioeconomic involvement to build a stronger Filipino American community. Pictured here are CORE members promoting books at their CORE Read Philippines program in 2011. (Courtesy of Venessa Manzano.)

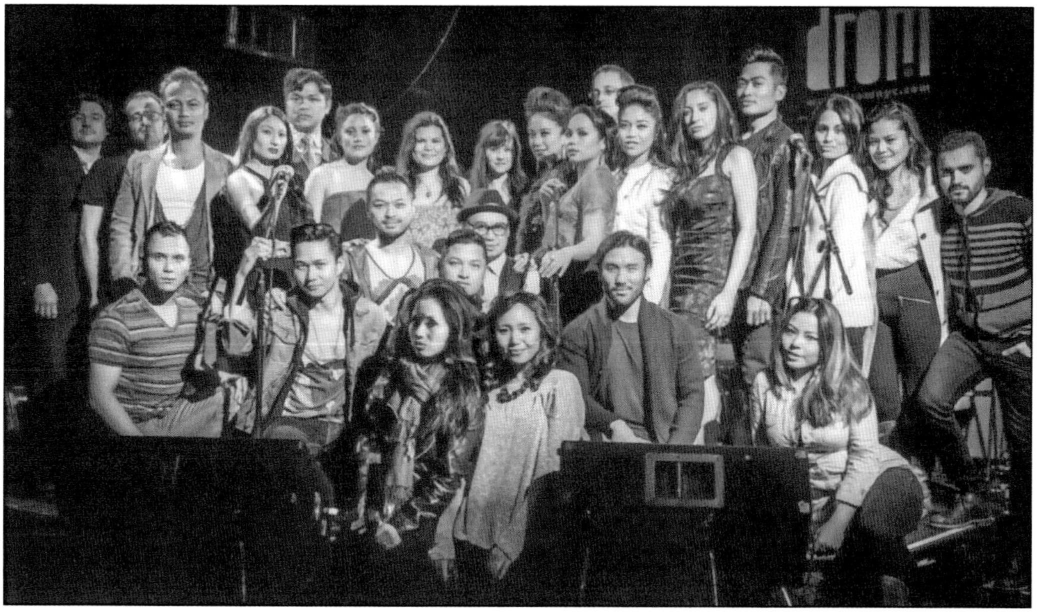

Cofounded by Liz Casasola, Billy Bustamante, and Brian Jose in the fall of 2009, Broadway Barkada is a collective of professional performers and artists whose aim is to meld their varied talents and backgrounds in programs that promote and deepen the Filipino sense of community. Pictured here are performers at their annual Valentine's Day concert in 2014. (Courtesy of Liz Casasola.)

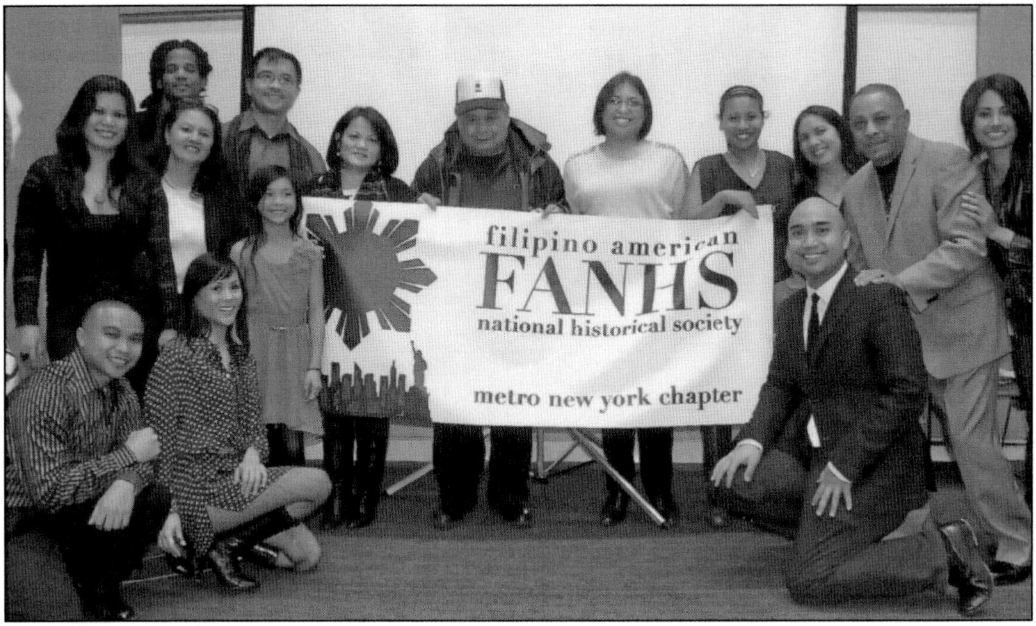

The Filipino American National Historical Society (FANHS) Metro New York Chapter was first established in 1992 and was the sixth established chapter of the organization. Pictured above is the FANHS Metro New York executive board with the legendary Joe Bataan and other featured performers. Below is the FANHS Metro New York executive board from 2012 to 2014. Pictured, from left to right, are (first row) Joey Tabaco, Jackie Tabaco, and Dr. Cecile Sison; (second row) Dolores Alic, Brenda Gambol, Lorial Crowder, Dr. Kevin Nadal, and RJ Mendoza-Nadal. Kilusan Bautista, Andre Dimapilis, Dr. Gail T. Prado, Alexandra Thomas, and Rose-Ann Ubarra-Cunanan are not pictured. The mission of FANHS Metro New York is to promote and preserve Filipino American History in the metropolitan New York area. (Above, courtesy of FANHS Metro New York; below, courtesy of the author.)

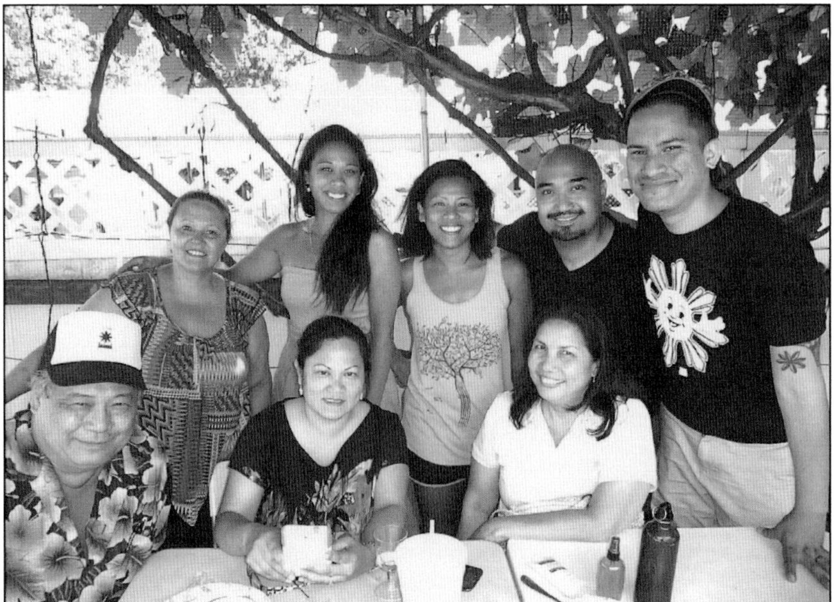

Six

Empire States of Mind
Notable Filipino American New Yorkers

There are many Filipino Americans who have contributed significantly to American society on both national and local levels. This section focuses on just a few of the Filipino Americans who have been successful in their various fields, from government to arts to civic engagement. Pictured here is Lorna Schofield, a US district judge for the District Court for the Southern District of New York. Judge Schofield is the first Filipino American in the history of the United States to serve as an Article III federal judge. In this photograph, Judge Schofield addresses a captive audience at the annual TOFA Award ceremony in 2013. (Courtesy of Arman and Joyce Andes-David.)

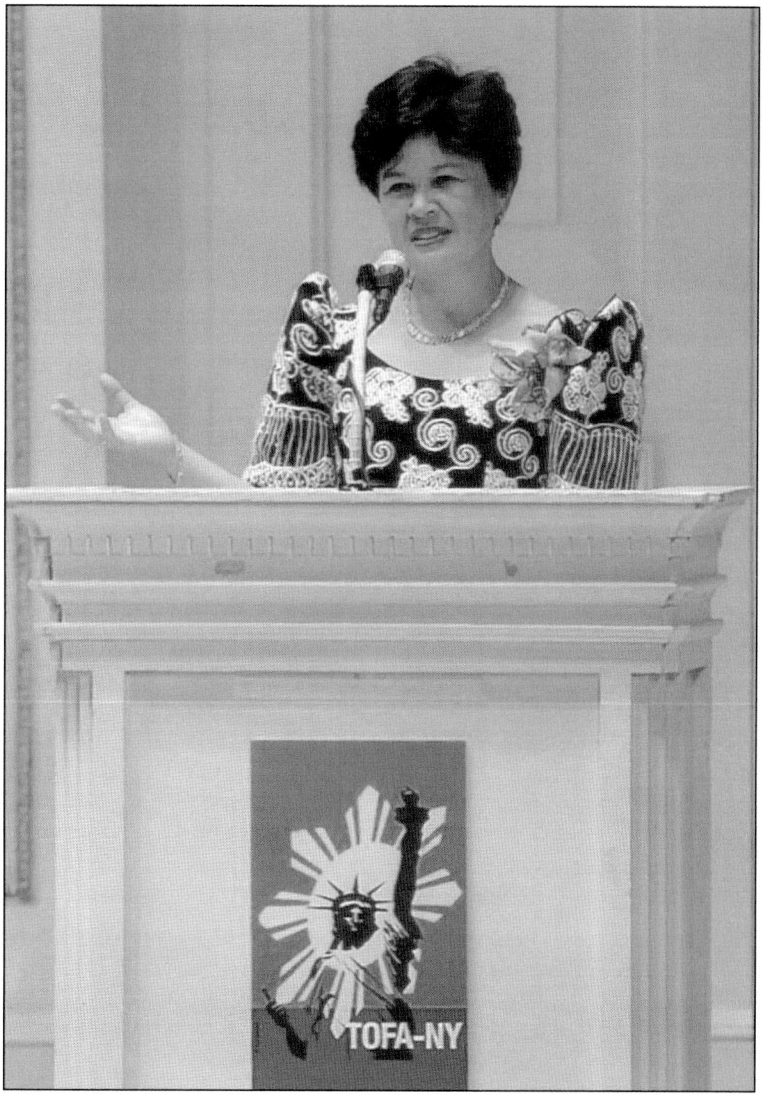

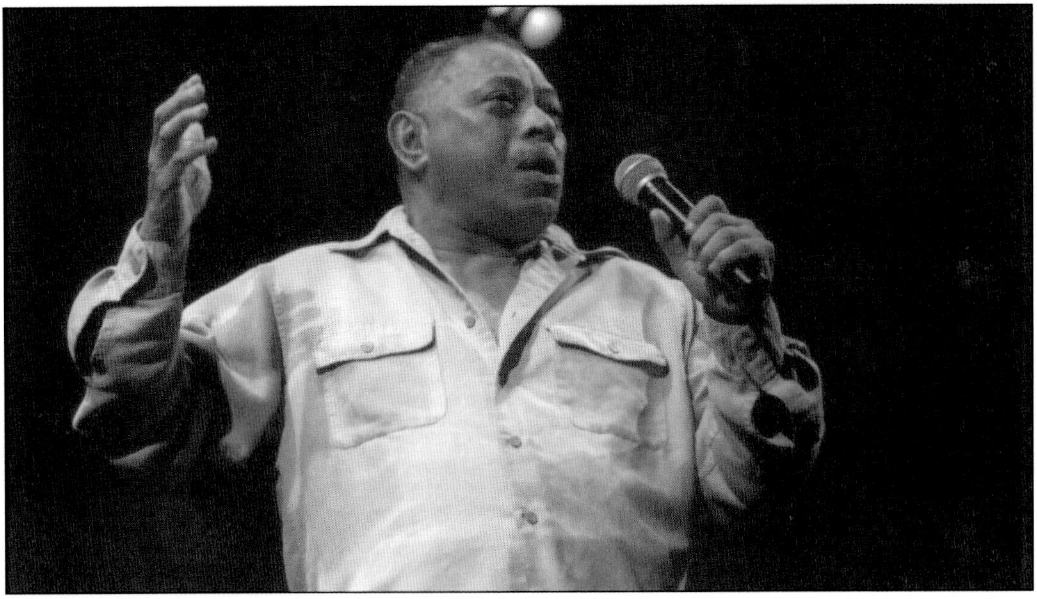

Also known as the "King of Latin Soul," Joe Bataan is a Filipino African American musician from New York City. Born to a Filipino father and an African American mother, Bataan had several hits in the 1960s and 1970s, including the romantic ballad "Ordinary Guy." He received the FANHS Metro New York Lifetime Achievement Award in 2012. (Courtesy of Chauncey Velasco.)

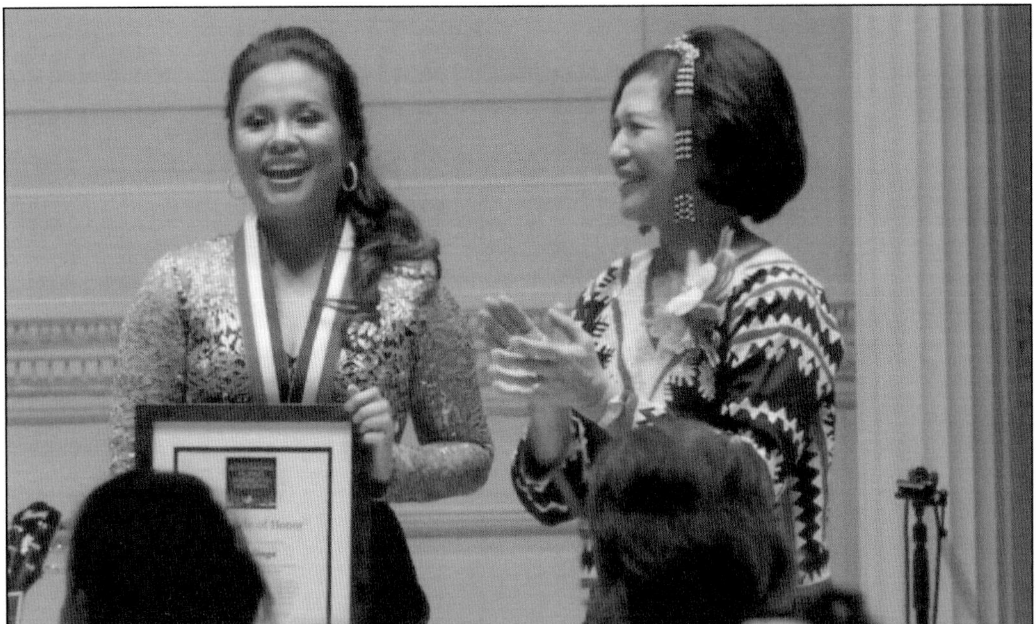

Lea Salonga first came to New York when she played the original part of Kim in the award-winning musical *Miss Saigon*. Since then, she also played the parts of Eponine and Fantine in *Les Misérables* on Broadway. An award-winning actress and singer, Salonga is pictured here receiving a TOFA Award from Loida Nicolas-Lewis in 2011. Nicolas-Lewis is an entrepreneur, attorney, civic leader, and philanthropist who served as chair and CEO of TLC Beatrice International from 1994 to 2000. (Courtesy of Troi Santos and Elton Lugay.)

Jose Llana is a Filipino American actor and singer who is best known for his roles on Broadway. Some of his credits include Angel in *Rent*, Jessie-Lee in *Streetcorner Symphony*, Wang Ta in *Flower Drum Song* opposite Lea Salonga, Chip Tolentino in *The 25th Annual Putnam County Spelling Bee*, and Ferdinand Marcos in *Here Lies Love*. (Courtesy of Randy Gener.)

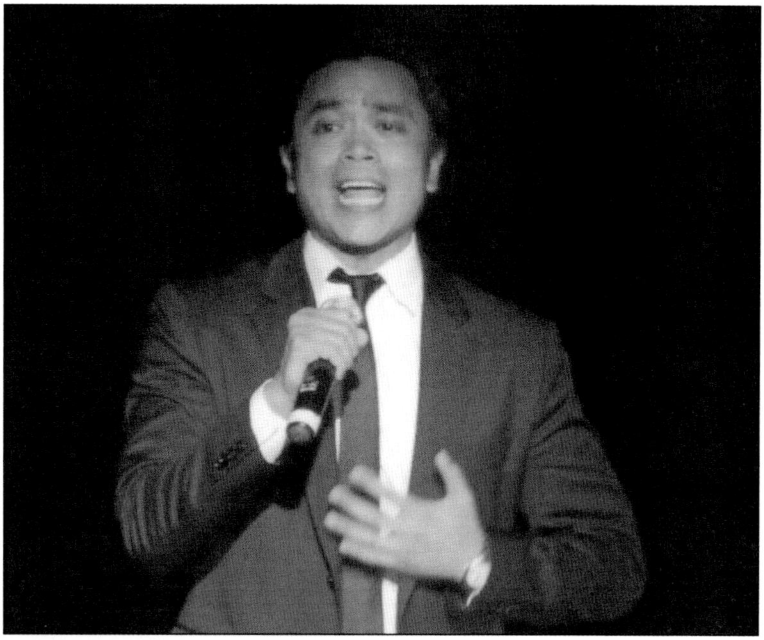

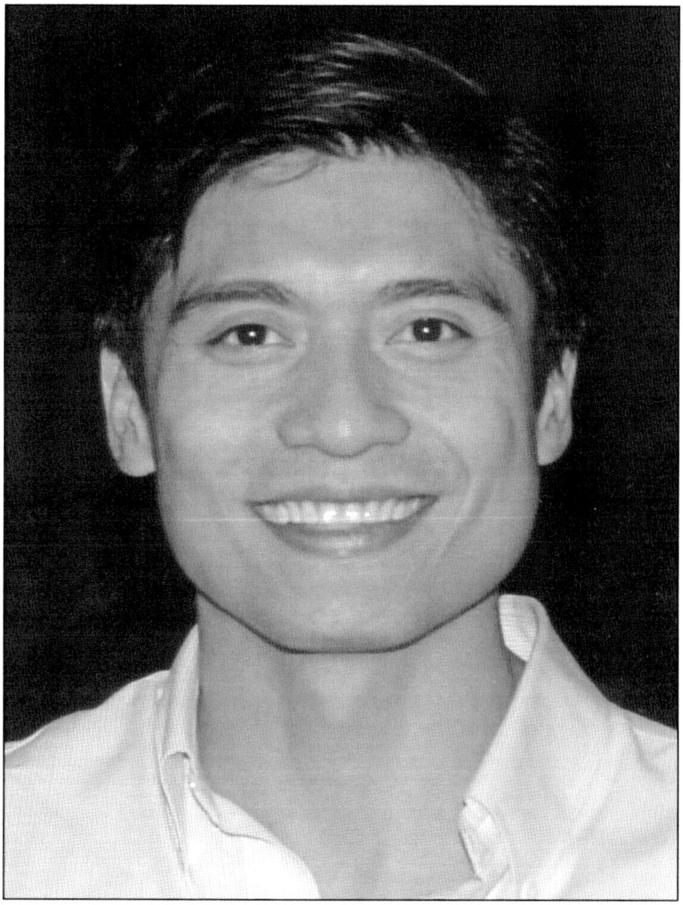

Paolo Montalban is a Filipino American actor and singer who is best known for his performance in the 1997 version of Rodgers and Hammerstein's *Cinderella* as Prince Christopher, opposite Brandy as Cinderella. On Broadway, he has starred in *The King and I*, *Pacific Overtures*, *Breakfast at Tiffany's*, and *Cinderella*. (Courtesy of Noel Calingasan.)

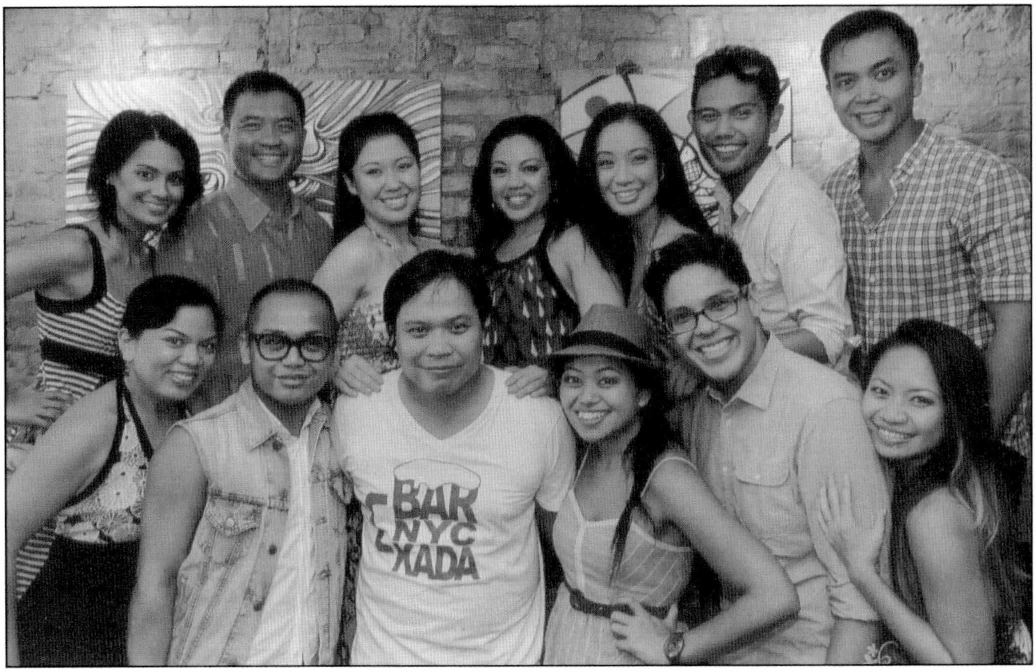

Here Lies Love is a rock musical, produced by David Byrne and Fatboy Slim, about the life of the former first lady of the Philippines Imelda Marcos and the People Power Movement in the 1980s. With an all–Asian American cast, the show has had two runs at the Public Theater. Starring Ruthie Ann Miles, Jose Llana, Conrad Ricamora, Jaygee Macapugay, and Melody Bitiu, the show received rave reviews from the *New York Times* and other prestigious outlets. Pictured is the cast of *Here Lies Love* in 2013. (Courtesy of Randy Gener.)

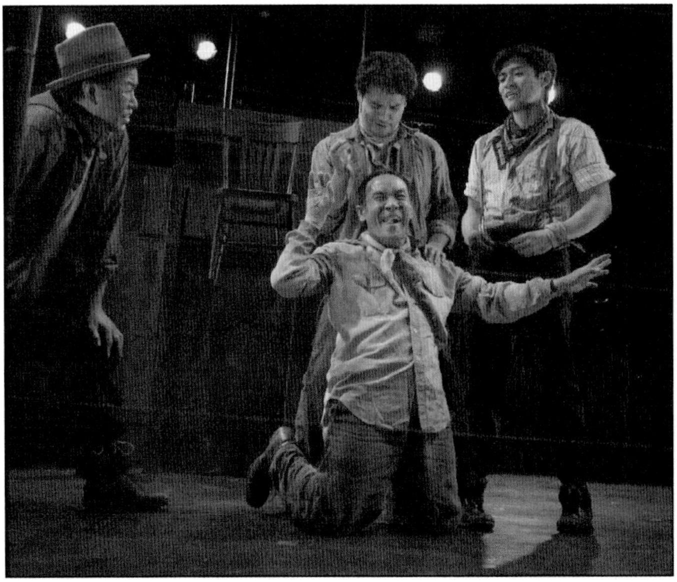

Founded in 1989, Ma-Yi Theater Company is a Drama Desk– and Obie Award–winning organization whose primary mission is to develop and produce new and innovative plays by Asian American writers. Ma-Yi has distinguished itself as one of the country's leading incubators of new work, shaping the national discourse about what it means to be Asian American today. Pictured here is a scene from *The Romance of Magno Rubio,* which ran in 2007. (Courtesy of Matt Zugale.)

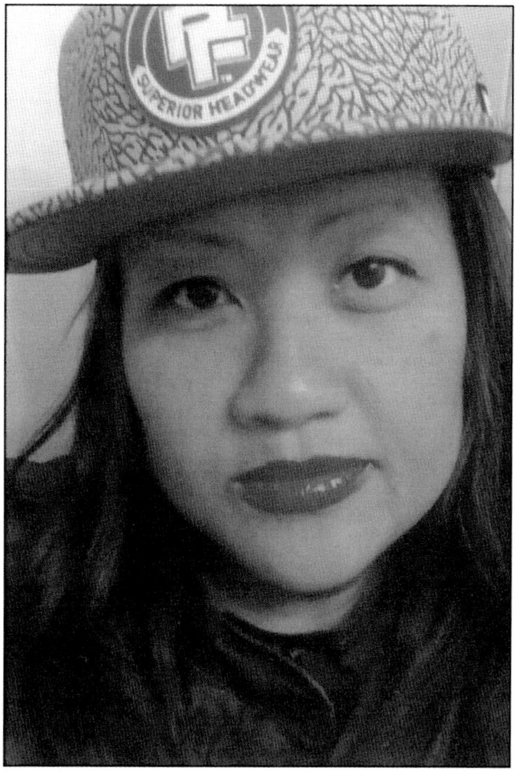

DJ Kuttin Kandi is one of the most respected DJs in the world of hip-hop. She earned a name for herself in 1997 and 1998, winning the ITF, Vibe Battles, and Rhythm Method DJ battles. She came out on top of the 1998 Source Magazine Championships and is the first female to make it to the DMC USA Finals. The artist has performed with big names Jay-Z, Busta Rhymes, LL Cool J, Wyclef, Mya, and Common. In addition to her DJ career, Kuttin Kandi serves her community as a lecturer and activist and has coauthored a book about Filipino Americans in hip-hop culture called *Empire of Funk: Hip Hop and Representation in Filipino America*. (Courtesy of Candice Custodio.)

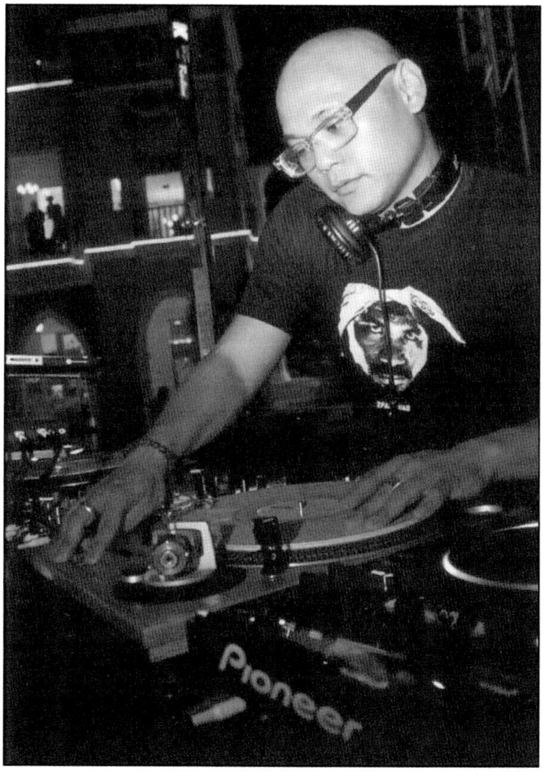

DJ Neil Armstrong is the founding father of the DJ Collective 5th Platoon and one of the most revered DJs in the world. Born and bred in New York City, he has performed alongside diverse artists—from De La Soul, the Roots, Company Flow, and Biz Markie to Kanye West, LL Cool J, Busta Rhymes, and Wyclef Jean. (Courtesy of DJ Neil Armstrong.)

J. Elaine Marcos was born in Burlington, Ontario, Canada, but moved to New York as a young adult to pursue her dreams of being on Broadway. She has been in eight Broadway shows, including *Annie* (Lily St. Regis), *Priscilla Queen of the Desert*, and *A Chorus Line*. Her favorite part about living in New York City is the glorious live theater scene and the Broadway community, which she calls her family. (Courtesy of J. Elaine Marcos.)

Ching Valdes-Aran is an actor and director who received an Obie Award for her performance in the Ma-Yi production of R. Pena's *Flipzoids*, directed by Loy Arcenas, as well as a Lucille Lortel nomination for Best Featured Actress in J. Hagedorn's *Dogeaters*, directed by Michael Grief and produced at the Public Theater. (Courtesy of Ching Valdes-Aran.)

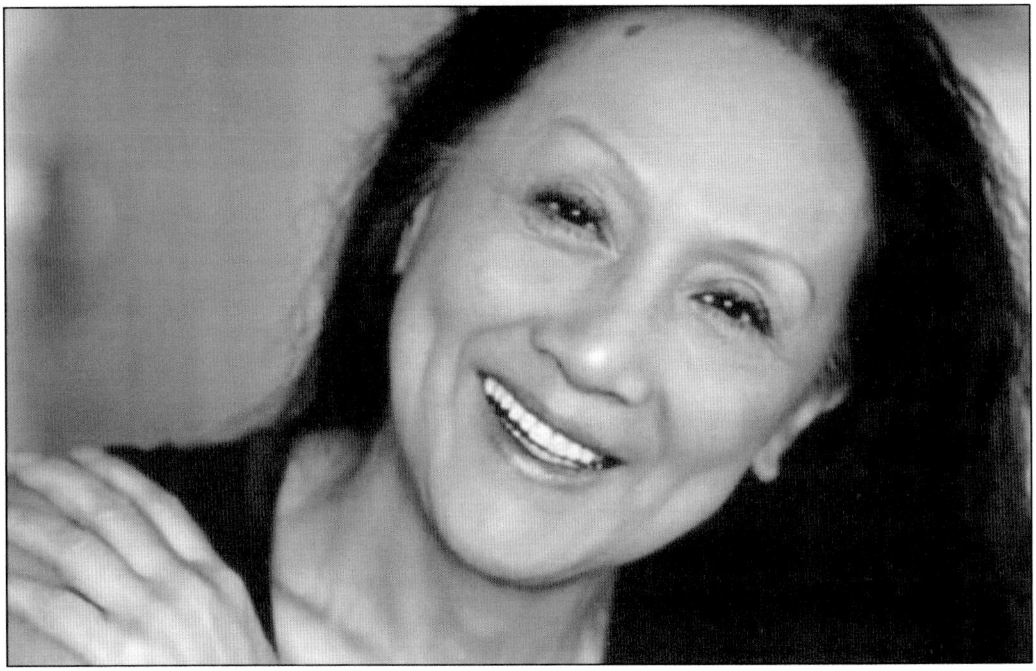

Michelle Aguilar Camaya started dancing at the age of four. A New York transplant by way of San Diego, California, she has appeared on stage, in movies, and on television. Her credits include Disney's *The Lion King* on Broadway, *Come Fly Away*, and *Kismet*. She is featured in the films *Enchanted* and *Memoirs of a Geisha*. In 2008, she was a finalist on Bravo TV's reality series *Step It Up and Dance*. (Courtesy of Katja Hirche.)

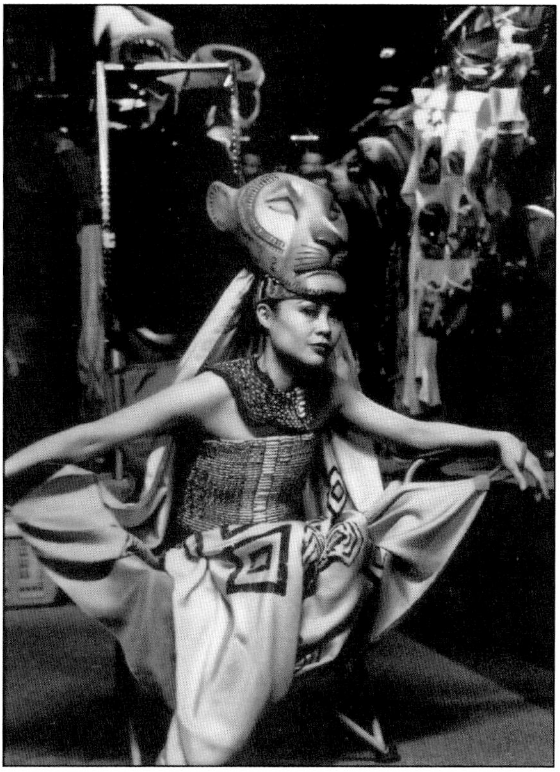

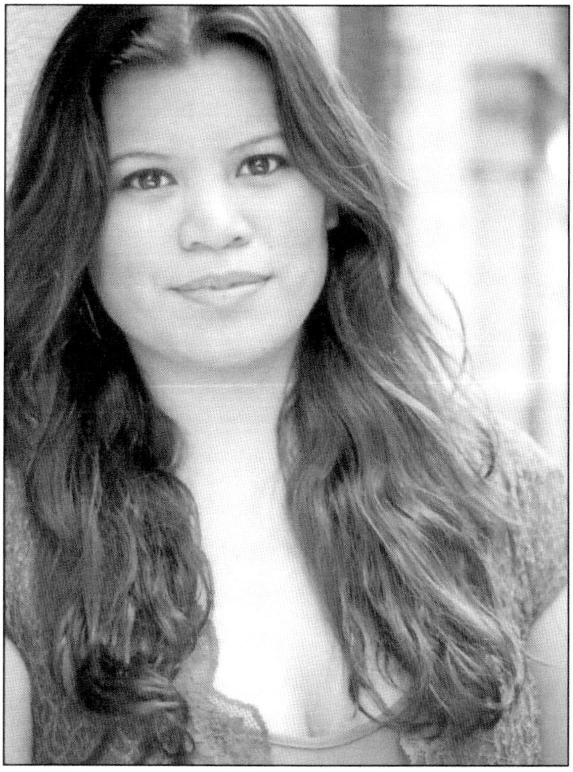

Liz Casasola is a singer, actor, and producer based in New York City. She had the honor of singing for the president of the Philippines Benigno Aquino III's inaugural ball. She has been seen in *Imelda: A New Musical*, *Miss Saigon*, *Dogeaters* at the Public Theater, and *Shout! The Mod Musical*. She coproduced Lea Salonga's sold-out concert at Carnegie Hall hailed by *Playbill* as one of the "Top 10 Best of 2005." Liz also produced the Filipino musical *Prison Dancer*—an award-winning 2012 New York Musical Festival production that was sold out for its entire run. (Courtesy of Diane Phelan.)

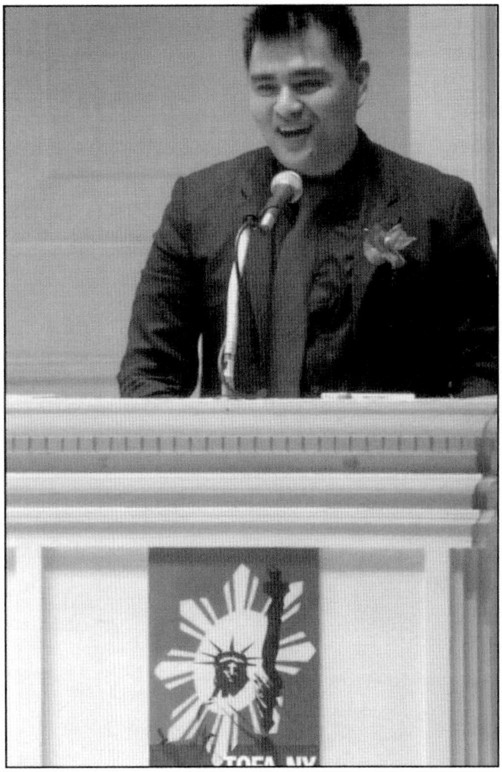

Jose Antonio Vargas is a Filipino American New Yorker who won a Pulitzer Prize for writing in 2008. In 2011, he became best known for writing about his experiences as an undocumented immigrant in the United States. Since then, he has become the face of the immigration rights movement, advocating for immigrants on Capitol Hill, on various national television programs, and through his produced documentary, *Documented.* Here he is pictured at the Outstanding Filipino Americans of New York ceremony in 2011. (Courtesy of Troi Santos and Elton Lugay.)

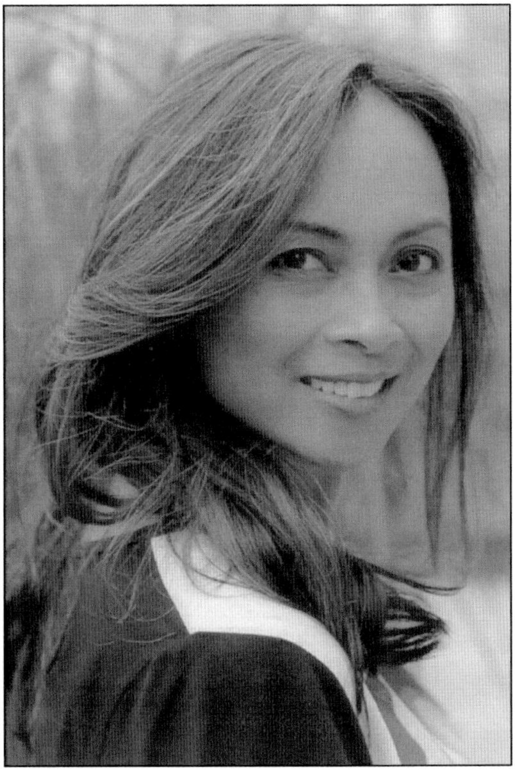

Ernabel Demillo is a television journalist who was a reporter and fill-anchor for FOX-5 New York's morning show, *Good Day New York*, from 1996 to 2005. Currently, she is the host and producer of CUNY-TV's new monthly magazine show, *Asian American Life*, which was nominated for a NY News Emmy for Best Community Affairs/Public Programming in 2014. (Courtesy of Laura Fuchs.)

Ryan Abugan, better known as Hydroponikz, is a hip-hop rapper who was born in Quezon City but raised in Queens. Heavily influenced by the 1990s New York hip-hop, he has produced and released several albums and performed his music all over the country. (Courtesy of Jeffrey Buenaventura.)

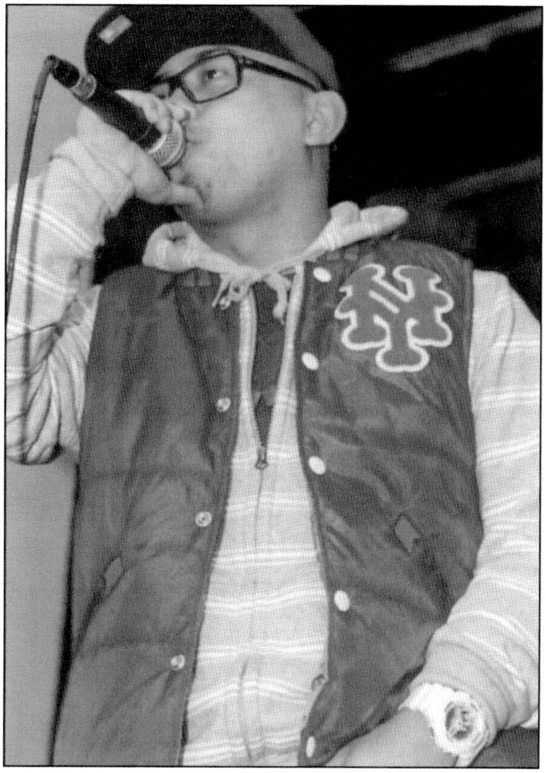

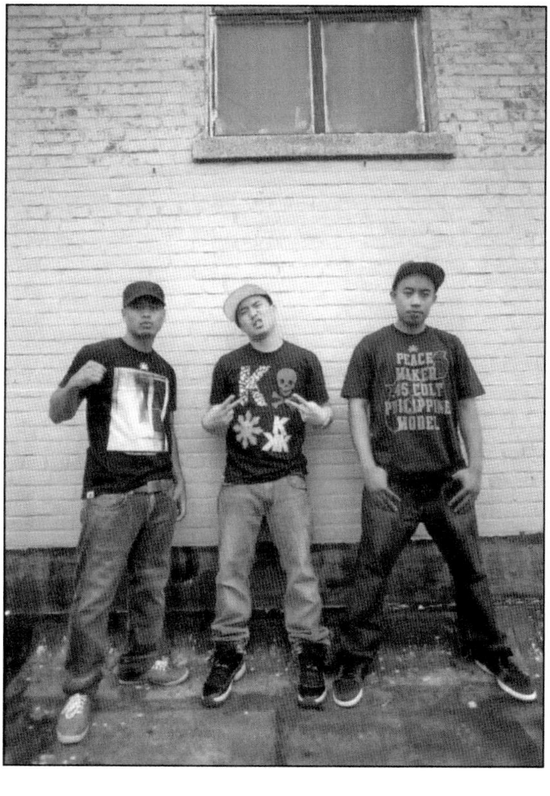

Deep Foundation is a hip-hop group that consists of three emcees representing Queens and New Jersey: CeeJay (Christopher Guiang), ILL Poe (Mark Malacapay), and MUG (Rosendo Pili). Deep Foundation has brought its 1990s-influenced hip-hop to domestic and international audiences since 2002. With the release of its debut album, *The First Draft*, and groundbreaking music videos for "Children of the Sun" and "Sleep," Deep Foundation has captured the hearts and imaginations of fans worldwide. (Courtesy of Ernie Peña.)

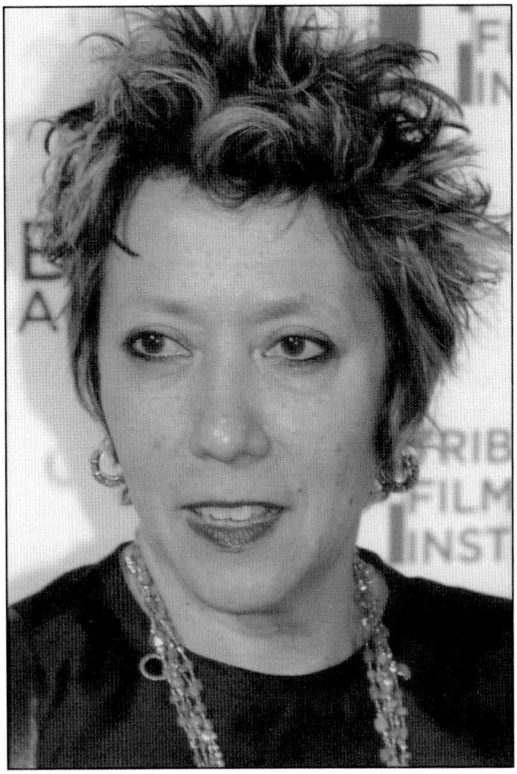

Jessica Hagedorn is the author of five books, including the novel *Dogeaters* (1990), which was a finalist for the National Book Award and winner of the American Book Award from the Before Columbus Foundation. She is the recipient of a Lucille Lortel Playwrights Fellowship, a Guggenheim Fiction Fellowship, an NEA-TCG Playwriting Residency Fellowship, and fellowships from the Sundance Theatre Lab and the Sundance Screenwriters Lab. Currently, Hagedorn is the Parsons Family University Professor of Creative Writing and director of the MFA writing program at Long Island University, Brooklyn. (Courtesy of Jessica Hagedorn.)

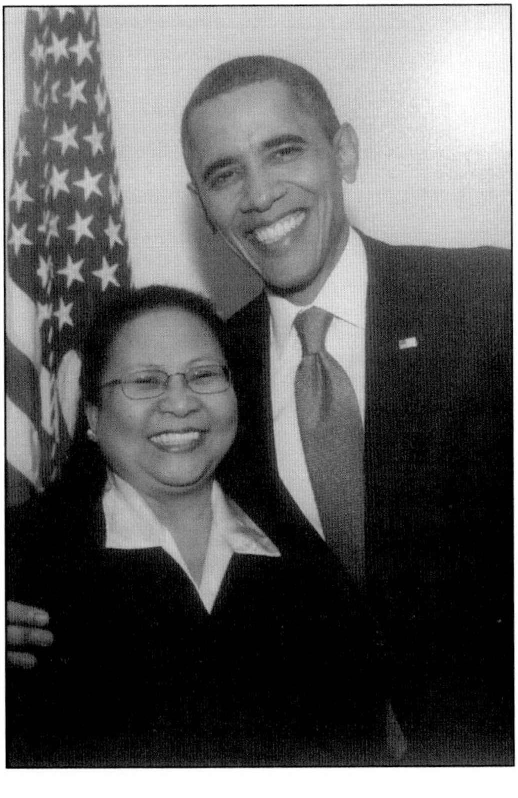

Menchu de Luna Sanchez has been a registered nurse for almost 30 years. She is best known for her heroic efforts during Hurricane Sandy in 2012. When the power went out at NYU's Langone Medical Center, Sanchez courageously initiated a plan to transport 20 at-risk infants to intensive care units around the city. Here she is pictured with President Obama in 2013, after he recognized her for her courage and conviction. (Courtesy of Menchu Sanchez.)

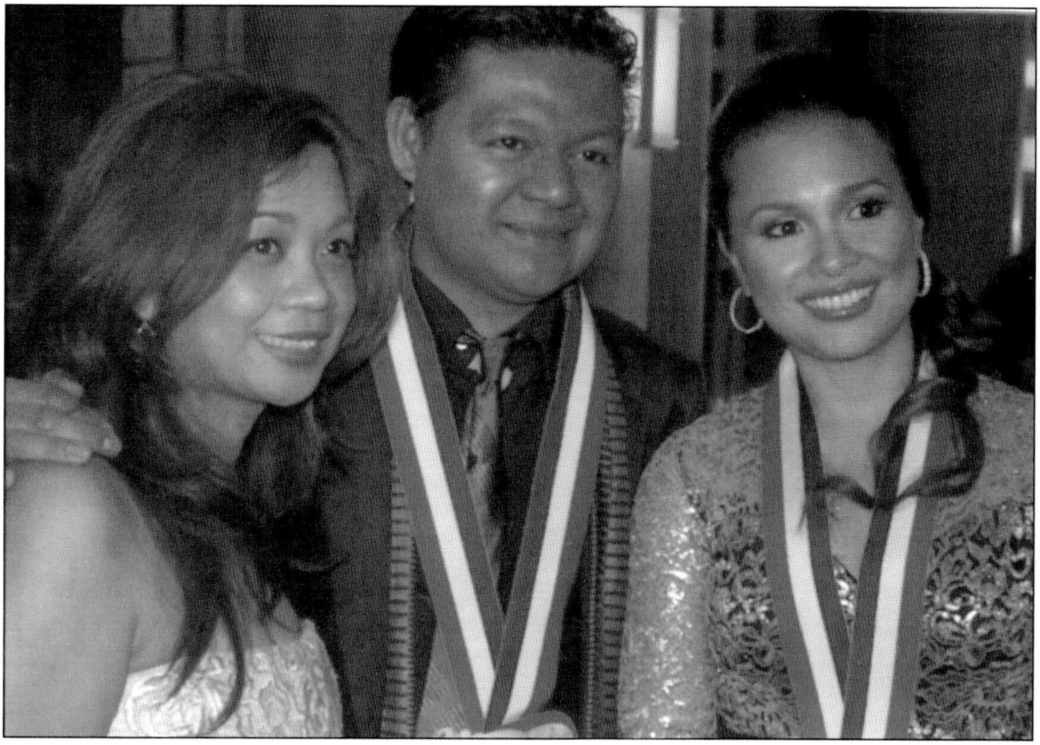

Pictured are, from left to right, Monette Rivera, Don Tagala, and Lea Salonga. Rivera is host and producer of NY Chika for the Filipino Channel's *Adobo Nation*. She has worked as a news correspondent for ABS-CBN since 2003. Rivera has been covering issues, people, and events surrounding the Filipino communities in Hawai'i, New York, and New Jersey. Don Tagala is an award-winning video journalist and the North American correspondent for *Balitang America* on ABS-CBN. He won the Bronze Award at the prestigious 33rd Annual Telly Awards for his Filipino Champion story "Armless Pilot" in 2012. (Courtesy of Troi Santos and Elton Lugay.)

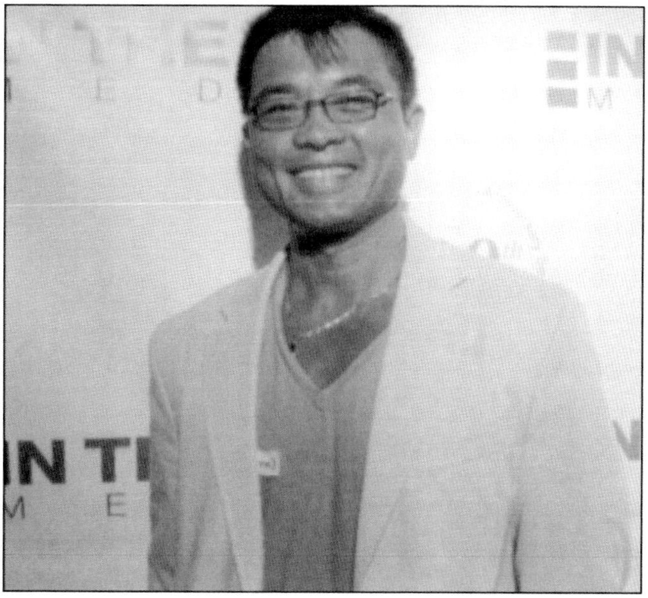

Randy Gener is an award-winning editor, writer, critic, and artist in New York City. He has had a significant record of reporting and writing for many major media outlets, including National Public Radio, the *New York Times*, *Newark Star-Ledger*, *Village Voice*, *New York Daily News*, *Time Out New York*, *New York Magazine*, and more. (Courtesy of Randy Gener.)

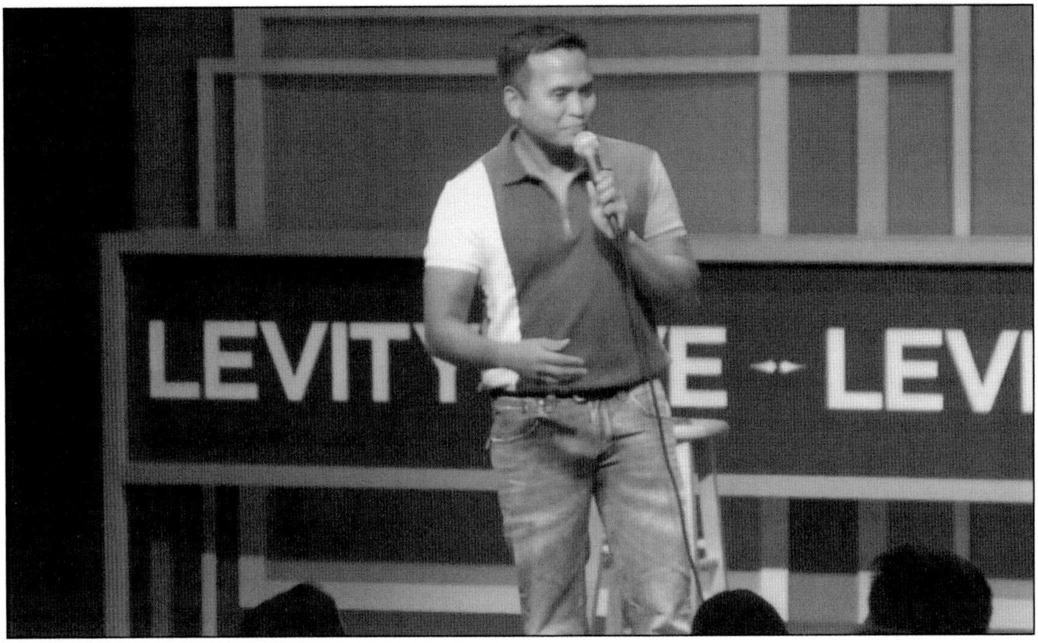

Air Tabigue is a comedian who was born and raised in Long Island, New York. He has performed at clubs and colleges around New York City and throughout the country. In 2004, Tabigue won the Eastern Division of the First Asian American Stand Up Comedy Competition held by Takeout Comedy. He has appeared on NBC and FOX, and has hosted the show *Asian America* on PBS. (Courtesy of Air Tabigue.)

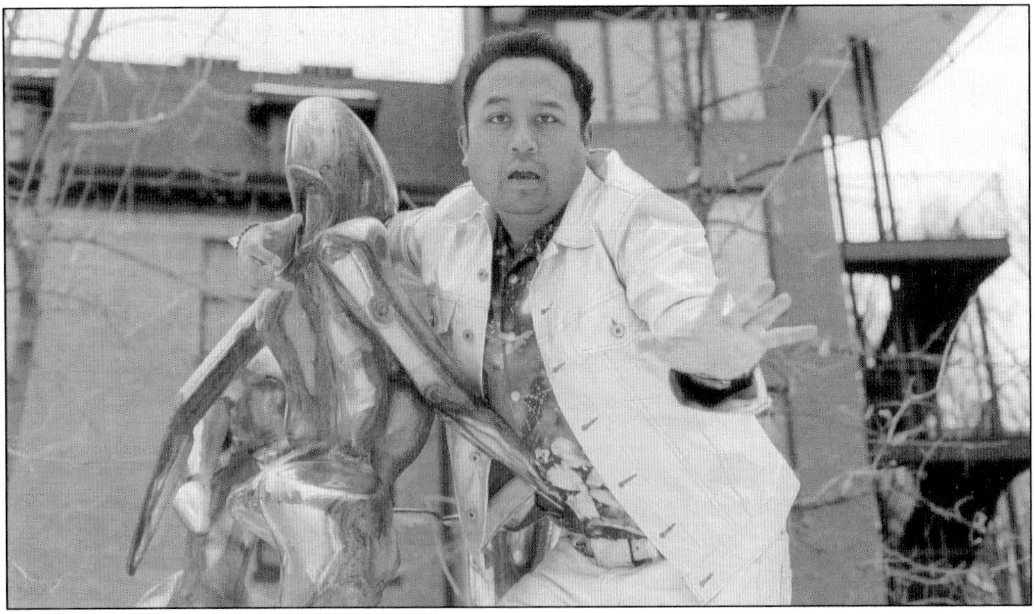

Regie Cabico is a pioneer of the spoken word and the first openly queer and Asian slam poet to take top prizes in the 1993, 1994, and 1997 National Poetry Slams. He is a former Nuyorican Poets Grand Slam Champion. He coedited *Flicker and Spark: A Contemporary Anthology of Queer Poetry and Spoken Word*, which was nominated for a 2014 Lambda Literary Award. Television appearances include HBO's *Def Poetry Jam* and NPR's *Snap Judgement*. (Courtesy of Les Talusan.)

Josie Natori is a fashion designer and the CEO and founder of the Natori Company. In March 2007, she was awarded the Order of Lakandula, one of the highest civilian awards in the Philippines. In April 2007, Natori received the Peopling of America Award from the Statue of Liberty-Ellis Island Foundation. She also served as a commissioner on the White House Conference on Small Business. (Courtesy of Elton Lugay.)

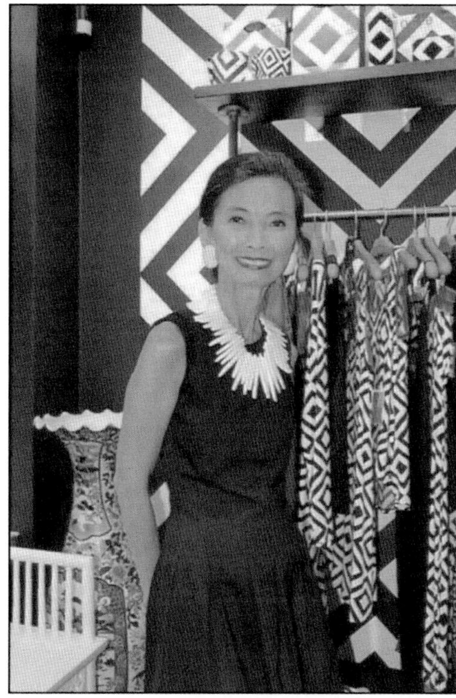

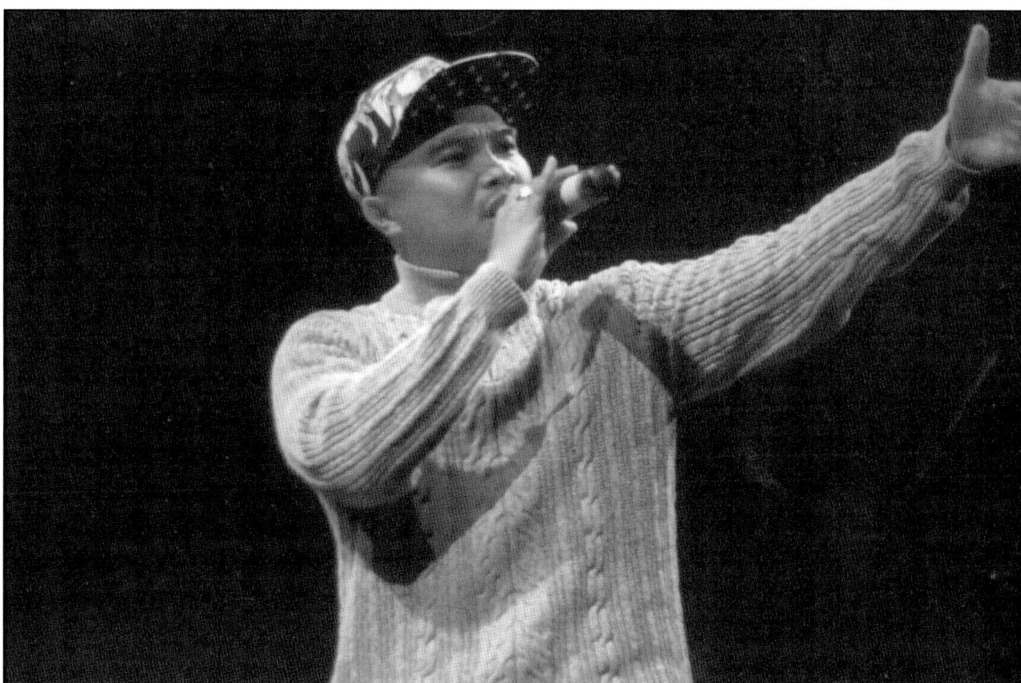

Kilusan Bautista is a performance artist who has performed UNiVERSALself, a solo multimedia production, all over the United States. In 2008, Bautista was featured on Showtime as the opening act for Nonito Donaire, the Filipino Flash, at Mandalay Bay Hotel in Las Vegas, Nevada. In 2005, he won the grand prize for a California statewide writing contest sponsored by the California Council for the Humanities and New America Media. (Courtesy of Chauncey Velasco.)

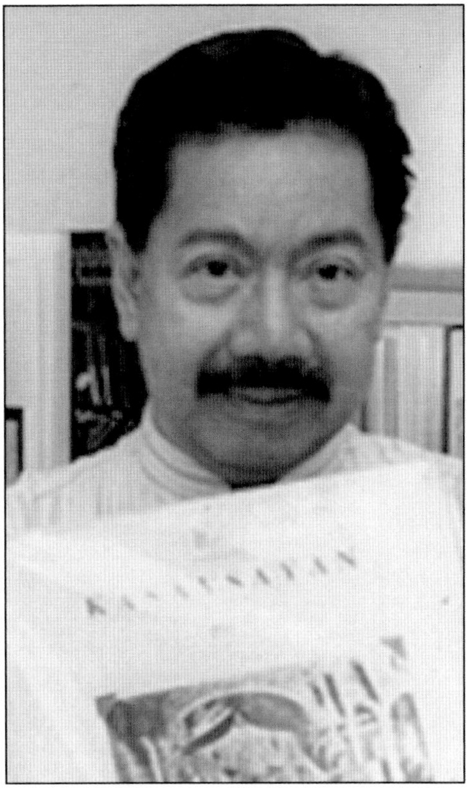

Reynaldo "Ronnie" Gamboa Alejandro was the founder of the Metropolitan New York Chapter of the Filipino American National Historical Society. He was the author of several books, including *Sayaw Silangan – The Dance of the Philippines*, *Philippine Dance*, *Philippine Cookbook*, *The Flavor of Asia*, and *Pinoy Guide to the Big Apple*, as well as the coauthor of the book *Pinoyork*. He was also a dancer, choreographer, director, dance and culinary historian, librarian, chef, party planner, and columnist. In 2009, he died in New York City at 67 years old. (Courtesy of FANHS National Archives.)

Filmed in Woodside, Jamaica, and Fresh Meadows, Queens, as well as Manhattan in 1996, *Waiting in the Wings* is a film about a Filipino American young woman who struggles with the pressures of her Filipino American family and has the dream of becoming a dancer. Director and producer Charles R. Uy received a student Academy Award and a Directors Guild of America Student Award for the film. Pictured here is the film's lead actress, Rona Figueroa, on the set of the film. (Courtesy of Charles Uy.)

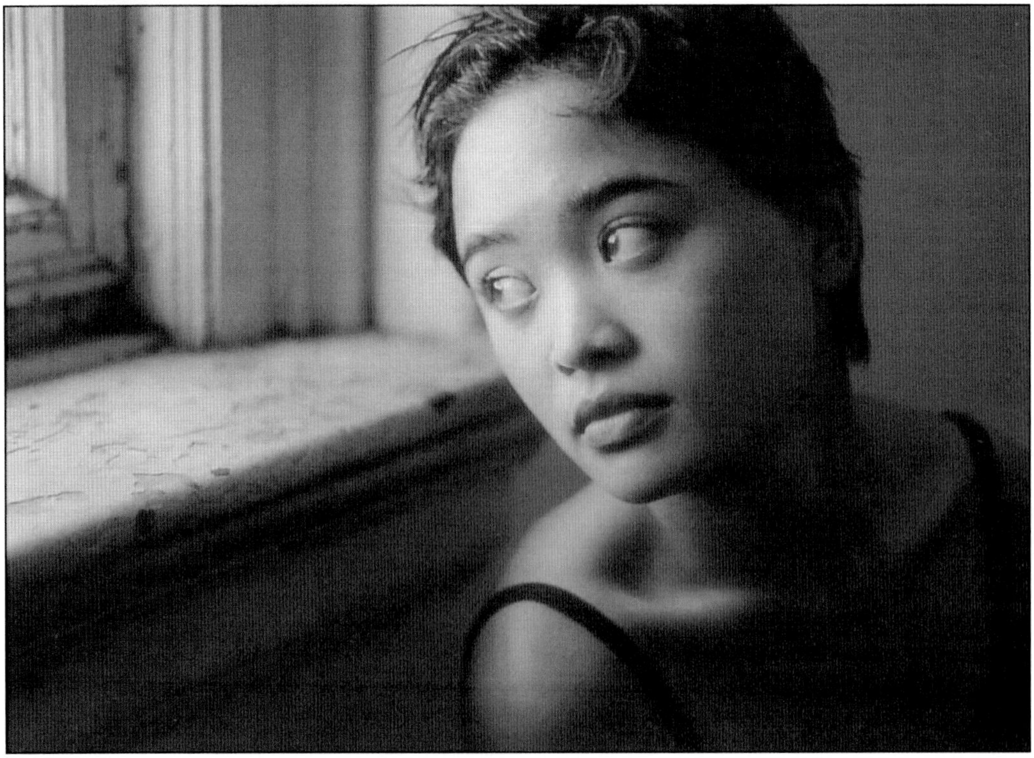

Luis H. Francia is a poet, journalist, and nonfiction writer. His semiautobiographical account of growing up in the Philippines, *Eye of the Fish: A Personal Archipelago*, won both the 2002 PEN Open Book and the 2002 Asian American Writers literary awards. He has written several poetry books and has written for the *Village Voice*, the *Nation*, and the *Far Eastern Economic Review*. On the board of trustees of the Asian American Writers Workshop and Kundiman Arts, he also teaches at New York University. Professor Francia received the FANHS Metro New York Lifetime Achievement Award in 2013 (Courtesy of Luis Francia.)

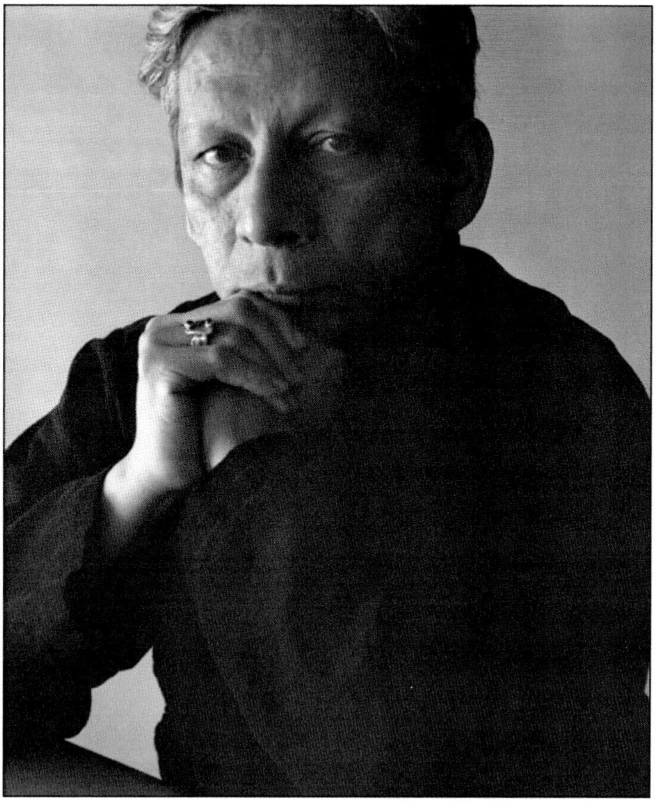

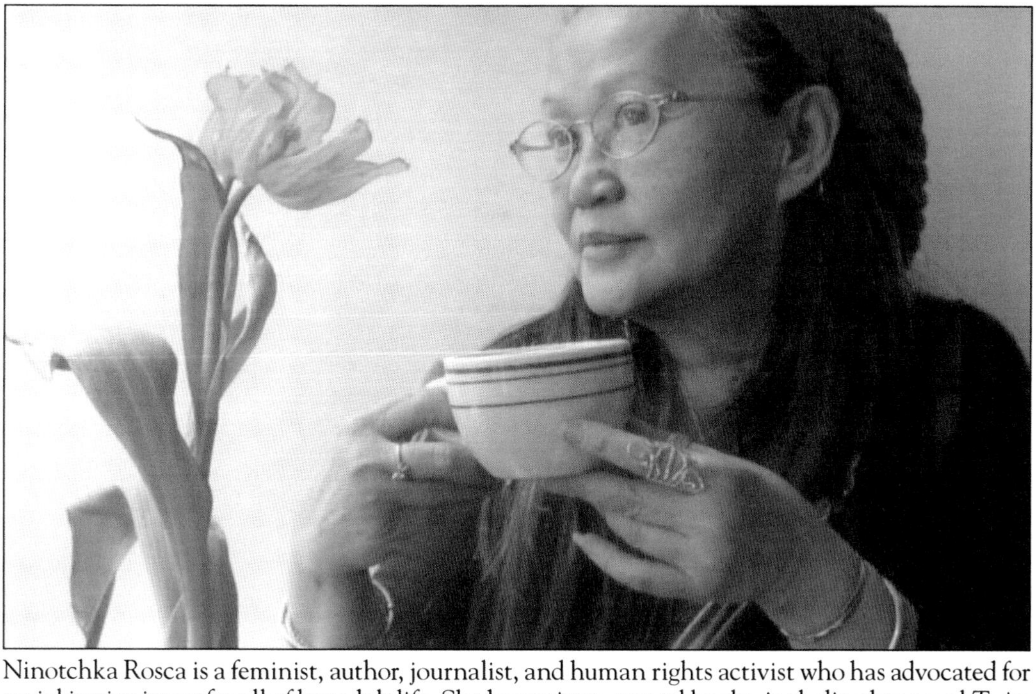

Ninotchka Rosca is a feminist, author, journalist, and human rights activist who has advocated for social justice issues for all of her adult life. She has written several books, including her novel *Twice Blessed*, which received the American Book Award in 1993. (Courtesy of Ninotchka Rosa.)

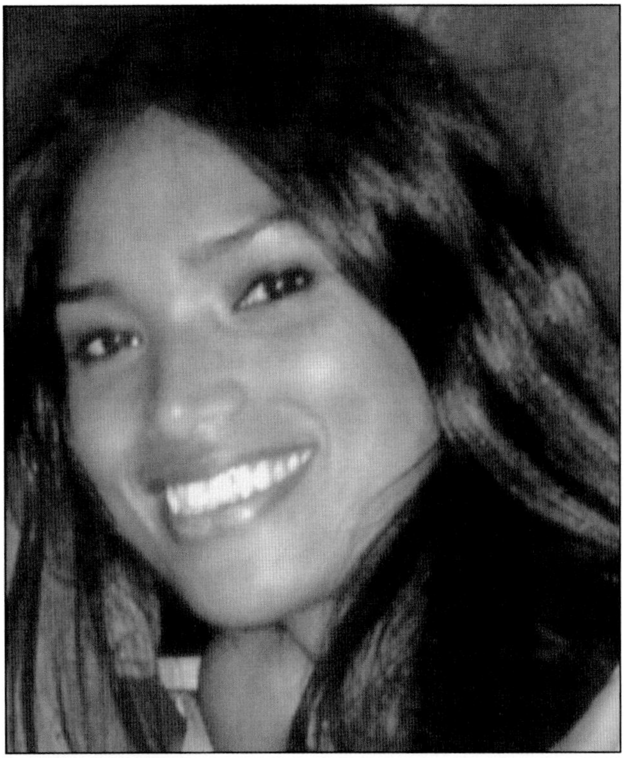

Geena Rocero is a professional model for fashion and beauty companies around the world. She immigrated to New York to pursue her dream of being a supermodel. In 2014, she came out as transgender during a TED talk, which was viewed over two million times in just a few months. Rocero founded the organization Gender Proud and has walked in several high-end runway shows. She has been featured in notable magazines, including an August 2014 spread in *Elle*. (Courtesy of the author.)

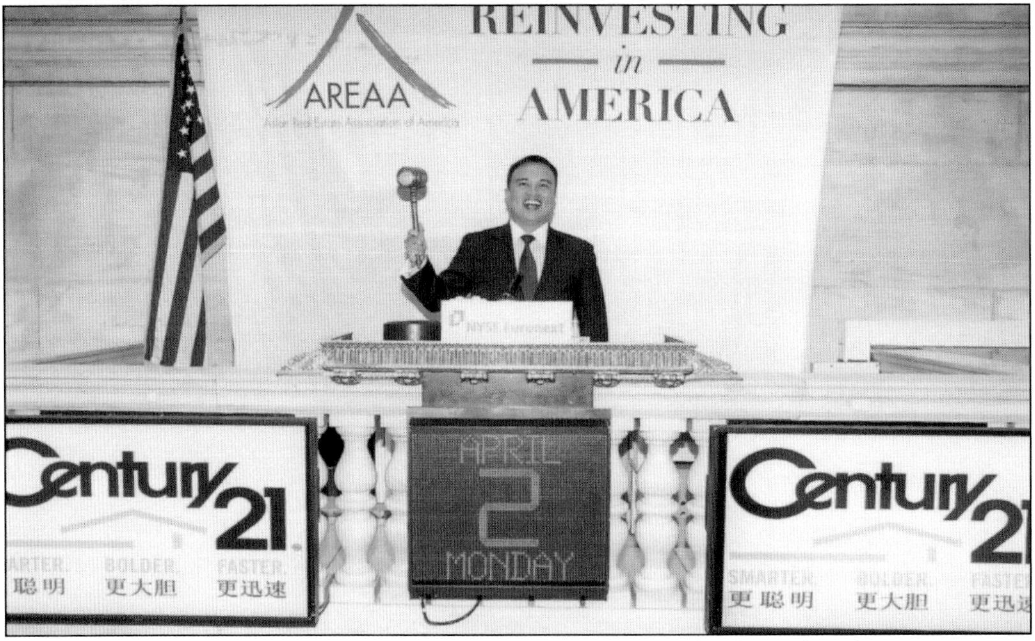

Rio Guerrero is an immigration attorney and revered community leader in the Filipino American community of New York. In 2012, the National Asian Pacific American Bar Association (NAPABA) presented Guerrero with the coveted "Best Lawyers Under 40" national award. He is the founder of the Asian American Bar Association of New York (AABANY) Immigration and Nationality Law Committee. Here, he is at the New York Stock Exchange in 2012. (Courtesy of Rio Guerrero.)

Seven

I Heart NY
Historical and Contemporary Images of Filipinos at New York Landmarks

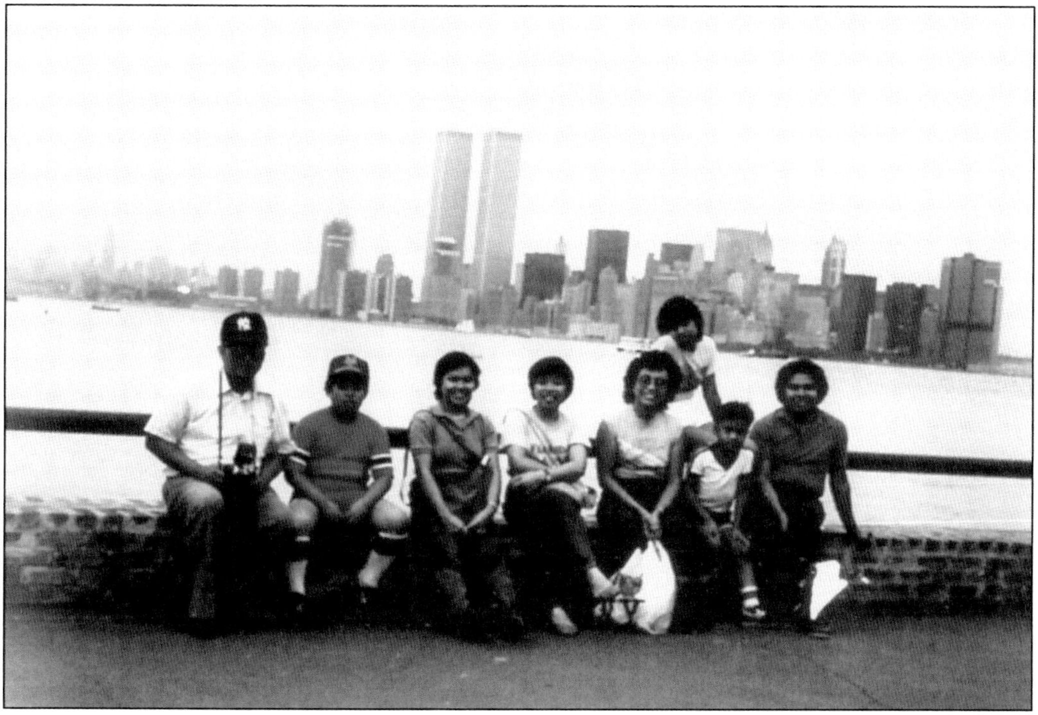

The Manhattan skyline is arguably the most recognizable in the world. From the Empire State Building to the Statue of Liberty, New York City monuments are often viewed as symbols of American freedom. Tourists travel from all over the world to have their photographs taken at places like the Brooklyn Bridge, Rockefeller Center, and Times Square. In this c. 1985 image, a Filipino family sits along the Brooklyn Heights Promenade, with the Lower Manhattan skyline behind them. Notice the World Trade Center Twin Towers still soar above the rest of the buildings. (Courtesy of the Prado family.)

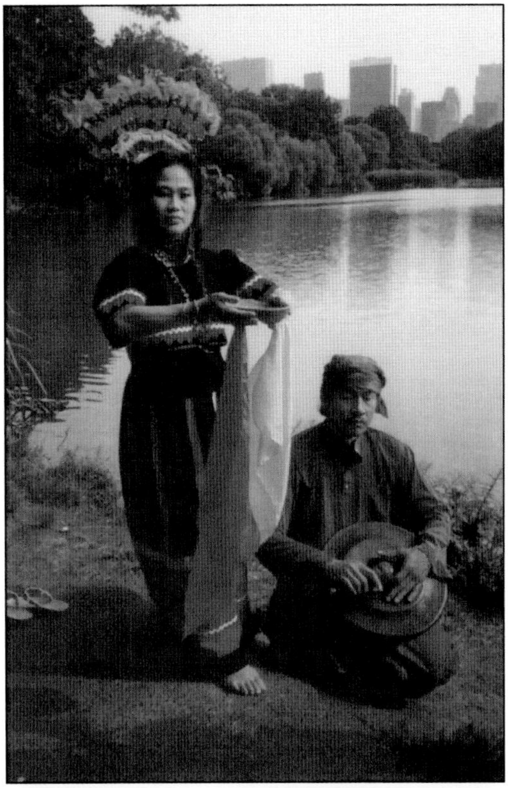

Potri Ranka Manis, RN, is a nurse, a community health worker trainer, and the founder of Kinding Sindaw, a not-for-profit dance group established in 1992. Here, Manis (left) is in Central Park with a fellow dancer in 1993. (Courtesy of Kat Palasi.)

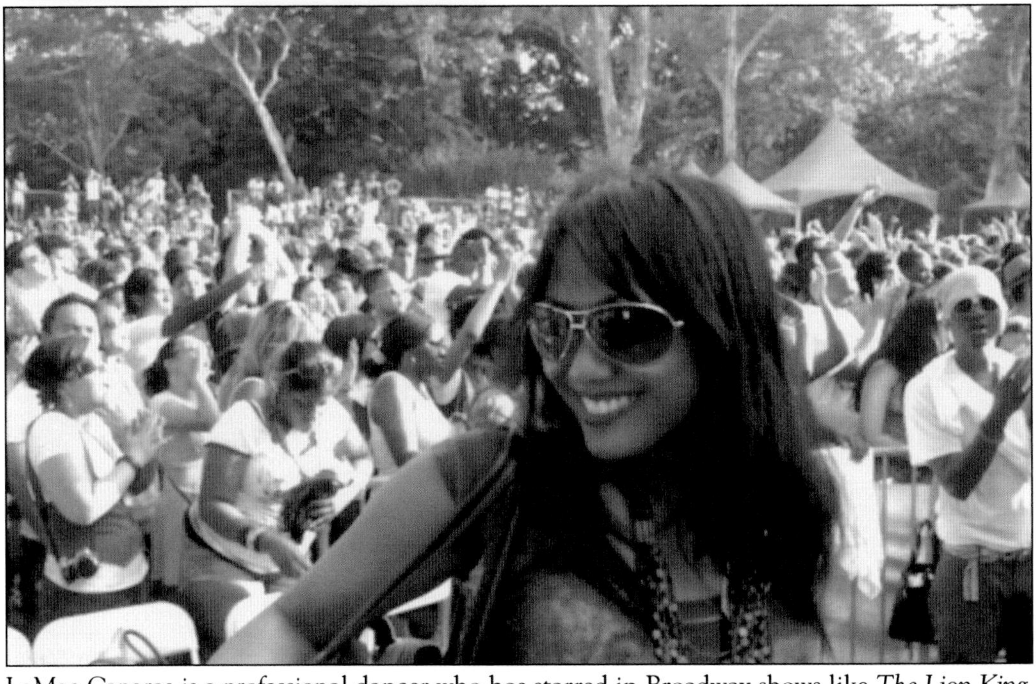

LaMae Caparas is a professional dancer who has starred in Broadway shows like *The Lion King*, *Fosse*, *Miss Saigon*, *The King and I*, and *South Pacific*. Here, she is at a concert in Central Park in 2009. (Courtesy of LaMae Caparas.)

Melissa Cariño, a community organizer, takes a selfie while on the Brooklyn Bridge in 2011. The bridge is one of the oldest suspension bridges in the United States, with its opening in 1883. A sketch of the Brooklyn Bridge was found in the diary of Jose Rizal, presumably from his visit in 1888. (Courtesy of Melissa Cariño.)

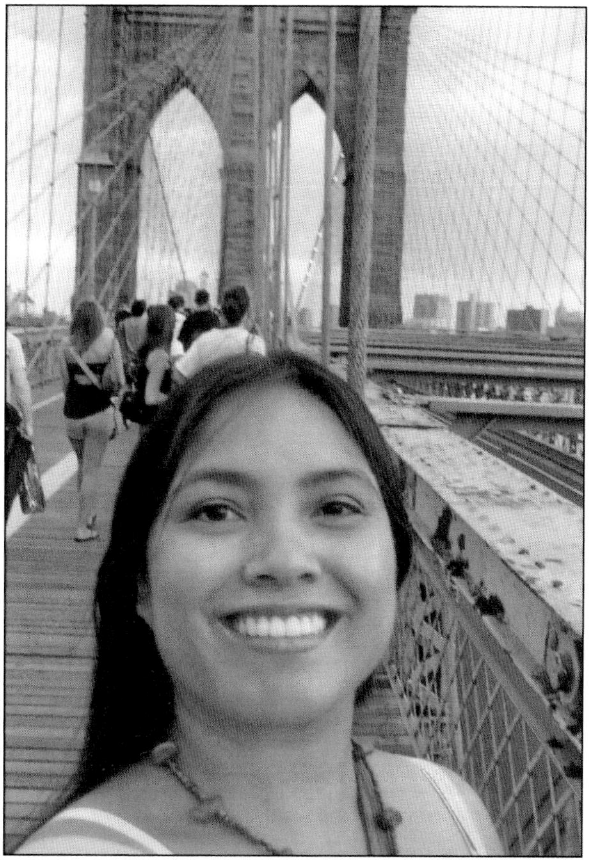

Pamela Tamayo and Ryan Abugan pose in front of the Brooklyn Bridge in 2013. Pamela is a graphic designer, and Ryan is a hip-hop emcee and digital artist. (Courtesy of Ian Tamayo.)

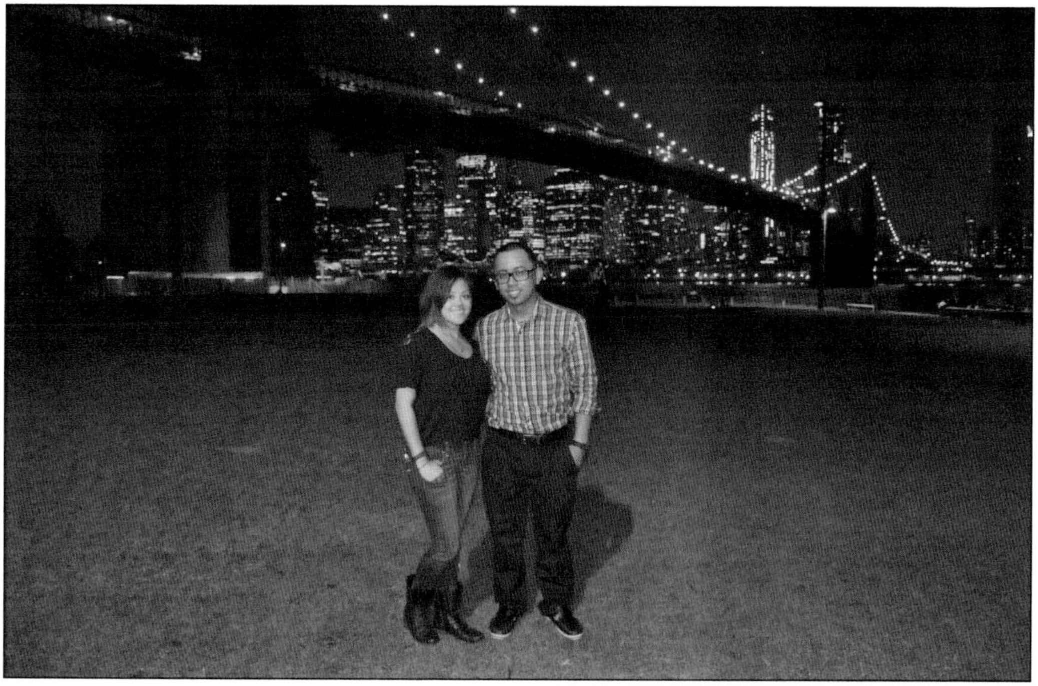

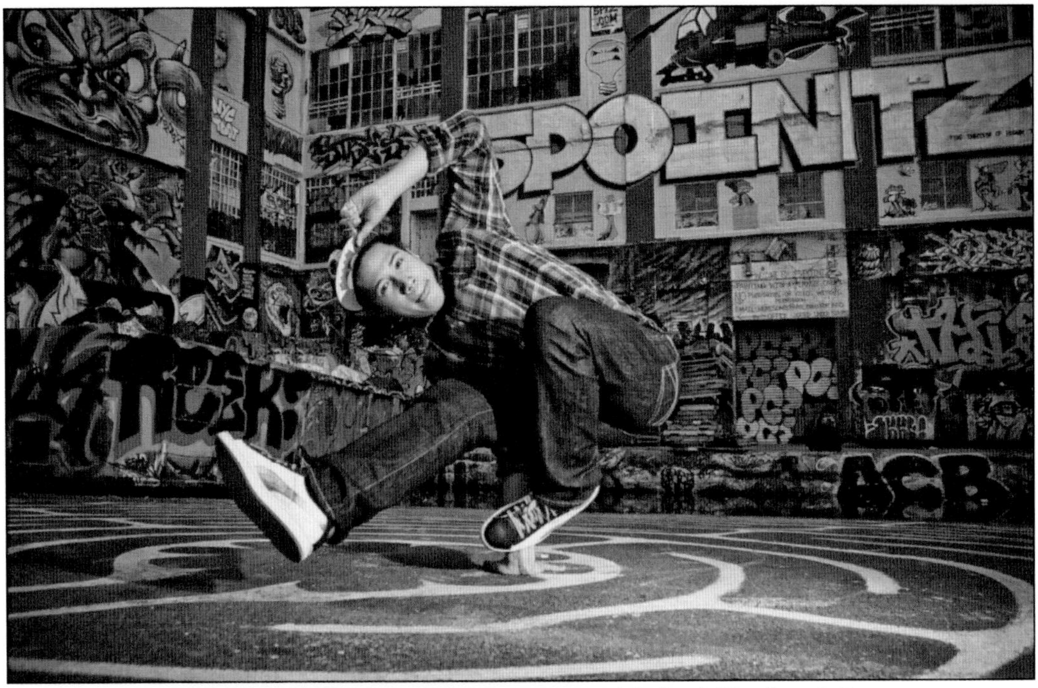

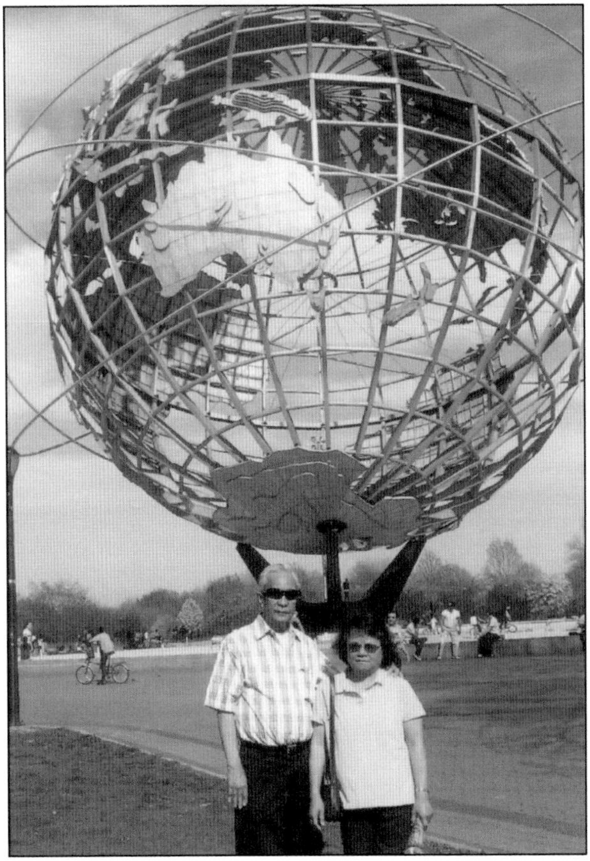

Michael "Suitkace" Capito is a registered nurse and an award-winning break dancer/B-boy. Here he is in 2009, posing in front of 5 Pointz, an outdoor art exhibit space in Long Island City, Queens. It was considered to be the world's premiere graffiti mecca before its closing in 2014. (Courtesy of J.R. Peña.)

Fabio and Neri Quijano enjoy a day in front of the famous Unisphere at Flushing Meadows Park in Queens in 2005. Also known as Flushing Meadows–Corona Park, the site was the location of world's fairs in New York in 1939–1940 and 1964–1965. (Courtesy of Frederick Quijano.)

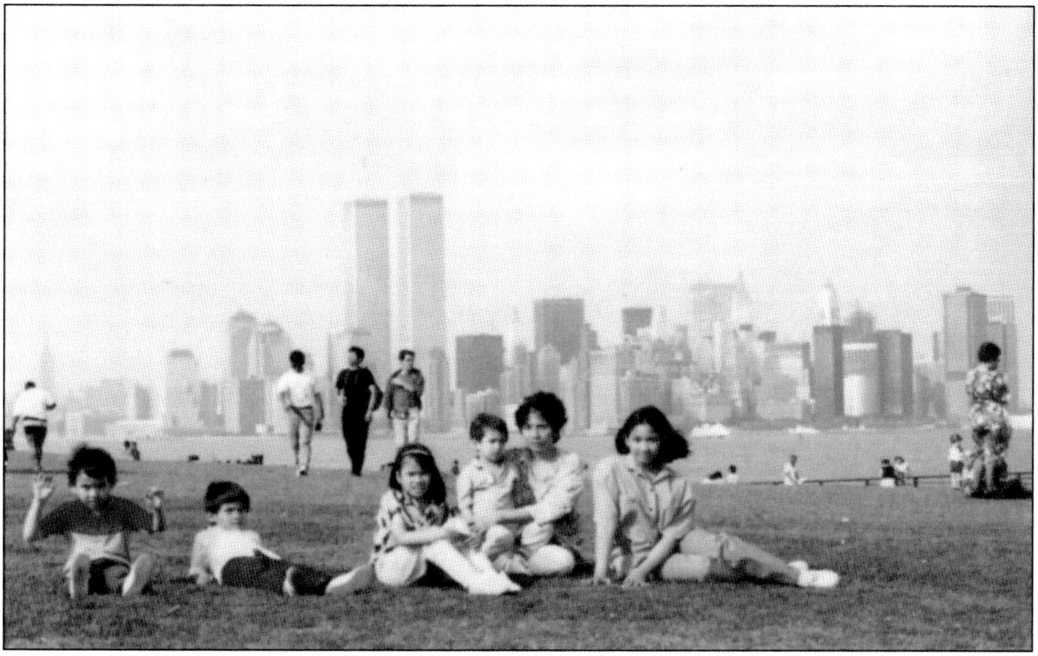

In 1983, the Sriken family relaxes on the Brooklyn Heights Promenade with the Manhattan skyline in the background. (Courtesy of Julie Sriken.)

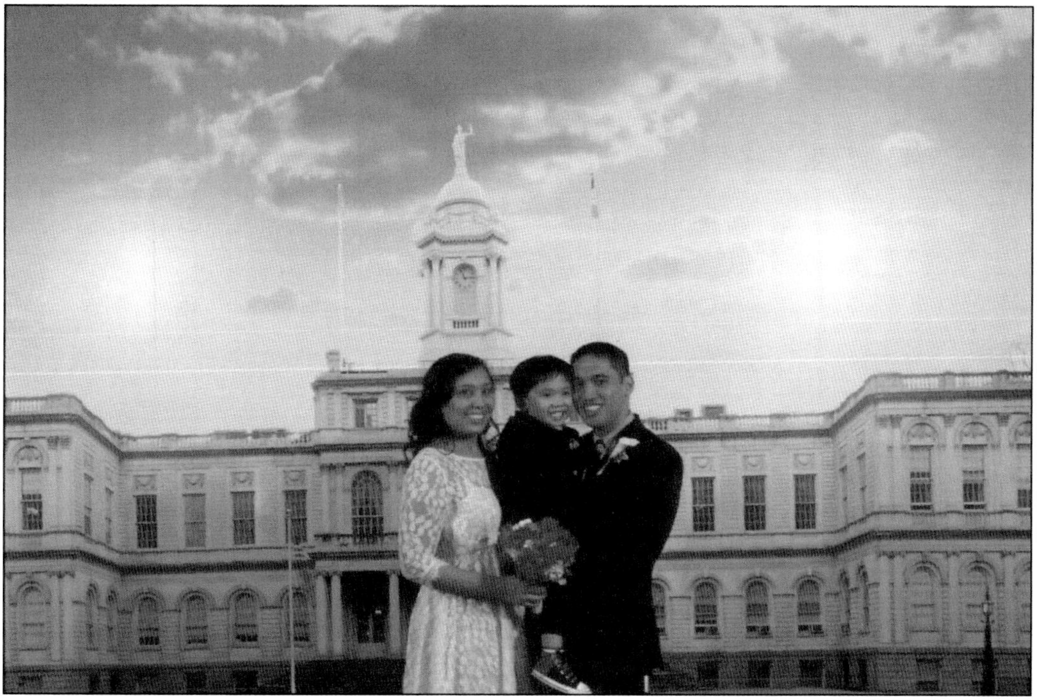

Greg Tuballes and Christina Rodriguez were married at city hall with their son Tristan as a witness in 2011. (Courtesy of Christina Tuballes.)

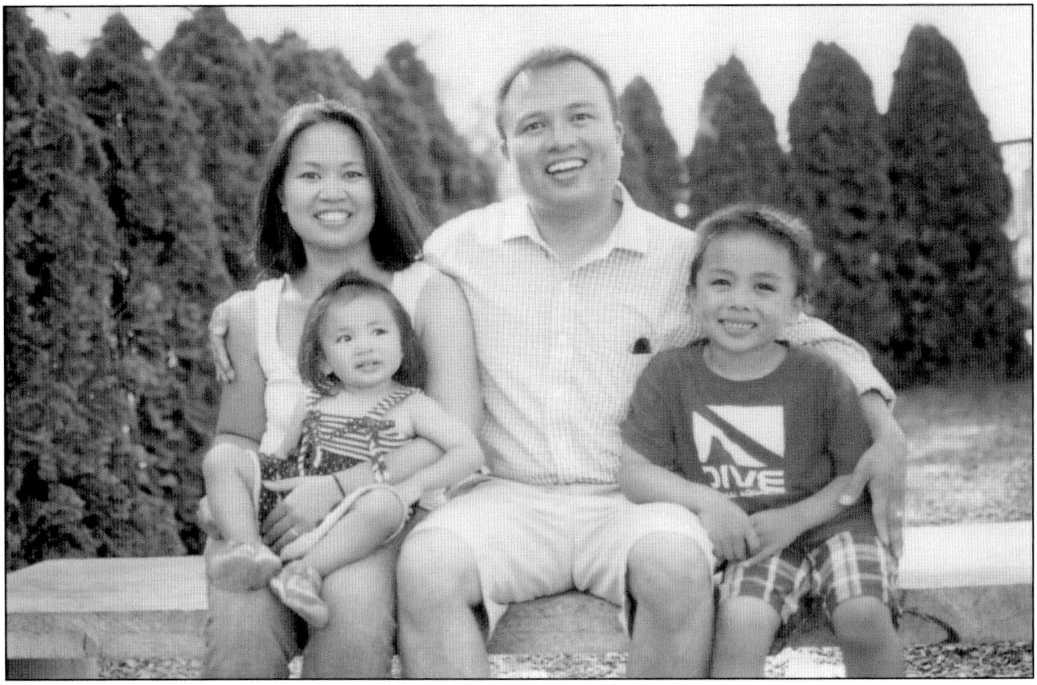

Rio Guerrero takes his wife, Joan, and children, Carina and Vincent, for an outing at the Brooklyn Botanic Garden in 2011. (Courtesy of Rio Guerrero.)

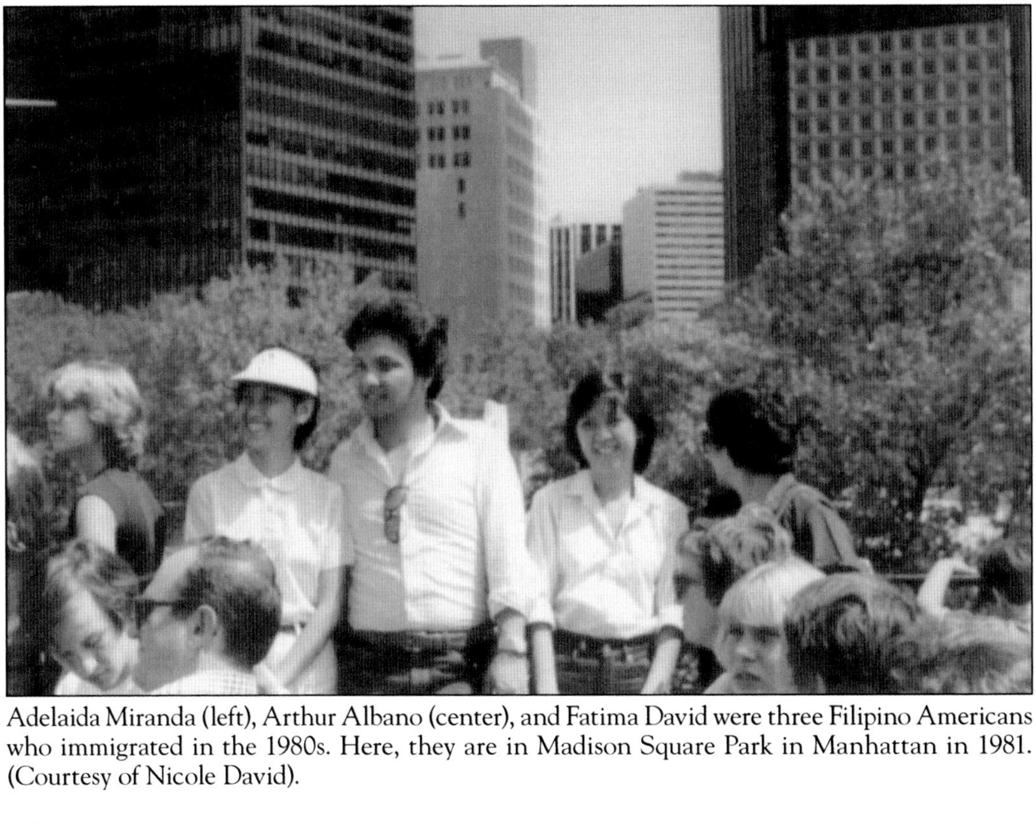

Adelaida Miranda (left), Arthur Albano (center), and Fatima David were three Filipino Americans who immigrated in the 1980s. Here, they are in Madison Square Park in Manhattan in 1981. (Courtesy of Nicole David).

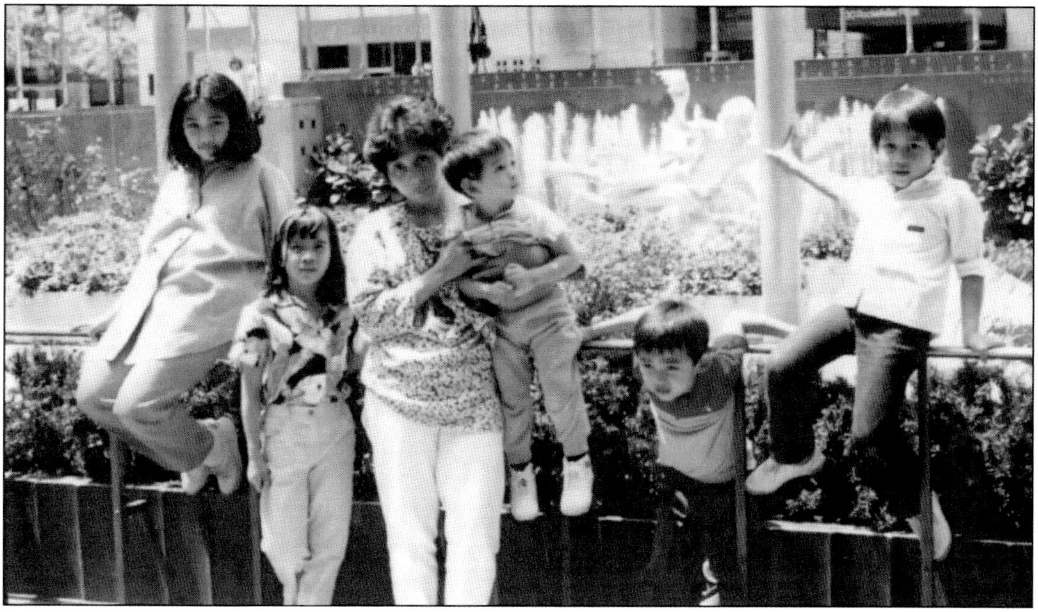

The Sriken family poses in front of the famous *Prometheus* statue at Rockefeller Center in 1983. (Courtesy of Julie Sriken.)

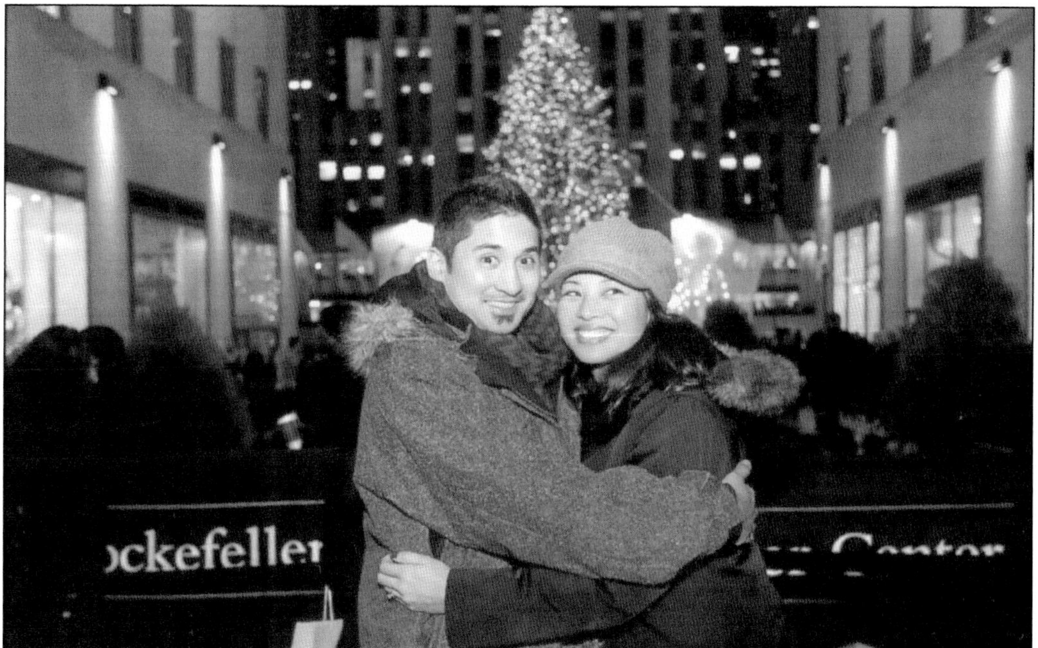

Marq Romero and Chriselle Buendia share a moment in front of the Rockefeller Center Christmas tree in early 2013. (Courtesy of Sean Guzman)

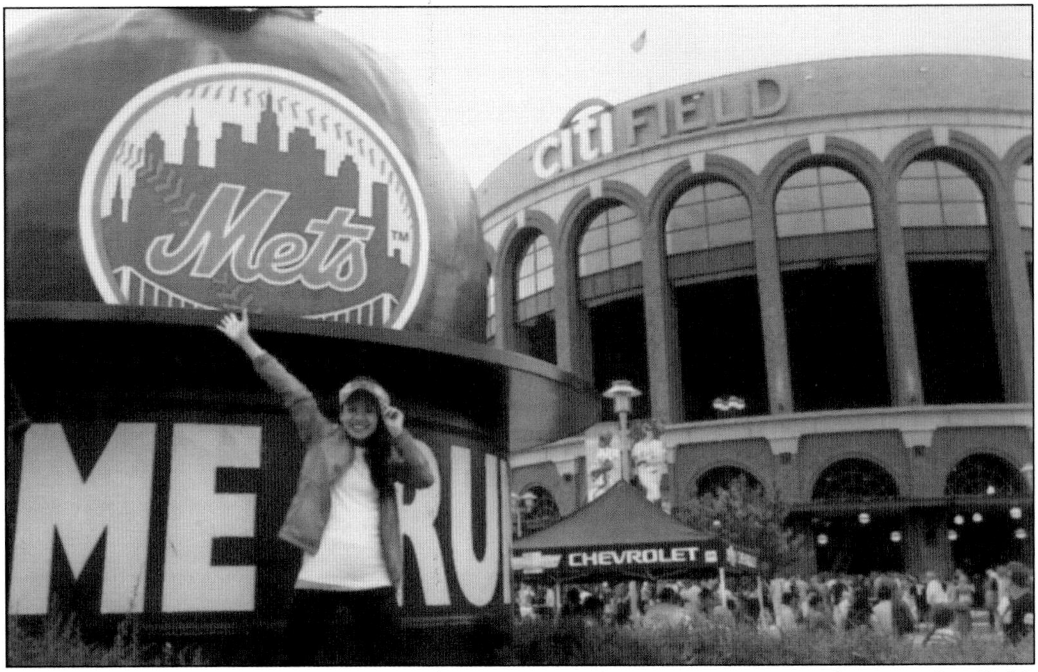

Mia Fulgado-Tyler, an attorney who was born and raised in Queens, is excited to visit Citi Field, the new stadium for the New York Mets, in 2012. (Courtesy of Mia Fulgado-Tyler.)

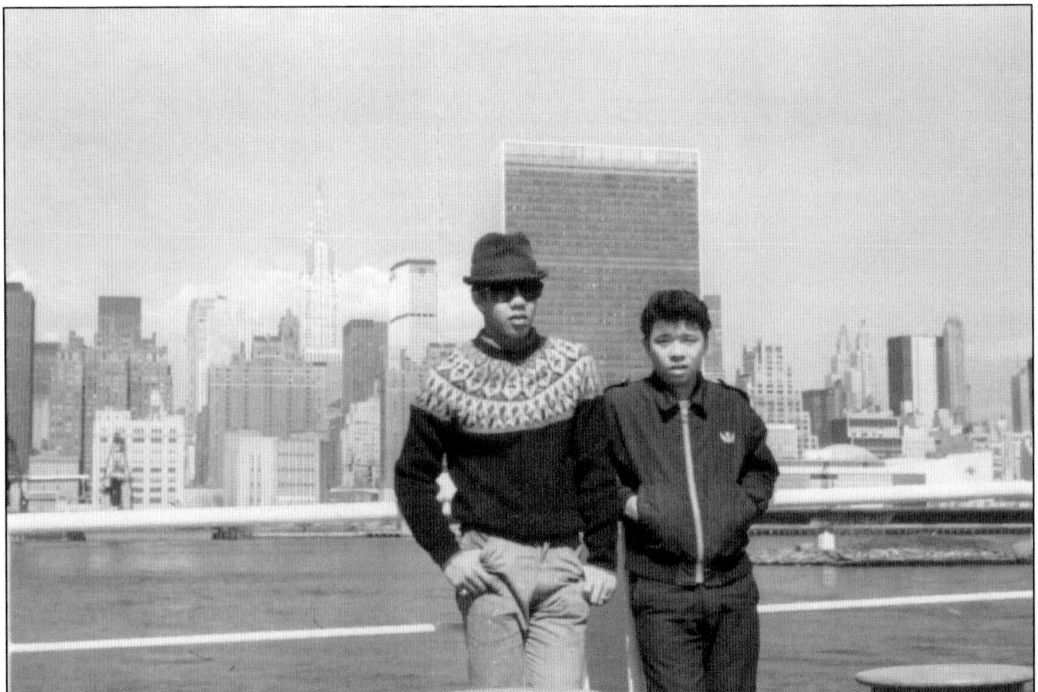

Pete Gipilano (left) poses with his friend Dennis across the East River from the United Nations and midtown Manhattan in 1966. (Courtesy of the Alic-Fernandez family.)

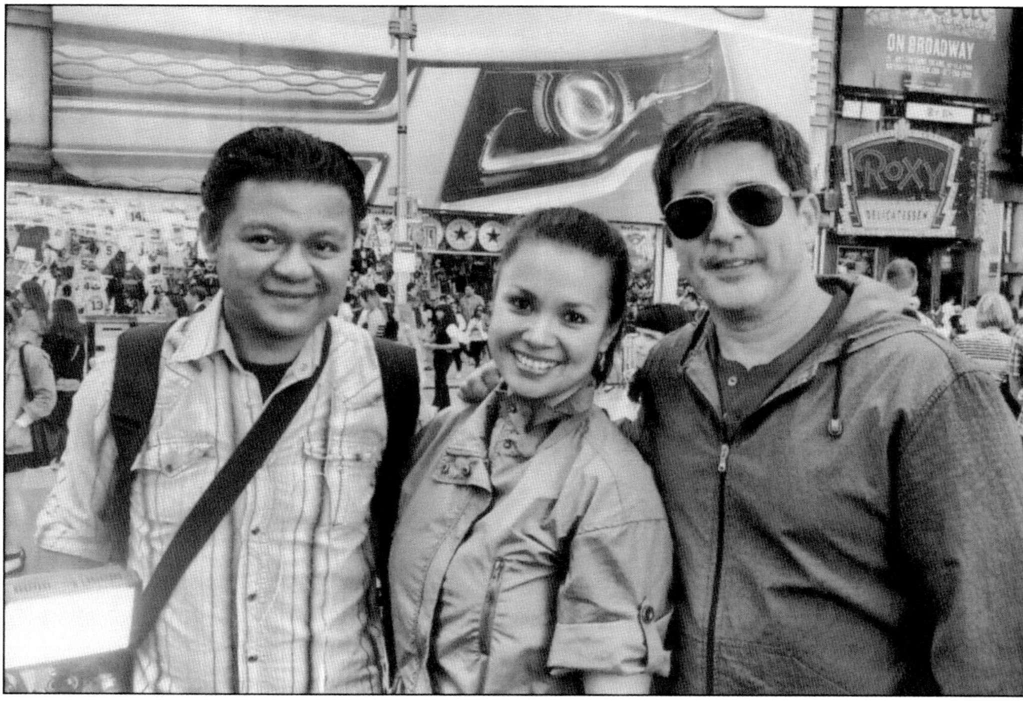

Don Tagala (left) visits Times Square with Filipino celebrities Lea Salonga and Aga Muhlach in 2012. (Courtesy of Don Tagala.)

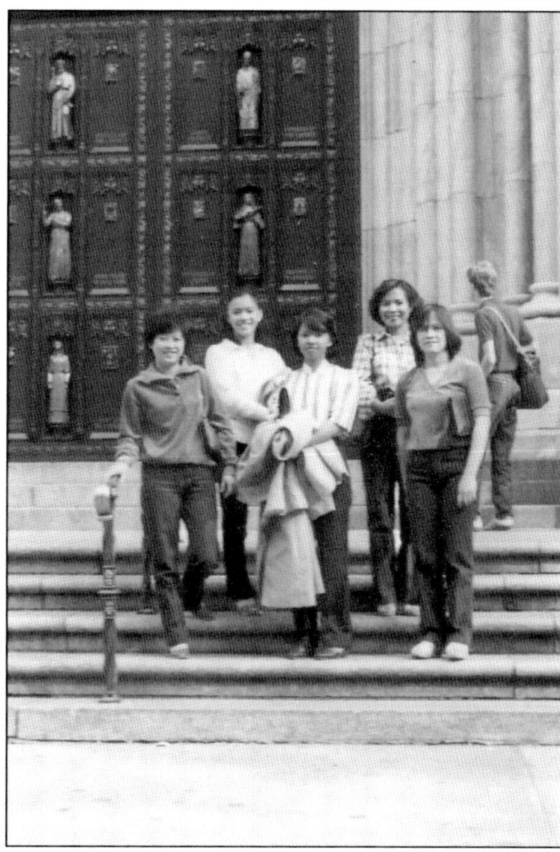

Evelyn Mercene Tamayo (a registered nurse who immigrated to Hollis, Queens) takes her friends to visit St. Patrick's Cathedral in Manhattan in 1982. (Courtesy of the Tamayo family.)

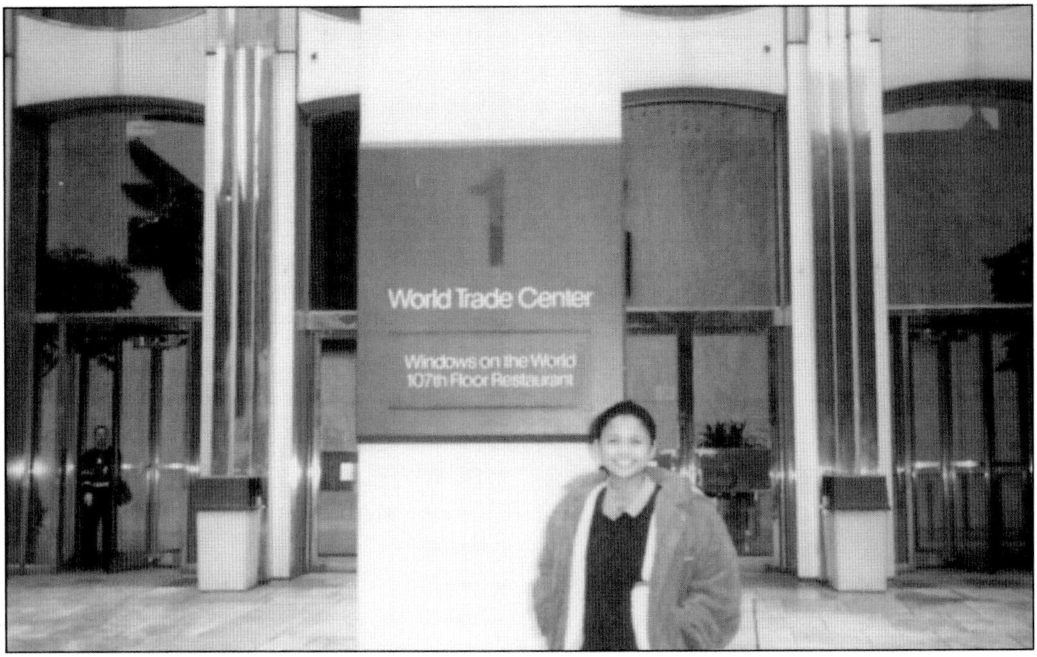

Gladys Magpily De Leon is a tourist who visited the World Trade Center in 1999. Given the tragic events of September 11, 2001, any photographs made in front of One World Trade Center or the second tower are now priceless. (Courtesy of Gladys De Leon.)

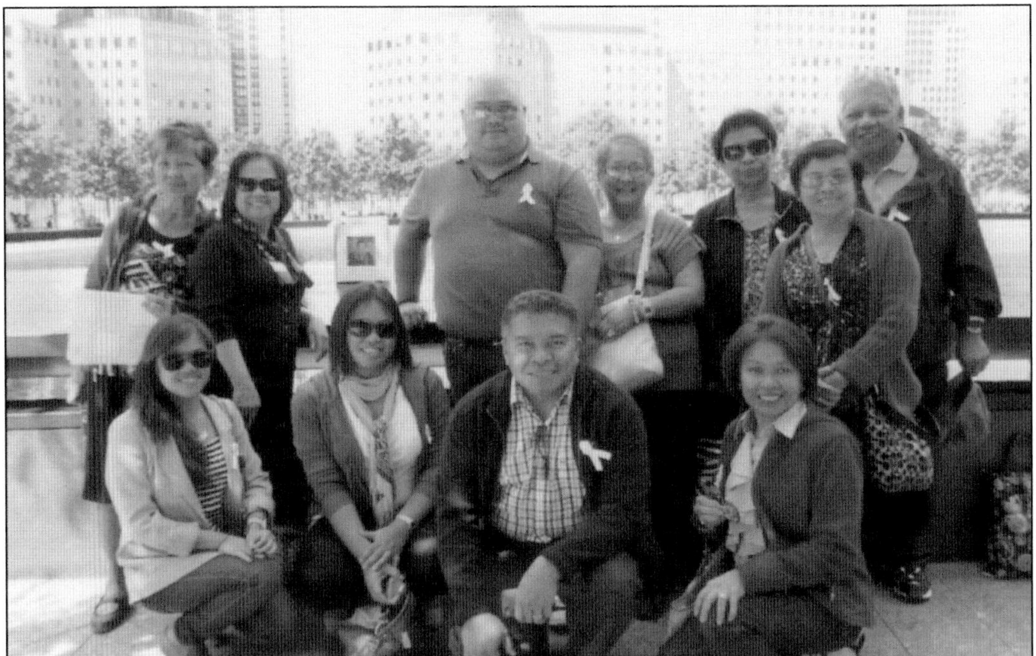

The Tamayo family visits the new World Trade Center in 2012. Pictured here are, from left to right, (first row) Pamela Tamayo, Gail Prado, Luther Tamayo, and Sheila Tamayo Punzalan; (second row) Rexy Tamayo, Evelyn Mercene Tamayo, Julian Tamayo, Wilhemina Reburiano, Elna Tamayo Prado, Eva Tamayo Iquina, and Severino Tamayo. (Courtesy of Sheila Tamayo Punzalan.)

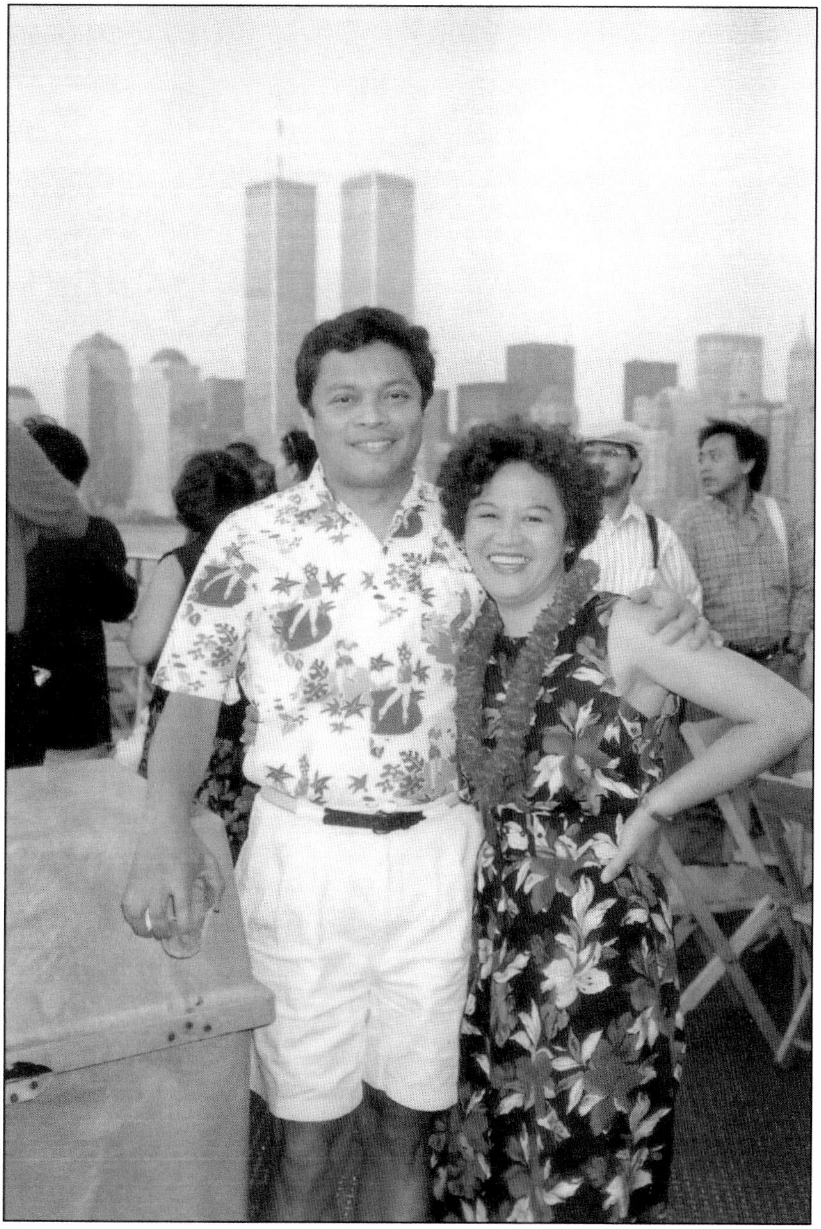

September 11, 2001, will forever be known as one of the most tragic days in American history. Thousands were lost on that day, including several Filipino Americans who died at the World Trade Center, the Pentagon, and the hijacked flights. Pictured here is Hector Rogan Tamayo with his wife, Evelyn, in 2000. Hector was an engineer who had been working on a project on the 86th floor of the second tower for just a few months before that tragic day. This book ends by recognizing the other known Filipino Americans who passed on that day. Rest in pinoy power to Grace Alegre-Cua, Cesar A. Alviar, Marlyn C. Bautista, Cecile M. Caguicla, Jayceryll M. deChavez, Benilda P. Domingo, Judy H. Fernandez, Ronald Gamboa, Ramon Grijalvo, Frederick Kuo Jr., Arnold A. Lim, Manuel L. Lopez, Ruben S. Ornedo, Carl Allen Peralta, Maria Theresa Santillan, Rufino Conrado F. "Roy" Santos, David Marc Sullins, Larry Sumaya, and Cynthia Betita Motus Wilson. (Courtesy of the Tamayo family.)